The Asbury Theological Seminary Series in Christian Revitalization Studies

In this landmark study, Martin Dignard brings capable historical and theological assessment to bear on a little understood but highly influential forerunner of the twentieth century charismatic renewal, Agnes Sanford. It represents the first comprehensive treatment of her innovative approach to the Christian ministry of healing, viewed in her life and times in the first half of the twentieth century. Influences include being raised in a Presbyterian mission home in China, a developing commitment to an Anglican understanding of sacramental healing, with an outlook influenced by her serious study of the twentieth century New Thought movement in science and religion. Dignard finds her to be maintaining a biblical and highly Christological approach to healing which makes use of the language and metaphors of contemporary science (including electricity) to convey healing grace. His study seeks to interface Sanford's intent to relate healing to the completion of God's purposes in creation, which found practical expression in a highly influential ministry of intercession for the sick and for healing of aberrations of nature, including seismic shifts causing earthquakes.

The anointed and influential ministry of Sanford, which was conducted within the context of mainline Anglicanism, has now received its long awaited and empathetic treatment in this research volume which here appears in the Pentecostal and Charismatic Studies sub series of the Asbury Seminary Series in Christian Revitalization Studies.

J. Steven O'Malley
General Editor
The Asbury Theological Seminary Series in Christian
Revitalization Studies

Sub-Series Foreword

Pentecostal and Charismatic Studies

Pentecostalism has, arguably, made the most significant impact on global Christianity of any movement to have emerged out of the renewal traditions. The beginning of the 20th century saw a theologically and spiritually distinctive tradition beginning to develop in numerous centers around the world (India, Chile, and Korea, for example) but this revival erupted into an explosive movement as a result of the catalytic Azusa Street Revival in Los Angeles, California, in 1906. The Pentecostal movement became a global one from that time onward and within one hundred years it was widely acknowledged that Pentecostalism, including the related Charismatic and neo-Pentecostal movements, had become the fastest-growing movement within Christendom. It is now believed that there are an estimated 600 million adherents worldwide, representing 25% of all Christians. In North America, Europe, and especially in the majority world, Pentecostals are noted for their vibrant worship services, marked by lively music and preaching, charismatic manifestations, such as speaking in tongues (glossolalia) and prophetic speech, and for their belief in miracles, including healing.

The Charismatic Renewal's beginning, normally marked as April 3, 1960, occurred fifty-four years after the beginning of the Azusa St. Revival. On this date, Dennis Bennett, rector of St. Mark's Episcopal Church in Van Nuys, California, announced to his congregation that he had experienced a baptism in the Spirit and had spoken in tongues. This began a wave of spiritual activity in Protestant churches outside of the classical Pentecostal boundaries. In 1967, the wave crossed the boundaries of Roman Catholicism, when a group of students at Duquesne University became overwhelmed by the Spirit and began speaking in tongues. By 1971, that wave had spread to eleven countries. Within a decade, then, the Charismatic Renewal, had made significant impact on both Protestant and Roman Catholic Christianity.

What is not often noted is that *prior* to these 1960s beginnings, the daughter of Presbyterian missionaries to China and the wife of an Episcopal rector, Agnes Sanford, had already begun providing what would become the primary texts for these Charismatic Christians who would begin practicing the ministry of healing. Agnes Sanford first published the classic *The Healing Light* was first published in 1947. It is Sanford's life and theology that are the subject of this volume in the Pentecostal and Charismatic Sub-Series, providing the first comprehensive study of this important pioneer of Charismatic healing ministry and, most importantly, analyzing her theology, as well as the influences upon her.

The late Fr. Peter Hocken, ecumenist and historian of the Charismatic Renewal, noted the value of this study of Sanford, especially in light of her influence on Charismatic healing ministries in North America and beyond. Fr. Hocken's examination of the dissertation from which this volume arises, occurred in the last year of his life. I was grateful to be able to work with him on that examination. As had always been my experience in conversations and work with him, his insights were keen and constructive. At the same time, even in the rigor of dissertation examination, Fr. Hocken was pastoral and led by the Spirit.

—Kimberly Ervin Alexander
Sub-Series Editor

REVEALED ORDERS:

Agnes Sanford's Theological Journey

Martin L. Dignard

Asbury Theological Seminary Series:
The Study of World Christian Revitalization Movements in
Pentecostal/Charismatic Theology

EMETH PRESS
www.emethpress.com

REVEALED ORDERS: Agnes Sanford's Theological Journey

Copyright © 2018 Martin L. Dignard

Printed in the United States of America on acid-free paper. All rights reserved. No part of this book may be reproduced, or stored in a retrieval system or transmitted in any form or by any means, electronic, mechanical, photocopying, recording, scanning or otherwise, except as permitted by the 1976 United States Copyright Act, or with the prior written permission of Emeth Press. Requests for permission should be addressed to: Emeth Press, P. O. Box 23961, Lexington, KY 40523-3961.
http://www.emethpress.com.

Library of Congress Cataloging-in-Publication Data

Names: Dignard, Martin L., author.
Title: Revealed orders : Agnes Sanford's theological journey / Martin L. Dignard.
Description: Lexington : Emeth Press, 2018. | Includes bibliographical references and index. |
Identifiers: LCCN 2018027805 (print) | LCCN 2018032737 (ebook) | ISBN 9781609471293 | ISBN 9781609471286 (alk. paper)
Subjects: LCSH: Sanford, Agnes Mary White. | Spiritual healing. | Healing--Religious aspects--Christianity.
Classification: LCC BT732.56.S26 (ebook) | LCC BT732.56.S26 D54 2018 (print)
  | DDC 234/.131092--dc23
LC record available at https://lccn.loc.gov/2018027805

"Cover art is by Agnes Sanford, used by permission of William DeArteaga"

DEDICATION

This work has to be dedicated first and foremost to Leanne Payne, who first introduced me to the works of Agnes Sanford. I am not sure who or where I would be had it not been for her. Second, to Clay McClean, who recognized and blessed the gifts and calling from God in my life. Third, to Kovu, who offered me a glimpse into what Agnes understood better than most—the love God has for all of His creation.

Contents

Preface / ix

Acknowledgement / xi

1 An Introduction to Agnes Sanford / 1

2 A Biographical Sketch of Her Life ./ 7

3 Principal Influences on Her Theology / 43

4 Understanding Her Healing Prayer Model / 73

5 A Decidedly Christian Theology / 95

6 Assessing Her Influence and Critics / 129

7 The Significance of Her Ministry and Theology / 161

Appendix 1 / 169

Bibliography / 197

Index of Terms and Persons / 215

PREFACE

My journey to understand healing began as a child in the Roman Catholic Church. I heard that saints could do miracles because they were holy and, therefore, God listened to their prayers. I began attending an Assembly of God church as a teenager and learned that ordinary people could pray for healing for someone else. When a healing took place, it was one of those rare events indicating God cared about someone. A few years later, I went to a Word-Faith church and heard that faith meant believing what God says even when circumstances or feelings disagreed. I was told healing was for everyone who knew God and had faith in His Word. When I went to college, I joined a Vineyard Christian Fellowship. I was excited to hear John Wimber talk about "doing the stuff" and having faith in God's willingness to heal without rejecting emotional healing or being in denial about our health. Each insight took me one step closer to gaining an understanding of those moments in time when God's reality breaks in upon our daily life. However, it was not until after I heard Leanne Payne speak about Agnes Sanford at one of her conferences that things truly began to come together.

When I first read *The Healing Light*, it spoke to me. I have always been a scientist at heart, similar to Agnes. She wrote about faith in simple and practical ways that made it real and concrete. There was no condemnation when a healing did not happen, but there was still humility to accept responsibility for our human limitations. Never before had I heard that the faith of a person praying for the sick mattered as much as the faith of the one getting prayer. I was too aware of my own doubts to presume that my prayers were all-sufficient in faith, and learning that there were actually things I could do to improve the effectiveness of my prayers for others was almost more than I could hope. People began to be healed when I prayed for them. With responsibility came a great sense of freedom.

As I entered my doctoral program and began to study the theology and history of Christianity, I realized the full extent that the contemporary Church needed to consider the simple things Agnes taught—things she wrote about more than a decade before the Charismatic Movement ever began. Sadly, I discovered that very little has actually been written about her, and nothing in any comprehensive way. I decided I wanted to write my dissertation on her theology. The last four years of my program focused on the different aspects of her life, ministry, influences, and contributions. Almost every paper I wrote for my courses somehow contributed to this final work.

In this book, I made the editorial decision to refer to Agnes by her first name throughout instead of her last. I decided this would not only be clearer to the reader but also reflect the significant impact she made upon the twentieth century as a woman during a time when women were often very limited in ministry.[1] I also strove to keep my discussion of her works and theology—as well as my evaluation of secondary sources—as unbiased and objective as possible. This is not always easy for any author or scholar, and I knew it would be difficult for me when I had a favorable opinion of her. I made the decision to face everything I found even when I did not like it. This meant I had to accept that Agnes believed and accepted some things that I really wished she had not. (I remember being extremely depressed for almost two weeks when I first began reading a few works on New Thought, wondering how Agnes could be associated with *those people*). Surprisingly, I was able to find a place where I could respect and value the positives without denying the existence of the negatives—a policy that every honest historian must embrace when evaluating and discussing human beings. (Indeed, even the heroes of the faith in the Bible were less than perfect). Nevertheless, I know my objectivity was tested when I had to discuss some sources that intentionally misrepresent Agnes's writings; I hope the reader can overlook any failures due to my weakness. Overall, I hope that as you read this work, you will be able to get a glimpse of the real Agnes Sanford.

Notes

[1] Using 'Agnes' instead of 'Sanford' was necessary not only to distinguish between Agnes and her husband Ted, who also had a ministry to the sick and is discussed in the text, but also to recognize her accomplishments as a woman in a position of ministry. I first encountered this approach in Jennifer Miskov's biography of Carrie Judd Montgomery where she explains, "I chose to apply some contributions of Feminist Standpoint Epistemology in my area of historical research because this approach seeks to give voice to a forgotten figure as a means of empowering. In this I refer to her as 'Carrie' instead of 'Montgomery' because her first name has a softer and more feminine feel." See Jennifer A. Miskov, *Life on Wings: The Forgotten Life and Theology of Carrie Judd Montgomery, 1858-1946* (Cleveland: CPT Press, 2012), p. 2, n. 4.

Acknowledgments

This extensive work has only been possible through the physical, emotional, and spiritual support of a multitude of people in my life. Although I cannot mention them all, there are a few who deserve special mention for the roles they played.

I want to thank Donnie Staggs, who not only encouraged me to apply to the doctoral program but also convinced me I was up to the challenge. He also reassured me during those times when I doubted I could finish. If it had not been for his prompting and motivation, that work leading to this book would not exist. I also owe a great deal to Corrine Paige for being a listening ear during the times I needed to vent. Only God knows how often she patiently let me express my frustration over issues related to revisions, schedules, sleep, finances, and countless other topics. In addition, I may not have made it without the repeated affirmations from Suzanne Luna, continually telling me "you can do this!" I heard you.

Gratitude must go to three professors who got me to this point. First, to Dr. Peter Prosser, who showed me history could be interesting; had it not been for his teaching me about the past, I would not have learned about the present. Second, to Dr. Wolfgang Vondey, who helped me to see that knowing what someone believes may not be quite as enlightening as understanding why; he helped me to look beyond doctrines to see how people actually saw God. Third, to Dr. Kimberly Alexander, who constantly gave me the encouragement and motivation to believe I had something to offer; had it not been for her support, I would have given up long before this book was done.

Finally, special mention needs to be given to Fr. Peter Hocken, who provided excellent feedback through his formal examination of the dissertation that was revised for this book. Sadly, he passed before this manuscript's completion; I hope it reflects his goals.

Chapter 1

An Introduction to Agnes Sanford

Agnes Mary White was born on the Presbyterian mission field in Hsuchoufu, China, shortly before the turn of the twentieth century. She spent the majority of her childhood there except for short periods in the United States for family furloughs and college. After earning a certificate in teaching, she returned to China and taught English at an Episcopal school for boys. While there, she met and married Edgar (Ted) Sanford, an Episcopal priest. The Sanfords subsequently moved to Moorestown, New Jersey where Ted became rector of a small congregation. While there, Agnes witnessed her son being healed of a chronic ear infection when another priest prayed for him. She became interested in healing and learned how to pray for the sick with noticeable effectiveness. She began to receive offers to speak and teach about healing, which led to the publication of her first book, *The Healing Light*. After its publication, she became a speaker at numerous conferences promoting the baptism in and gifts of the Holy Spirit to numerous groups within the mainline Protestant and Roman Catholic denominations. With her husband, Agnes eventually founded the School of Pastoral Care. During her life, she wrote fifteen books and a few short publications, most of which focus on healing.

Agnes holds a significant place in Christian history of the twentieth century and was influenced by the ever-changing theological landscapes in which she found herself. These influences will be more thoroughly explored in a subsequent chapter. She was also a primary influencer and change-agent, as will also be examined. As a child in the Presbyterian Church, she was taught the doctrine of cessationism, which was based on Calvin's *Institutes of the Christian Religion* and had declared that all miracles—especially healing—had been "temporary" for the New Testament Church and then had "immediately ceased."[1] Through her ministry and writings, she demonstrated to an audience previously influenced by cessationism that miracles and healing still occurred. Additionally, Agnes is recognized as the founder of the inner healing movement, a type of prayer geared toward healing of memories and emotions. In these respects, Agnes became a significant and foundational part of the Renewal Movement in the first half of the twentieth century.

Because of her membership in the Episcopal Church, recognized as a liturgical mainline denomination, Agnes's books had a profound effect upon Christians who might not otherwise accept the validity or existence of the baptism and gifts of the Holy Spirit. Her first book, written from a scientific and metaphysical perspective, became a primary source for the Charismatic Movement, recognized as "the penetration of Pentecostalism into the mainline Protestant and Catholic churches" where the proponents "have received the Baptism in the Holy Spirit and have chosen to stay within their own churches."[2] Of course, there are notable variations among scholars on the definitions of "Pentecostal" and "Charismatic" and their related movements. In this book, the term "Charismatic Movement" is commonly used to describe "the occurrence of distinctively pentecostal blessings and phenomena . . . outside a denominational and/or confessional pentecostal framework."[3] Agnes had a profound influence on the early Charismatic Movement.

Agnes published her primary book, *The Healing Light*, more than a decade prior to the day that Dennis Bennett announced to his congregation he had received the baptism in the Holy Spirit, an event associated with the emergence of the Charismatic Movement. Agnes's book had already circulated enough by then to be considered by some the movement's main source for a practical theology of healing prayer. As such, the argument can be made that her healing theology formed a significant part of the healing ministry used in a majority of Charismatic churches. Additionally, her Episcopal affiliation gave her significant credibility with mainline churches where classical Pentecostals would likely have been viewed with suspicion; testimony from someone in a historically liturgical denomination undoubtedly provided a sense of safety. As such, she played an instrumental role in convincing many churches to reject cessationism and to accept the validity of the Charismatic experience, both of the baptism in and gifts of the Holy Spirit. Perhaps more than any other reason, however, Agnes's expansive paradigm appealed to her audience. Her incorporation of science and medicine into her theology connected with those seeking a balanced, mediated position. These factors together resulted in her having a foundational impact on the early Charismatic Movement.

The Need for this Research

Of course, influence and impact do not necessarily equate to a volume of material being written on a subject. Little has been written about Agnes's theology and influence on the Charismatic Movement compared to the numerous books she wrote and her impact on early Charismatics. Literature connected with Agnes can be divided into three main categories: primary sources written by her, secondary sources written about her, and tertiary sources using her as a reference.[4] She authored at least twenty one publications: five books on healing, one of which was written for children; seven novels, five for adults and two for children; an autobiography, describing her life and involvement in the healing ministry; a selection of meditations, encouraging the reader to develop a positive image of God; an apologetic text on the environment, describing a Christian perspective on ecology; five small articles and excerpts for publication, presenting her thoughts on healing; and a small academic booklet, instructing students in effective ways to study and learn. Additionally, she wrote at least two works never published: a theatrical play, describing the life of Saul and David, and a handout for the School of Pastoral Care participants, outlining prayer for the healing of homosexuality. Other unpublished handouts are lost to history along with copies of some stories she wrote as a child that were published in a Shanghai newspaper under an unknown pseudonym.

Of Agnes's numerous works, her instructional books on healing dominate most discussions although they comprise less than a third of her total publications. Sources discussing Sanford are comprised of three books, a handful of graduate-level theses and dissertations, and a small collection of journal articles; additionally, she is briefly discussed in a limited number of interviews, articles, and book references. Sources referencing Agnes as a source do so predominantly in the field of psychology and counseling. However, none of the sources discussing her provide a comprehensive examination of her background, influence, theology, and contributions to the Charismatic Movement and Renewal in the Church.

A critical examination of the available source material mentioning Agnes Sanford along with an extensive analysis of her published works will reveal several very significant conclusions: her works and teaching were instrumental in many churches accepting the Charismatic message and its related renewal experience during the early years of the Charismatic Movement; her healing theology and prayer model formed the foundation for a healing paradigm in most churches affected by the twentieth-century Movement; and her theology and works offer significant insight along with a comprehensive understanding of a Spirit-infused reality that holds value for Renewal Theology.

The examination and evaluation of source material involves a critical but affirmative position in which the source texts are understood to have clear and specific meanings that directly reflect their authors' motivations and intentions; therefore, care has been taken to reveal those motivations and intentions as accurately as possible in light of limitations related to the interpretive distance between the authors and the readers. Source material published by Agnes or focused on her is examined and evaluated to identify her theology and its implications and ramifications for Renewal Studies. At the present, all material relative to Agnes Sanford in this study is available in English with no language translation required. For works prior to 1980, care has been taken to identify any variations in grammar and word usage that would indicate any differences in meaning.

Of the three books and handful of graduate works on Agnes's theology and influence on healing ministry, none are comprehensive. Two of the books represent extremely biased perspectives, one by a pastor whose ministry developed from Agnes's and the other by a doctor who considers inner healing an inherently occult practice; the third book focuses narrowly on Agnes's work combatting cessationism. The doctoral dissertations and graduate theses qualify as scholarly but often reveal bias or do not evaluate the potential of her theology for Renewal Studies or new understandings for healing ministry. The journal articles discuss her life and ministry in limited contexts, providing minimal insight into her overall significance. A further contribution is required to combine in one work the background and influences that formed her worldview, the benefit of her teachings as they relate to theology, Christology, and Pneumatology as well as physical and inner healing, and the potential of her works for future dialogue in Renewal Studies.

Agnes' Contributions to Christian Theology

Agnes held a theology that can be shown to be congruous with Christian orthodoxy even though it was clearly informed by metaphysical, psychological, and scientific convictions. She describes God as a Being consisting of a Trinity of three relational Persons—Father, Son, and Holy Spirit—while commonly using terms associated with energy, force, and thought. She affirms Jesus Christ as the only avenue of salvation but explains His redemptive work on the cross in notably therapeutic terms. She promotes the baptism in the Holy Spirit as a primary means for the Christian to live a holy, holistic, and empowered life yet recognizes that people can operate in the gifts of the Spirit independent of the baptism. Agnes viewed Scripture as the divinely inspired Word of God although she often relied on science for interpreting and explaining it. She also held a sacramental view of the Christian faith, affirming supernatural experiences related to God's transcendence and immanence. Additionally, she understood healing as inherently connected with God's nature and His creation of the universe. Agnes combined her many beliefs into a coherent and cogent theology that affirmed Christian orthodoxy.

A pioneer in healing ministry for the twentieth century, Agnes not only provided a groundbreaking prayer model for physical healing but also originated the ministry of inner healing through her discussion of the healing of memories. Through her ministry, she confuted the doctrine of cessationism by demonstrating that healing and miracles still took place, promoted the baptism and gifts of the Holy Spirit to leaders within numerous denominations and non-Pentecostal groups, and contributed to the theological and interdisciplinary foundation of the Charismatic Movement. Her blend of sacramental, metaphysical, and interdisciplinary approaches to healing laid a strong foundation for future dialogue and discussion in the field of Renewal Studies. Agnes affirmed the validity of psychology in healing ministry during a time when it was almost unanimously condemned within Western Christianity, and her teachings on forgiveness and the healing of memories are considered seminal by some in the fields of psychology and counseling. Through her numerous speaking engagements, published works, and personal interactions with others, numerous ministries have arisen to shape and influence the Charismatic Movement of the twentieth century. Notably, she accomplished all these achievements in a largely indirect manner and as a wife and mother during a time period when women were only minimally affirmed in positions of leadership in the Christian Church. In these respects, Agnes's contributions to Christianity deserve recognition.

Outline of the Book

Chapter Two describes Agnes's biographical background. Although her works form the foundation for this chapter, some secondary and tertiary sources are also incorporated to supplement her subjective perspective. The biography intends to examine key influences and circumstances within her life and identify some of the potential relationships between her personal experiences and her developing theology and ministry paradigm. Although the majority of the chapter relies on Agnes's autobiography, *Sealed Orders*, it also incorporates information from *The Second Mrs. Wu*, a novel based upon her childhood, and other sources independent of her own publications.

Chapter three describes the significant ideologies, theologies, and methodologies that influenced Agnes's healing paradigm, worldview, and theology. Based upon her own accounts and statement in her autobiography and first book, the foundation of Agnes's theology and methodology were initially formed by her religious background, first from her childhood in the Southern Presbyterian Church and then her adult life as a member of the Episcopal denomination. As she became aware of the ongoing existence of healing and miracles, she began to examine some of the metaphysical ideologies of the early twentieth century. Paralleling the practices of many of the early Pentecostals of the time, she accepted and incorporated many of the concepts promoted by New Thought and Unity Christianity. Additionally, she affirmed several aspects of science and incorporated the scientific method into her healing model. When her ministry further developed, she was introduced to Jungian Psychology through her pastor, Morton Kelsey, and her son, John Sanford. She incorporated some of Jung's concepts, along with principles from other psychological theories, into her theology and healing model. These influences are examined and discussed, relying primarily upon material presented in *The Healing Light* to provide a clear understanding of their effects upon her worldview and theology.

The next two chapters analyze her contributions. In the fourth chapter, the healing prayer model she espoused in her books is described. This chapter is important for clarifying what she actually taught as compared to what many people have attributed to her. Chapter five relies heavily upon *Behold Your God* to describe the core aspects of Agnes's theology. Although that chapter is unable to comprehensively describe her theology in full, it clearly affirms her Christian faith and disproves critics' charges of Pantheism, Spiritism, and the New Age.

The final two chapters move toward an examination of her impact and influence. Chapter six relies on secondary and tertiary sources to identify her potential impact upon various groups within the Christian church. The chapter concludes by giving special attention to authors critical of her works, both to understand their positions as well as to identify any improper interpretation or attribution of her material. Chapter seven then outlines the major implications that arise from her ministry and theology. The section includes discussion on recommendations for incorporating more effective practices of healing prayer in contemporary churches, the significance of Agnes's use of scientific language and the scientific method in *The Healing Light* for interdisciplinary discussions between science and religion, and the implications of her work for the theological discussion of the role of women in ministry. After delineating the findings of this research, the section finishes with suggestions for further study, such as outlining the full extent of her impact on the Charismatic Movement as well as the field and study of Renewal Theology.

Notes

[1] James Robinson, *Divine Healing: The Formative Years, 1830-1890; Theological Roots in the Transatlantic World* (Eugene: Pickwick, 2011), 3.

[2] Vinson Synan, *The Century of the Holy Spirit: 100 Years of Pentecostal and Charismatic Renewal* (Nashville" Thomas Nelson, 2001), 8; Vinson Synan, *Aspects of Pentecostal-Charismatic Origins* (Plainfield: Logos International, 1975), 1.

[3] Peter D. Hocken, "Charismatic Movement" in *The Dictionary of Pentecostal and Charismatic Movements*, edited by Stanley M. Burgess, Gary B. McGee, and Patrick H. Alexander, 130-160 (Grand Rapids: Zondervan, 1988): 130; also, *The New International Dictionary of Pentecostal and Charismatic Movements*, edited by Stanley M. Burgess and Ed M. Van der Maas, 477-519 (Grand Rapids: Zondervan, 2002): 477. Due to the length of these titles, they are often referenced as DPCM and NIDPCM, respectively. See also Allan Anderson, *An Introduction to Pentecostalism* (Cambridge: Cambridge University Press, 2004), 1; Harvey Cox, *Fire From Heaven: The Rise of Pentecostal Spirituality and the Reshaping of Religion in the Twenty-First Century* (Cambidge: Da Capo, 1995), 106-7; Amos Yong, *The Spirit Poured Out on All Flesh: Pentecostalism and the Possibility of Global Theology* (Grand Rapids: Baker Academic, 2005), 18.

[4] See Appendix 1.

CHAPTER 2

A Biographical Sketch of Her Life

Any biography of Agnes Sanford must primarily rely upon material found in her own autobiography although additional sources provide valuable insight into her life. Several secondary works provide a listing of biographical facts about her, but data alone produces only limited results. Modern historiography considers objectivity a nonexistent illusion of reality and subjectivity the unavoidable elimination of truth; the former becomes impossible while the latter becomes inescapable. Nevertheless, for the biography of Agnes's life to aid in understanding her theology and ministry, ascribing some levels of significance and meaning to specific events became necessary. Doing so requires care, for an overly complimentary evaluation lacks critical analysis while an excessively disparaging one lacks credibility. Therefore, incorporating primary and secondary sources in conjunction with conscientious citation practices safeguards the quality and validity of any assessments and interpretations. A chronological format provides the most effective and expedient framework for discussing Agnes's life, proceeding from her childhood through her adult life and ministry and concluding with her death.

Background

Agnes lived the majority of her early childhood outside the United States. She entered the world on November 4, 1897 as Agnes Mary White, born to Hugh and Augusta White, Southern Presbyterian missionaries in Hsuchoufu, Kiangsu, China.[1] Although both came from Virginia, they met, married, and lived most of their lives in China. Missionary work at the end of the nineteenth century required exceptional dedication and commitment. Foreign missionaries often lived in complete and total isolation from contact with their own cultures. In his popular book on missions, Agnes's father, Hugh White, poignantly describes this sense of separation, presumably based on his own personal experience:

> The pioneer missionary, as he walks before his barrow in the early morning, having left at a distance the only ones in all that land who can fully share his thoughts and feelings, seeing the scores of villages in sight, knowing that to every soul therein he is a misunderstood and hated man, with perhaps one man, his helper, who can understand him at all, and he by reason of race-instincts, heredity, and lack of development, intellectually and emotionally separated from him, feels in a partial measure what Jesus must have felt.[2]

Two other American families living at the station could not completely negate this sense of isolation. According to Francis Baltz, they were the only Americans "within a territory of 10,000 square miles."[3] The Whites gave up a great deal for their mission work in China.

These missionaries often sacrificed their health or even their lives for their calling. The "primitive means of transportation" in rural areas often left them "short of help" and "at the mercy of famine [and] disease."[4] Precisely because of the widespread illness in the rural areas, medical services formed a significant avenue for sharing the gospel in these locations. In his work on Presbyterian missions in China, James Bear describes one missionary doctor treating more than 8000 patients in a nine-month period and simultaneously caring for her baby while her husband was away trying to prevent thousands from starving.[5] These circumstances often resulted in sickness among the missionaries themselves, sometimes even resulting in personal loss of life.

During this period, widespread distrust and animosity existed toward foreigners—especially Christian missionaries. Persecution occasionally arose for both political and economic reasons. In his book on missions, for instance, Hugh White recalls,

> When missionaries were opening work at Yencheng, Kiangsu Province, China, in 1911, they met bitter opposition. From past experience and an intimate knowledge of the facts in the case, they knew the origin of this opposition. A rich, influential man, named Mr. Gold, was accustomed to make large profits by forcing impoverished property holders to sell to him at ruinous rates. The missionaries leasing properties and paying reasonable amounts would interfere with his monopoly. Hence he hired men, at five hundred cash per day, to instigate opposition.[6]

He had personal knowledge of the situation, for he personally started this specific work.[7] Propagated rumors and superstitions had led many Chinese to blame missionaries for droughts and famines, sometimes resulting in mass hysteria; the anti-foreigner hostility increased until it eventually erupted in massive bloodshed.[8] Although the Whites were not victims of the violence, they experienced ongoing hostility throughout their time in China; nevertheless, they persevered through the turmoil, continuing the ministry at the station, and shortly before the worst of the violence, they gave birth to their first child.

Childhood

Agnes was born at the Hsuchoufu mission station. In her autobiography, she describes the first incident she recalls as affecting her life occurring when she was one year old. The Whites had just arrived in the United States for a brief furlough, which unexpectedly became extended to three years due to the Boxer uprising.[9] She describes being terrified by the loud trains at the station. She writes, "Up to this point, my travels had been by sedan chair, mule cart, canal boat, and steamer."[10] Whether or not she had a personal recollection of those earlier travels, she found the foreign trains unknown and frightening. When her mother tried to comfort her by saying God would protect her, she asked, "Where *is* God? . . . Baby want to *see* God!" [Ellipsis and emphasis are in the original].[11] Agnes describes this incident significant and her response as being representative of her life: seeking God, finding Him, and seeing Him work in and through His creation.

Although this account may have come from her mother later describing it to her and not from her own memory, it provides important insight into her life and worldview. The sight of the trains shocked Agnes because she had only known Chinese culture up to that point. Even at an early age, she identified more with Chinese than American society, and she remembered only a few things about those early three years in Virginia: "My only memory of these years was not of my parents nor of a baby brother born during this time, but of my grandparents."[12] However, she describes in vivid detail her memory of her father, weeping as they traversed the frozen fields immediately upon their return to China; she does not explain why her father wept, but based upon other comments, it likely involved his love for the Chinese people and grief over the ongoing wars and famines—along with his own foresight that American missionaries would eventually be expelled from China.[13] Some significance can be ascribed to her first recollection of her mother being when they left China and her first memory of her father being when they returned: China had become her home and the place she associated with life and family.

Although Agnes viewed China as her home, the ongoing hostility toward most foreigners prevented her from forgetting they were not actually Chinese. Nevertheless, instead of the cultural animosity toward her and her parents breeding in them bitterness or defensiveness, it fostered an acceptance and respect for cultural differences. She writes,

> We did not in any way suffer from being a minority group, nor did we resent it. We *were* different. No wonder they called us "foreign devils" and spat at us occasionally on the street (but usually missed). Everyone was different—all peoples

and races, all men and women within the races, all animals and plants and growing things. No one had ever told us that all people were the same, so we were spared the stultifying effect of that false doctrine. We accepted inequality and thought nothing of it.[14]

The Whites accepted themselves as aliens and assimilated to Chinese culture instead of expecting the Chinese to understand and accept American ways. In *The Second Mrs. Wu*, a novel Agnes based on her own childhood, she describes her family regularly using Chinese phrases, even in their private conversations, and following the local social customs of etiquette. Agnes clearly considers the book as an accurate depiction of her life, for she identifies it as "the story of my own life, actually. There is only one thing in the book that isn't absolutely, literally true, and that is the incident about Valerie. All the rest of it really happened, just like I wrote it."[15] In the novel, her parents respect the local customs and believe in empowering the Chinese to oversee their own churches—a perspective that was considered radical for missionaries of the time.

Agnes eventually regarded growing up in China as a pivotal part of God's plan for her life. She believed that it significantly enhanced her ministry by giving her a perspective on other people and other cultures that she likely would have missed had she grown up in the United States or another western culture. In her autobiography, she explains the unique result growing up in China during that time period had on her view of people:

> Why, I have often wondered, was I born in China? As I write this, I can see one reason which I never realized before: it is because, from infancy, I knew and accepted the fact that people, both individually and racially, are not identical but are delightfully different. They are not 'equal,' as we love to say, but vary tremendously in every way—by God's own decree and for His own purpose. Understanding this has made it possible for me to deal with all kinds of people and not to feel superior or judgmental. I understand that they have as much right to be themselves as I have to be myself, and I seek, therefore, not to conform them to me, but to help them to be themselves.[16]

By developing in her an inherent respect for personal and cultural differences, she saw that her life in China prepared her to reach people where they were and speak to them on their level.

As Presbyterian missionaries in Hsuchoufu, her family accepted austere conditions to serve the locals. The station contained a small chapel, a boy's school, and a medical clinic, with someone assigned to oversee each of them; the only other buildings consisted of separate houses for the three missionary families and two small homes for servants. The station was inside the city wall, which separated the compound from land commonly used for executions and considered haunted.[17] Nevertheless, Agnes had good memories of her early years there. She recalls, "there was much love and joy among these three families, and peace among their children, and Jesus was very real to all of us."[18] Her account of her early experiences provides important information about her theology.

Agnes' description of her early relationship with Jesus provides insight into her theological background. Agnes describes not remembering a time when her family did not begin every day with devotions, and this led to her personal knowledge of God:

> Every morning after breakfast we had family prayers. Dada, Mother, myself, Henry Martyn (or H.M., as he was always called), and even the little girl, Junia. We studied the Bible from Genesis 1:1 to Revelation 22:21 and then turned back to Genesis 1:1 and started through again. ... I was also caused to memorize Bible verses every day, and to become adept in the Shorter Catechism, and surely all of this is good, for I knew Jesus—and I knew myself.[19]

However, her statement requires clarification. In a Camps Farthest Out (CFO) meeting, she says, "I was born a Christian, I reckon; I don't remember a time when I first knew Jesus" but then moments later mentions being "converted" on furlough when she was nine years old; this apparent contradiction between already knowing Jesus before having a conversion experience is also repeated in her autobiography.[20] Her language here seems to reflect her understanding of the Christian faith. She did not view a personal relationship with God as being solely dependent upon a conscious conversion experience; a person could know Jesus *on some level* from childhood. This does not indicate pluralism or universalism but reflects her early Presbyterian teaching as well as her later Episcopalian theology.

Unlike most Evangelical denominations, the Presbyterian Church did not maintain exclusive revivalist positions on conversion. In particular, infant baptism was practiced to confirm the spiritual state of children prior to personal faith decisions. They historically viewed children of believers as being—and becoming—believers in the fullest sense of the word. Lewis Schenck explains this as the official position of the time. He begins by affirming the work of Horace Bushnell, stating that a baptized child of believers would "grow up as a Christian and never know himself as otherwise."[21] He makes this statement in reaction to revivalist teachings that overemphasized conscious conversions.

After referencing Calvin's Catechism, a foundation for Presbyterian doctrine, Schenck writes, "children of believers are included with their parents in the promise of God," and "on the basis of God's promise, [children of believers] are also included in his church, since they too are regarded as presumptively true children of God."[22] Therefore, children of believers were baptized and viewed as believers. Schenck quotes from both the *Larger* and *Shorter Westminster Catechisms* as proof: "infants descending from [believing] parents ... are in that respect within the covenant, and to be baptized," and "baptism is not to be administered to any that are out of the Visible Church, till they profess their faith in Christ and obedience to him; but the infants of such as are members of the Visible Church are to be baptized."[23] In this respect, children of believers were expected to grow up as Christians and never know themselves as anything but believers, children of God, and people who knew God. This doctrine certainly informed Agnes's understanding, but it may not fully explain her comments about her own conversion.

As missionaries in the field, the Whites strongly held to the core teachings of the Presbyterian Church on baptism. Agnes herself describes learning the Shorter Catechism from as early as she could remember. Being baptized and growing up in a Christian family, she was considered a Christian and viewed herself as one—at least until she became old enough to make her own decision. Even after marrying Edgar Sanford and becoming Episcopalian, her theology remained consistent. According to *The Book of Common Prayer*, baptism is

> a sign of Regeneration or New-Birth, whereby, as by an instrument, they that receive Baptism rightly are grafted into the Church; the promises of the forgiveness of sin, and of our adoption to be the sons of God by the Holy Ghost, are visibly signed and sealed . . . [and] the Baptism of young Children is in any wise to be retained in the Church.[24]

As a child, Agnes had an elementary relationship with Jesus, and when she later heard the gospel, her theology confirmed her personal decision to respond.

Because Agnes and her siblings were schooled at home by their mother, she did not have many friends during her early years at the mission station. In her autobiography, she describes having only one friend around her own age: Isabel, the daughter of another missionary family at the compound. When not with Isabel, she would usually be off by herself. However, she did not believe this solitary lifestyle negatively affected her personal identity development, for she writes,

> To this day, I marvel at people who join groups and classes in order to find out who they are. I never had the slightest doubt as to who I was. And why should I? There I was, alone for the most part, with the elm tree and the crows and King Whitetoes, my cat, and Chang Sao, my dear old nurse. Also, much of the time, I had one friend, Isabel, about my own age, the daughter of the Reverend Donald Grier and his wonderful wife, Dr. Grier, a tiny woman who was the only doctor for hundreds of miles. I did not have to conform to a peer group. There was no peer group, only Isabel and I, and I thought faster than she did. There were no Brownies or Girl Scouts or—anything. I considered myself too old to play with the "children," my younger brother and sister and Isabel's. When not with Isabel, I thought my own thoughts and dreamed my own dreams, no radio or television to interfere with them.[25]

The frequent solitude along with being a firstborn child likely precipitated Agnes becoming an independent person. Her independence undoubtedly facilitated her later ability to persevere in ministry even when promoting uncommon or unpopular positions.

The first major change in Agnes' life occurred when she was six years old. She recalls it as the time she developed "the most troublesome fear that I have ever known" precipitated by "a change in my father's life . . . referred to vaguely as a nervous breakdown."²⁶ This condition apparently afflicted numerous missionaries during this time. Although conditions on the mission field contributed to poor health, Hugh White says,

> It is the man who is in a run-down condition, his nerves worn out, his body insufficiently nourished, that yields to these causes. Two-thirds of the breakdowns could be traced to the nervous system. Young missionaries do not believe the older man who tells them they cannot work so hard on the field as they did at the University. They usually have to have each his own spell of nervous prostration before they will believe it.²⁷

Although he does not confirm it, he likely wrote this warning from personal experience, hoping to help other missionaries to avoid a similar condition.

Reflecting on the situation after several years in ministry, Agnes identifies a slightly different reason for her father's breakdown. She writes, "Very likely no one knew the cause of his collapse ... [but] looking back now from the vantage point of many years, I can see a cause that they never saw: he was doing the work of the Holy Spirit without the full power of the Holy Spirit."²⁸ She does not make this evaluation lightly but bases it upon her own experience in healing ministry. She explains her position in the very next paragraph:

> The Holy Spirit worked *through* him, yet not quite in him, just as for many years while I did the works of prayer and healing in Jesus' name, the Holy Spirit was obligated to push His way, as it were, through all the burdens and fears of this world. I did not know then that the outburst of power called the baptism in the Spirit was available today just as it was on the Day of Pentecost, and so I had not received this infilling of power that awakens within one the wellspring of life. Yet the miracles that God did through me, as recounted in *The Healing Light*, were real and true, and their results remained. And the healing of souls and the forgiveness of sins that Our Lord accomplished through my father were real and true. But since the wellspring of God's power had not been awakened within him, the toll on his own strength was great, and the nerves of his body could not stand it.²⁹

At the time, however, she simply noticed her father losing weight, becoming pale, and getting weak. His condition became serious enough that they were ordered to take a year-long sabbatical at a small mission-owned cottage in the Kuling Valley of China in 1904.

During her first year at Kuling, Agnes developed a great fear, precipitated by her father's illness as well as her mother's latest pregnancy. As she explains it,

> My father and mother would go out in the afternoon for a walk or for a cup of tea with other families marooned upon this island of coming darkness. Our faithful servants were with us, but for some strange reason, I felt myself vaguely responsible both for them and for "the children." I must never let them know that I was afraid, lest they should be disturbed. As evening drew on, I would

watch at the front window for the darkening figures of my father and mother to come slowly up the road, my father strangely weak and thin, my mother big with child. Fear would grip me with such a strangling hand of terror that I would be actually sick and even my body would react with nausea and diarrhea. . . . What then did I fear? I feared that my father would not come home at all, but would die in the snow on that lonely road.[30]

Due to her father's illness, she became inordinately anxious over the health and safety of him along with everyone else in the family—a heavy burden for a young child. This fear followed her throughout a significant part of her life. She admits, "I have always been rather free from reasonable fears . . . but waiting for a loved one to come home has been the agony of my life, and only now is it being healed."[31] Living with her own fear as a result of early life events made Agnes sensitive to the role childhood traumas have on emotional and psychological health, and it certainly informed her inner healing model.

Although the houses at Kuling consisted of bare stone—perhaps more primitive even than the homes at Hsuchoufu—and despite her growing fear, Agnes immediately fell in love with this new location. She exclaims, "I loved it and still love it more than any place on earth, for there the earth was my own, and it communed with me and I with it," and "never have I seen such beauty!"[32] She found herself enraptured by the landscape throughout the changing seasons. Agnes often found great joy in nature, most especially in flowers, and the first purchase she ever made with her own money consisted of four rosebushes she bought as a small child.[33] This became one of her favorite places to be, and she often looked forward to their time at Kuling. Throughout her life, Agnes believed that God often ministered to her through nature, and the last book she wrote, *Creation Waits*, details her incarnational—and evangelistic—view of the earth and creation.

Agnes maintained profoundly positive memories of Kuling. She recalls, "There was nothing to harm or to hurt upon those mountains: no poisonous snakes, no poison ivy, no evil-thinking man. In great freedom I roamed where I pleased, intoxicated with beauty, so caught up in the ecstasy of life, that I was living, it seemed, in another dimension, not that of earth," and "Amid all this beauty, my little sister Sara was born and was a comfort and joy, a pledge, as it were, of new life to the family. And new life did return to my father, the strength of resting and of the healing earth—but not completely."[34] The Whites then returned to Hsuchoufu to continue their mission work.

The order of events becomes uncertain at this point. In Agnes's autobiography, she simply states, "We returned to our mission station, and my lessons continued as briskly and vigorously as ever. H.M., being four years old, was added to the school."[35] However, other sources indicate a slightly different chain of events. According to Baltz,

> In 1904, Hugh White became ill, and the Whites stayed at the beautiful vacation spot for missionaries at Kuling. They remained there until 1906. Because his

health did not improve, the Whites returned to the United States in October 1906 where he received medical treatment at Johns Hopkins Hospital in Baltimore. In February 1908 after his complete recovery, they returned to Hsuchoufu.[36]

Agnes does not mention the additional year at Kuling or the trip to the United States. However, important additional information is provided by Bear, the source utilized by Baltz, in the "Personnel" subsections of his research on Presbyterian missions in China:

> In the spring [of 1904], Mr. White had a serious illness and the Mission Meeting authorized his staying on in Kuling after the summer for a year.... The Whites were still in Kuling [the next year], and the 1905 Mission meeting gave them permission to remain for another year.... In February, 1906, Mr. White asked permission to go to Japan or North China for a few months, as Kuling was not helping him. He went to Chefoo, and then the 1906 Mission meeting at the recommendation of the medical committee, approved of his going to the States on a health furlough. The Whites left China in October, 1906 and did not return until February, 1908.[37]

This latter material, not described in Agnes's autobiography, indicates her father's breakdown required treatment and kept them from the mission field for almost four years.

Bear's account adds clarity to some of the gaps in Agnes's account. She writes, "During the next two summers we spent our vacation time, not at Kuling, but for reasons that I do not know, at Chefoo, a seashore resort in North China," and also describes being "converted while on furlough at the age of nine."[38] Apparently, her parents did not explain the extent of her father's illness or the ongoing need for treatment to Agnes, presumably to spare her from anxiety and stress. She perhaps considered the second year at Kuling simply to be due to her sister's birth and the trip to the States to be a furlough, which all missionaries took occasionally. So far, her account fits Bear's mission records.

Possibly one of the most significant events of Agnes's childhood occurred after they returned to the mission station, and it forms the plot of her novel *The Second Mrs. Wu*. The issue was whether or not the Chinese should have authority in their churches:

> My father, who was in charge of country work and the training of Chinese ministers, wanted to give them more freedom and authority. He even said that the time would come when the Chinese church, if it survived at all, would have to stand on its own feet. The other missionaries did not share his vision. The Chinese, they said, could not be entrusted with authority, and a time such as my father proclaimed would never come at all. For who could imagine the church persecuted and the missionaries driven away?[39]

This difference of opinion formed a major rift between the families at the compound. For missionaries already separated from their own culture, division within the group could be significantly traumatic. This was certainly the case for Agnes and her family. She recalls,

> My little world crumbled and fell apart. The glory of sunset and morning, of tiny flowers in the grass, and laughing crows holding a caucus in the elm tree faded away and was gone. The flowers no longer spoke to me of God's love, nor did the crows rejoice my heart. For the peace of our little group was darkened and put out by bitterness and anger. This break in our loving relationship was caused by a difference of opinion about the work itself.... None of this was told to me at the time. But night after night, I lay awake and heard low, heartbroken voices in the living room and trembled at the sound of my mother's sobs. Before this, I had never known her to weep. Neither flood nor famine, illness nor death, could shake her... nothing but this breaking of the bonds of love. [The second ellipsis is in the original].[40]

The unity of the group deteriorated from this point onward and never fully recovered.

The issue had peaked after another minister at the Hsuchoufu station, Mark Grier, baptized a family of converts in which the husband had two wives—a custom accepted in China at the time but forbidden by Presbyterian teaching. Some leaders within the Southern Presbyterian missions wanted the man to divorce his second wife or be put out of the church. Hugh White chose to support the minister's original decision, relying on points he published in an article for *The Christian Observer* in 1906: the Presbyterian resolution against polygamy forbade believers from entering that type of union but did not address new believers already in that state; the restriction in 1 Timothy 3:2 applied to men becoming church leaders—not to every member of the congregation; and divorcing the second wife would reflect negatively on the mission work by forcing her to choose between suicide, prostitution, or starvation.[41] In Agnes's novel, the issue is resolved by the man re-identifying the woman as his first wife's chief maidservant and wet-nurse.

Although Agnes's father supported him in doing the baptism, Grier subsequently used the situation to undermine White's position that the Chinese should oversee their own churches, and the conflict resulted in a division forming between the churches they each oversaw. Grier then sent a letter to the mission board, explaining the division and asking them to decide the issue. The mission board responded in the Fall of 1909 by sending a replacement to assume leadership of all the planted churches, reassigning Grier to oversee the school and restricting White to continue with evangelistic work in the country; the next year, three new missionary families were appointed to take over the Hsuchoufu station, and the Whites were assigned to start a new mission station in Yencheng, China.[42] Agnes's parents remained at this new station for the rest of their time in China. Agnes recounts that her father was so loved by the local believers in Hsuchoufu that at least thirty of them followed him to the new location.[43] Nevertheless, the damage done by this rift remained largely unhealed so that their leaving the station involved a profound sense of grief over the loss in the work they did among the Chinese.

This division significantly affected Agnes. In *The Second Mrs. Wu*, she describes the beginning of a prolonged struggle with depression as well as hatred toward the other leader. Additionally, she began to feel disillusioned with Christianity. She explains,

> Somehow I lost faith not only in those missionaries who had been my father's friends and closer than brothers and who now appeared as his enemies—I lost faith also in God. For these people were "completely Christ-centered and Bible-centered," as they loved to say. Their God was real, and Jesus was their loving Savior. Therefore, Somebody Up There should have been able to help them. My parents would have said that I had no right to think this, but I knew that I did have such a right. I, too, knew Jesus. I had been converted while on furlough at the age of nine.[44]

Walking in unity became a core concern for Agnes in her ministry. She repeatedly mentions in all her works the vital importance of forgiveness and love not only for anyone desiring to operate in healing, miracles, or any of the other gifts of the Spirit but also for everyone serious about knowing God. Many of her books also describe in detail the destructive results of unforgiveness on a person's spiritual, emotional, and physical health. Although she based her position on taking the commands of Jesus in the gospels very seriously, her personal experiences undoubtedly informed her understanding.

Agnes does omit some noteworthy material from her autobiography. According to *The Second Mrs. Wu*, the initial suggestion that the Whites should leave the mission station came from Grier. From her viewpoint as a child, he caused the rift forcing her family to move, and throughout most of the book, she struggles with hatred toward him. Additionally, one night shortly after his recommendation, a minor earthquake shook the area, filling her with fear. In the novel, Mary Lee, the character representing Agnes, lay "frozen with terror" and "trembling so that even the bed was shaken," and she describes subsequent nights when her father found her talking in her sleep, shouting "Earthquake!" as well as "hate him, hate him" about Mr. Bligh, the character representing Grier.[45] She does not mention the earthquake in her other books, but in *I Prayed, He Answered*, the author explains how Agnes recognized a major earthquake in California as the originating event in a young man developing paranoid schizophrenia.[46] After briefly speaking with him, she identified the cause and was able to successfully pray for his healing. It is possible her personal experience may have given her insight.

Agnes also became disillusioned with Christianity and the Church over the doctrine of cessationism, claiming miracles no longer take place. Several denominations embraced the position, but she related it to the only Church she knew. She explains,

> In fact, never in my life do I remember doubting His reality. *But there was something wrong* [emphasis hers]. And if it was not in Jesus and not in the Bible, then it must be in the church. I hit upon it one morning while my mother was curling my hair while I, as usual, recited those Bible verses that I had been caused to learn. "Verily, verily I say unto you," I recited, "He that believeth on me, the works that I do shall he do also" (John 14:12). And I asked my mother, "Then why don't we do them?" "Because the age of miracles is past," she told me. "This is a new dispensation." I made no reply. One did not argue with one's mother who was also one's schoolteacher, and thus had total authority. But I thought, "Either the Bible is lying—or she is, she and all of them—these missionaries."[47]

Even as a child, she found cessationism inconsistent with an otherwise systematic and faithful reading of the Bible. This led her to begin questioning many of the other claims being taught as biblical truth. However, Agnes did not doubt the commitment and the faithfulness of the missionaries—just their knowledge and their understanding. She says,

> They were as good and as completely consecrated people as one could find. They were not consciously lying. But they had been misinformed. . . . And when they thought that God could no longer do the smaller miracles of healing of the body, how could they believe that He could do the greater miracle of the reestablishing of love? Thus the ancient enemy defeated them. For he could not tempt them to steal or to kill or to commit adultery. But he could tempt them toward hate.[48]

The discrepancy between what she saw in the Bible and the lifestyles of the believers around her, first in their divisive attitudes toward each other and then in their lack of power in prayer, resulted in a crisis of faith that impacted her for several years.

During this time, a wave of sickness hit the compound, keeping the children quarantined from each other for several months. Agnes could not see her best friend, Isabel, who subsequently lost her younger brother to diphtheria when the medicine did not arrive in time. Agnes "could not help a feeling of being rejected by God and man . . . especially as about this time, I contracted trachoma in its virulent Chinese form and was forbidden to use my eyes in reading, writing, or drawing for three months."[49] Although she completely recovered with no loss of sight, all the children then contracted measles one after another. By this time, it was too late in the year for the Whites to visit Kuling, so they spent a few weeks in a temple guest house outside the city. Shortly after they returned to the compound, the White's one-year-old daughter, Virginia, contracted amoebic dysentery and died due to their inability to get the medicine.[50] These events certainly increased Agnes' sense of isolation, depression, and disillusionment, and her novel describes that period as seeming like a dark shadow was resting on the compound.

Another incident during this period may have had some type of an effect on Agnes's later life as well as her theology. The temple where the Whites stayed for three weeks included a cave containing the third largest Buddha statue in the world.[51] Up to this point, Agnes had never given much thought to the numerous Chinese idols she saw, considering them nothing more than stone statues. However, in light of her growing disillusionment at the time, she began to wonder if idols were as powerless as her parents had always claimed. One day when she had visited the temple and found it empty, she decided to try praying to the giant statue to see if anything would happen. She recalls,

> I folded my hands together, bowed before the serene gilded idol, who apparently paid me no attention whatsoever, and murmured "O-me-to-fu" as the monks did. Nothing happened. Or did it? I wonder. For gradually there came to be within me another voice, sneering, despising, scorning me. I thought little of this inner dialogue, assuming that everyone as they grew older had within them two voices, one of which continually denied or derided the other one.[52]

Agnes devotes only a few short paragraphs to the incident and does not mention it in her other books, so she likely did not consider it a major event. However, she later concedes it may have been "opening my mind to a power that was not God," resulting in demonic oppression that became, at least partially, a source of her depression; she later describes someone discerning "a sort of Chinese demon" behind her and commanding it to leave.[53] Her suggestion that a seemingly minor event may have affected her later life reflects her belief that minor childhood incidents can have repercussions; this became a core aspect of her inner healing paradigm, and this incident may have informed her larger theology.

Shortly after the long period of illness at the compound finally ended, the Griers sent Isabel away to a boarding school in Shanghai. Agnes greatly missed her one friend, and the loss increased her disillusionment and bitterness. She says in her autobiography,

> It might be expected at this point that in my loneliness I turned to the Lord. No, I didn't. I was rather fed up with the Lord, if the truth must be told, although I would never have said it or even admitted it to myself for fear of being cast into hell. Not that I ceased to believe in Jesus! I do not remember a time when I did not believe in Him. But I felt that He had rather forgotten me and my family and that He was a bit careless about fulfilling His promises of giving us His peace and joy.[54]

The fear, anger, and grief had a visibly negative effect on her health. Her parents thought her weight loss was due to an illness and had her examined by a doctor.[55] Agnes knew the real reason but said nothing for fear of increasing the burden on her parents.

Possibly due to the doctor's recommendation, Agnes began to sleep outside on the porch under a mosquito net. Although she enjoyed sleeping under the stars, it did not help resolve her emotional issues. She recalls, "night after night I lay awake until one or two o'clock, and when I did sleep, strange thoughts and pictures were apt to float up into my mind and start me quaking and perspiring in utter terror."[56] One specific nightmare frequently returned to torment her even though she did not understand it: "it had popped into my mind full-grown, a composite mental picture, when I was studying the history of the ancient Greeks, particularly their methods of human sacrifice."[57] In her later healing ministry, Agnes came to highly value psychology for its insights into the meaning of symbols and imagery that surface from the unconscious mind; she knew from experience that people sometimes struggle with issues that defy easy and clear identification.

Agnes began painting to fill the lonely hours after Isabel left. While painstakingly copying a picture of a yellow rose from a catalog, some of the dark cloud lifted from over her heart: "in giving my whole attention to it hour after hour, I sensed some of its perfected glory enlightening my inner being. It impressed upon my subconscious a picture of perfect beauty that I have never forgotten."[58] In many of her books, Agnes describes seeing God's glory reflected through creation, especially plants and flowers, and *Creation Waits* outlines her incarnational theology of the earth. In this instance, she felt the the image brought some healing to her heart, and using the imagination to heal depression and emotional trauma eventually became a core part of her inner healing paradigm.

In her autobiography, Agnes again expresses some of her theology of salvation while relating this part of her story. Initially, she appears to contradict her earlier comment about being converted and knowing Jesus. She writes,

> As I sit in my California home looking out upon my own roses glowing in perfection before a background of wild and glorious mountains, I marvel again at the goodness of God who has returned to me a thousandfold all that beauty for which my starved heart yearned in childhood. I did not know Him then. I had heard of Him with the hearing of the ears, and I had given my heart in love as best I knew how to His Son Jesus Christ, but I did not know Him.[59]

This statement by Agnes about not knowing Him does not necessarily negate her conversion at nine years old. On the one hand, it could reflect a sentiment in which a new, deeper intimacy with God lead her to view any prior relationship with Him as superficial or incomplete; on the other hand, she may have been trying to indicate that her childhood relationship with Jesus had not yet developed into the intimate knowledge of God the Father that she later knew as an adult.

Agnes apparently forgave Grier before they left Huschoufu and started the Yencheng station. She writes about this not in her autobiography but in *The Second Mrs. Wu*.[60] During this period of stress, she often would be awake until well past midnight. She describes being awake one night and seeing a lone figure walking through the compound toward the area where they had buried her young sister, Virginia. Going out to investigate, she found Grier standing over the grave of his infant son, Isabel's brother. At that point, they both recognized the grief and loneliness in the other, and it brought understanding to each of them. Grier realized how lonely she was with her best friend gone, and he recognized that her health issues were caused by fear and not a physical illness—something her own parents had missed. His attitude toward the Whites softened somewhat, and he not only advocated for Agnes to be included in more of the discussions between the families at the compound but also gave her a collection of Shakespeare he had won in college and had planned on giving to his son.[61] On her part, Agnes understood his pain and fear, and she forgave him, both for causing the rift between the families and for sending Isabel away.

Agnes reports that she received freedom from the fear of death and the nightmares shortly before they left Hsuchoufu. While the Whites were staying with some missionary friends in Haichow, it occurred to her one night before bed to ask God to remove the fear from her. Kneeling by the bed, she prayed for Him to do so. As she remembers it,

> I slept and dreamed that I was dying—the most real and vivid dream that I ever had. I simply awoke in that bed in the dream, and knew that I was dying. And I was filled from head to foot with a radiation of God's power that I have since come to know. Then, I had no idea what it was; my whole body tingled in a thrilling manner, and I was filled with unbelievable joy. . . . I have never from that day to this feared death."[62]

Agnes regularly discusses the detrimental effect fear has on people, and her healing model is designed to counter fear and anxiety. Although she consistently proclaims healing as God's will, she often describes death as a glorious transition into eternity; this childhood experience provided a confidence in her theological doctrine of heaven.

A significant portion of Agnes' childhood contained traumatic events, beginning when she was seven years old. Her autobiography and her novel reveal an independent-but-sensitive child who enjoyed life while simultaneously carrying the full weight of her family's burdens. In her later ministry, Agnes promoted the sacrament of confession for healing internal struggles and painful memories; however, she did not have that option as a young Presbyterian in China, so she suffered alone and in silence. Leaving the station at Hsuchoufu marked the closing of the door on her childhood.

Teen and Early Adult Years

The Whites left Hsuchoufu and founded the new mission station in Yencheng shortly after having another boy and prior to Agnes turning fourteen years old. Still alone, she describes beginning to retreat "into a dreamworld wherein I was princess and heroine, undergoing untold pain and danger in order to save and rescue prince and hero"; she recognized the danger of separating herself entirely from reality, however, and decided she should do something with the fantasies. She explains,

> Before this dreamworld became more real to me than the real world, however, some inner sense of rightness warned me that I should give these dreams flesh. I should write them down and weave them into stories that might someday be published.[63]

Some of her stories were later published in the children's section of a Chinese newspaper, the Shanghai *Mercury*. According to Baltz, she received one Mexican dollar for the first published story.[64] This would be a significant amount to a child in 1911. Although she describes the stories as "worthless," she attributes her later creativity to the concentration she had invested into learning how to write at this young age.[65] She also began to practice photography, but writing clearly became the significant part of her life and directly contributed to the effectiveness and impact of her ministry.

At the new location, Agnes spent much of her time reading. The mission received a large collection of inspirational books when a nearby church closed. However, she liked the classics instead of the overtly evangelistic stories. She says, "I read Dickens and Scott and other adventure novels, which I greatly preferred to the holy books of the Sunday school. In fact, there gradually developed in my mind a certain cynicism concerning piosity, a cynicism which lasts to this day."[66] Agnes distrusted faith that was not followed with practical actions and relates this cynicism with cessationism. She admits,

> This attitude of cynicism, indeed, tended to spread to Christianity in general. I did not doubt the reality of Jesus Christ, nor the devotion and consecration of my missionary parents. But *something was wrong somewhere* [emphasis hers]. There was Jesus, and he had said, "The works that I do shall ye do also"—but they were not being done. I had analyzed this when I was eleven years old, and my mother had told me that the age of miracles was past. But I forgot my own analysis and knew only that here was this thing called Christianity, but it didn't work.[67]

She perceived Christianity as internally inconsistent. Her father was actually performing exorcisms by this time, eventually writing a book on the subject.[68] His involvement in what would later be called deliverance ministry indicates a departure from the prominent cessationism of his tradition. It also raises questions about Agnes's later assessment of his ministry and its lack of spiritual power, discussed earlier. However, even this dynamic ministry of her father's did not satisfy her doubts. She confesses, "Up to this point, then, Christianity *did* work [emphasis hers]. And I felt rather guiltily that I should be satisfied with this quite real and evident salvation. But I was not."[69] For her, the inconsistencies she saw outweighed the one visible exception.

Another inconsistency revolved around the hypercritical attitude among the missionaries. Although she had forgiven Grier, she remained sensitive to division and strife within the Church. That year, the Whites went to Kuling, and Agnes saw Isabel again. Although she enjoyed the vacation, she came to dread Sundays. She writes, "There, for a season, one sat with eyes glazed with utter boredom, at a thing called Sunday school."[70] Considering her perception of

Christianity by that time as well as having grown up in a family that spent an hour every morning in Bible study, her attitude is not entirely surprising. However, the major problem for her involved the afternoon meals after church:

> But on the long homeward drag, my heart would sink, for I dreaded Sunday dinner. Conversation at dinnertime was reserved for the grown people, which was fair enough considering that we young ones had the run of the house at other times. The grown people's Sunday sport was the tearing apart of the sermon, phrase by phrase, and argument by argument. Dr. Harry Emerson Fosdick once visited China and preached at our church, and fragments of his sermon were scattered over every course brought in by our beaming table boy, Wang Er. Dr. Fosdick preached on Christian love, but he was not *sound* [emphasis hers] because he did not mention the Blood of the Lamb in about every third sentence. This went on and on until finally I burst into tears and left the table, to the utter consternation of my parents, for such a thing I never did.[71]

The judgmental attitude by Christians toward other Christians distressed her immensely, for it did not coincide with her understanding of the gospel. In her books, she repeatedly stresses the need for believers to practice love and unity if they desire to pray effectively.

During this vacation at Kuling, Agnes decided she would not live in fear of the unknown. She would take risks and enjoy life instead of walking only on the safe paths to avoid dangers that may never actually happen. She explains,

> There was nothing to fear upon those mountains unless it might be a snake hidden under the bushes or in the high grass. I made a decision in those early days from which I have never wavered: I would not go all of my life in the bondage of treading only a known path lest I step upon a snake. I would go through untrodden country toward the goal of my choice, whether or not I trod upon a snake.[72]

This also became her philosophy when she began learning about healing: she would examine any source that offered insight into healing, not just those that came from the mainline denominations. Many sources refer to her as a trailblazer for this approach while others have criticized her for it. Her integration of these insights will be examined later—as will the critiques of it.

Agnes made another choice at this time that carried over into her ministry. As she roamed the mountains during the warmer months, she often collected flowers to decorate their bare home. After returning, she would not rest until after she had arranged them:

> These I would gather with reverence and love and bring them home, never to waste them, but to cherish them in beauty as long as they would live. One rule I made for myself: I would never sit down and rest on returning home, no matter how weary I might be, until I had arranged the flowers and cooled them in water and set them in vases about our living room.[73]

After Agnes began her teaching ministry, she often pushed herself and refused to allow weariness to prevent her from completing a task. This occasionally caused exhaustion or illness, which she associates with two incidents of breast cancer and an insistent cough that required medical treatment.[74] Although she regularly warned others against ignoring health issues, her passion for the ministry sometimes led her to disregard her own advice.

Agnes had two positive spiritual experiences at Kuling during that summer and the next. As mentioned, she often went off alone to explore the mountains. In these two cases, she recalled experiencing a supernatural communion with nature and an unexplainable joy:

> In some way that I could never recapture, I entered into a state of indescribable dreamy bliss wherein I was one with the tall crisp grass, and with the tiny creatures that lived within it, and with the high blue sky whence sunlight drenched my body with pure joy. There was no more time. It was yesterday and today and forever. And there was no more *me* [emphasis hers] as a separate being. I was part of [it all].[75]

Agnes did not understand the experiences at the time. However, she later realized "surely at that moment (or eternity) His Spirit communed with mine. . . . [It was] the uncreated essence of the Creator, His ever-living creativity, flowing into me from bamboo and from rock, from ferns and moss and tiny orchids hiding in the grass."[76] Although these two incidents seem somewhat incompatible with twentieth-century Presbyterianism, this kind of spiritual experience through Creation became a frequent, even normative, claim on her part and eventually became a significant aspect of her ministry and theology.

Agnes went to the new Shanghai American School that fall. While there, she saw her first play, *Romeo and Juliet*, and immediately fell in love with theater. After acting out some short skits at the school, she realized she had a talent for drama. She writes,

> This was a new part of me! I recognized it for the first time! I was an actress! Solemnly, I reconsidered my intent to become a writer. I had far more talent for acting than for writing, though where it came from, in a long line of Presbyterian divines, it would be hard to say. But also I was a young woman of fourteen, probably strongly influenced by the Chinese view of marriage and descendants though I was not aware of it, and I desired husband and children. . . . The raising of a family could be done better in conjunction with writing than with theater. Therefore I returned to my original intention of becoming a writer.[77]

Agnes later wrote and directed Christmas plays at the church her husband pastored. However, writing, rather than acting, certainly seemed to serve Agnes better in ministry.

At this point, her autobiography reveals a faulty recall of dates and events. She indicates she began at the Shanghai school when she was thirteen years old and left for college one year later, but this timeline does not coincide with some of her other statements. She describes leaving for the school "in my fourteenth year," seeing Romeo and Juliet with many of the other students as "a young woman of fourteen," and attending the Shanghai school for only a single year; she recalls,

> The Shanghai American school, only one year old and made up for the most part of a collection of missionaries' children, mother-trained, found it rather difficult to separate us into forms or classes. Some of my subjects were considered senior, and some junior course. But at the end of the year, I had gone as far as this delightful school could carry me, and it was time to go "home" as we fondly called that great unknown, the United States, to college.... I was fourteen going on fifteen when I embarked on the tiny Japanese freighter, the *Shidzuoka Maru*, for that far country, the land of the free and the home of the brave.[78]

These statements would seem to indicate she attended the Shanghai school from 1911-1912. However, she also says, "[The First World War] had begun while I was crossing the Pacific in 1914," which would make her sixteen, not fourteen, when she left for college.[79] In this case, incorrectly remembering her age more than five decades later is more likely than incorrectly remembering where she was when she heard about the war; also, being sent overseas by her parents to begin college seems less probable if she were only fourteen—but more reasonable if she were sixteen. She likely, therefore, started at the Shanghai American School when she was fifteen years old.

After a year of school in Shanghai, Agnes went to the United States to attend Peace College, a Presbyterian women's college located in Raleigh, NC. During the three-week trip across the Pacific, she had a spiritual experience, similar to the ones in Kuling. One night, she lay on her back in a lifeboat, looking up at the stars. As she recalls,

> How long I lay there I have no idea, for I slipped beyond the swing of time or place. I was one with the stars—I was one with the universe. I felt within me the life of the strange creatures within the sea and beneath the waves and flying above the waves. I was not myself, I was life. And yet, I was myself, and life was me. Words cannot say it nor can I now remember the actual feelings of that time between time and eternity—only that it happened.[80]

Agnes experienced this feeling one additional time when she heard Stokowski direct a Philadelphia Orchestra production of Debussy's *La Mer*; however, all later attempts to reproduce the experience by repeating any of the activities failed: "I have tried. It does not come. There is no use in your trying.... There is in the Creator such a passion for diversity that He cannot be standardized, He cannot be commanded. Our times are in His hands, and He will come to us as He wills, when He wills, but never in the same way twice."[81] She realized she could not manufacture or coerce Godly spiritual experiences and needed to allow Him to decide if, when, and where they would happen.[82]

Expecting to become a teacher, Agnes earned a certificate in education. She spent three years at Peace College, a Presbyterian school in North Carolina.[83] She did not actually become a school teacher as she expected, but the courses in dialogue and expression aided her in her later ministry. She usually stayed with extended family for the holidays, but she spent one Christmas with her roommate, Rachel, who had a brother with epilepsy. Agnes developed a crush on the boy, Oscar, and "determined to pray for him every day for seven years. This I did, and long before the seven years, he was healed."[84] However, instead of being encouraged by the result, she convinced herself that her prayers had nothing to do with the outcome; when she later returned to China, she became afraid to pray for others, believing that it must be dangerous and unorthodox.

The teaching certificate from Peace College only authorized Agnes to teach in North Carolina, so she continued her education at Agnes Scott College in Georgia for two more years. She had planned on earning a bachelor's degree in teaching, but when she learned she would have to take an entire year of math, science, and French—and be forced to miss courses on writing, poetry, and art—she chose to finish as a special student instead of earning the degree.[85] Doing so enabled her to take the courses she truly desired instead of those that were required. Although she worried for several years later that she may have made a bad decision, she eventually considered the choice was providential and gave her the skills she needed for her later ministry.

Agnes returned to China in 1919. Her time in the United States had not resolved her disillusionment with Christianity, and signs of depression began to show. However, two events reveal her possessing a notable level of what she would later see as spiritual discernment. First, World War I had ended on November 11, 1918, shortly after her twenty-first birthday; while everyone was rejoicing, she recalls, "suddenly the bottom dropped out of all my rejoicing. I knew that there was nothing to rejoice about. The world had not been made safe for democracy. Evil had not been banished from among men that righteousness could prevail."[86] She later came to wonder if she had somehow foreseen World War II. Second, she attended a group Bible study with her parents and other missionaries at the mission compound one day. When one of the missionaries stood up and testified that God had healed her from depression, Agnes immediately knew otherwise. She writes, "As I looked at her, I thought, 'But she is *not* healed! Why doesn't somebody *do* something?' I was right. She was not healed. Some months later she hanged herself from her bedroom window after trying to cut her wrists." [The italics are in the original].[87] Although she had seen her roommate's brother healed when she prayed for him, she had subsequently convinced herself she could not pray for the sick; nevertheless, she believed that she had discerned that the woman had not actually been healed.

Agnes began teaching her brothers and sisters at home to give her mother more freedom for missionary work, but her parents recognized that it minimized her skills and education, so they encouraged her to apply for actual teaching positions. She did so and was hired by Saint Mary's School in Shanghai, an Episcopal school for girls. However, she only taught there for a single year before being released. She says, "This did not distress me too much, for I knew I was failing in my relationships with the other teachers and in my attempt to teach French to Chinese girls."[88] She accepted a position teaching English literature and writing, a better fit for her, at the Soochow Academy, an Episcopal school for boys, and some of her joy began to return. While there, she met Edgar (Ted) Sanford, a visiting priest who taught at a nearby Episcopal school for boys. They fell in love rather quickly, and he often visited so they could take long walks and talk late into the evening. They eventually married on April 3, 1923.[89] Agnes left teaching in Shanghai and became the wife of an Episcopal priest in an Episcopal mission station in Changshu, China.

Marriage and Family

Agnes taught English at the Episcopal mission station where Ted continued to work. She became pregnant that summer, and their first child, Teddy, was born in April. Shortly after his birth, however, she fell into depression: "It was at this time that I felt the approaching footsteps of depression. I can remember looking out over the waves of hills and thinking, 'Why can't I feel anything?' For all feeling seemed to have left me."[90] By the time winter had arrived, the darkness had lifted from her mind, and her outlook had returned to normal. The timing of the onset and departure of the depression suggests she probably was experiencing postpartum depression.

Although Agnes had experienced significant childhood fear over her father's health, she felt none during these years. She describes an instance when she learned bandits had taken control of the boat Ted was traveling on from Soochow; instead of worrying for his safety, she took a nap, knowing he would be delayed in getting home. She explains, "This seems inconceivable now; I am apt to swallow a lump in my throat when an automobile is late in delivering children and grandchildren to my door . . . but in those days I did not know fear."[91] Her decision at Kuling seemed to stay with her.

Agnes's recollection or description becomes uncertain at this point. She records her son Teddy being born on the first day of the Ching Ming festival, April 4, 1924, and her then unhappily discovering she was again pregnant when he was "seven months old," which would place the date in November, 1924; however, their second child, Virginia, was born on October 1, 1925 while they were on furlough in Pennsylvania with Ted's family.[92] It is unusual for a pregnancy to last more than ten months, so her discovery may have been later. Alternately, this may have been her third pregnancy instead of her second. Because she was still nursing her first child and preparing for a trip overseas, she confesses, "I am ashamed to say that I rebelled strongly against my condition. . . . a more inconvenient time for childbearing could hardly be imagined. I did not know in those days that one's thoughts made any difference to oneself or to an unborn child."[93] She connects her emotional distress and internal resistance with Teddy subsequently running a high fever for several days before being diagnosed with diurnal malaria. It is possible she miscarried the earlier pregnancy from November, became pregnant again a few months later, and simply chose not to record it in writing—or did not realize it was a different pregnancy. In early 1925, they left for the United States, not realizing they would never again return to China.

During this time period, Agnes had little interest in God. She confesses, "God was very far away from me in those days, so far away that I did not even realize that He was gone," and "I had no thought about God, except that one went to church on Sunday to worship Him, because it was the thing to do."[94] Although she had seen deliverances as a child through her father's ministry and a physical healing at college through her own prayers, Christianity seemed powerless and inconsistent for practical life. According to De Arteaga, Agnes came to believe "certain elements of orthodox theology could be both totally wrong and stubbornly unscriptural.... Perfectly sincere Christians, such as the fellow missionaries who opposed her father, were all too ready to confuse conventional doctrine with biblical truth."[95] Cessationism certainly had some influence in her apathy toward God, but depression was becoming a significant factor at this point in her life.

After preaching occasionally in Pennsylvania, Ted was offered a position as rector of a small church in Moorestown, New Jersey. Agnes hated the idea of remaining in the United States instead of returning to China where she understood the culture and had the benefit of employed servants. She writes, "[I felt] my heart sink into my shoes at the desperate prospect of having to cook and clean and take care of babies and wash diapers and be a minister's wife as well. . . . [but] I looked at Ted's face and knew that I must go . . . so we went to Moorestown, my heart sinking lower and lower at every mile"[96] However, the rectory was spacious and so closely resembled the mission houses in China that she began to adjust to life in America. She notes, "If we could have stayed there, very likely I could have weathered the change and become as well-adjusted to American life as I had been to Chinese life."[97] However, an offer came shortly after their move to have a new church and rectory built for them at no charge in another location.

While the contractors built the new rectory, she and Ted moved into a temporary house. Agnes describes the worst of the depression starting immediately after they made that move. She recalls,

> Darkness crept upon me in that house. Shadows fell and would not move. All my senses deadened under a weight that I could not understand. For did I not love my husband and children? And did anything matter as long as I had them to love? Thus I would reason with myself, but reasoning did no good. I became utterly weighted down with dismal weariness.[98]

Initially, she associated the depression with the move itself, thinking it resulted from too many changes in a short period of time. However, she eventually came to believe it had to do with the actual house where they had moved:

> All of these years I have thought that it was simply this one more uprooting that upset me. But now I wonder.... Could it have been the house itself? Some years ago I would have thought this utter foolishness, but now I am not so sure. For old houses do develop an atmosphere that can affect those who enter into them. Some people call such houses haunted, but I am sure that name would not have applied to the innocent old house on Main Street. But now, looking back, I can understand that house. It was filled with memories, many of them sorrowful ones: memories of frustration and discouragement and fear.... But I did not know these things at that time, and the darkness of the Moorestown house grew upon me.[99]

Agnes did not lightly attribute problems to demonic sources, but she did believe a place could maintain a spiritual atmosphere according to its history. She later taught that people could pray over a house, blessing it in the name of the Lord, and change its atmosphere.[100]

After several months, they moved into the new rectory. Unfortunately, it was designed in a gothic style with small, draped windows, which resulted in reduced airflow and sunlight in the house. These—along with the stresses of keeping the house, taking care of family, and adjusting to American life—resulted in her depression becoming even worse. She notes, "The kind of person that I used to be was dead. And the new person, whom I was now forced to be, had much trouble in living."[101] Agnes hid the seriousness of the depression from everyone and continued to care for her house and family. She describes overwhelming difficulty with simple things, such as trying to make meals "when it was almost impossible to decide whether to cook rice or potatoes for dinner; when I would stand in the middle of the kitchen floor, head in hands, in an agony of indecision."[102] By the time her third child, John, was born in 1929, she had almost become suicidal. She explains, "For many months I could not go near an upstairs window without wondering when I would throw myself out of it. I did not want to do it; I merely felt dully that some day I would. I seldom peeled vegetables without wondering whether the kitchen knife was sharp enough."[103] Had she not received help, she likely would have committed suicide as had the young woman missionary in China who hanged herself.

Help appeared in 1930 in the form of Hollis Colwell, an Episcopal priest from a nearby town. He had dropped by to see Ted, who happened to be delayed that day. While waiting, he inquired about the children. When she mentioned her youngest, Jack, had had an ear infection and fever for six weeks, Hollis exclaimed, "I'll go up and say a little prayer for him," and seeing his joy, she "knew he had some kind of power."[104] To her complete amazement, the child was healed. Instead of convincing her about healing, however, the incident only increased her confusion concerning cessationism, healing, and Christianity. She did not understand why his prayers had succeeded while hers had not.

The Episcopal Church in New Jersey had some familiarity with healing ministry by this time. Healing prayer had already been introduced to this diocese through the work of James Moore Hickson, who had an active healing ministry in England during the late nineteenth and early twentieth centuries.[105] Feeling led by the Holy Spirit, Hickson began to travel the world in 1919, speaking on God's love and praying for the sick. One of his stops that year took place at an Episcopal Church in Boonton, New Jersey.[106] The rector of the church, Henry B. Wilson, was also involved in healing ministry. He had previously started a "Society of the Nazarene . . . to deepen spiritual life and to impart strength and health to the body and soul by prayer, the laying on of hands, or anointing."[107] When Hickson visited Wilson's church, the bishop for the diocese of New Jersey invited many of his clergy to attend the meeting; one of the clergy was Hollis Colwell. It is possible that Colwell first learned about healing prayer at that time and in that meeting.

Egan draws another connection between Agnes and the healing ministry of James Hickson. His ministry, founded in England, was directly influenced by the writings of Charles Gore, an Anglican bishop. Gore promoted views of God consistent with science, evolution, and even other religions, and he expounds an "incarnational theology" which "argues for a more rational, reasoned and historical approach to faith."[108] Some of Gore's teachings were clearly considered extreme at the time. Notably, however, he affirmed the continuation of the gifts of healing in the Church and believed that "if a person is sincere and faithful" in seeking God, the person would eventually find "the way of the light."[109] Although Agnes may not have read or even heard of Gore's works directly, it is likely Hickson promoted some of these views in his ministry, which Colwell would have heard. It is possible that Colwell became positively disposed to New Thought teachings because of some similarities he heard through Hickson's ministry. Either way, the Episcopal Church in the diocese of New Jersey had been positively impacted by the healing ministry of Hickson, resulting in a positive environment not only for Agnes's healing but also for the healing ministry she eventually founded.

Although seeing her child healed brought her some comfort, it did nothing for her own depression. In fact, she found that the darkness she felt on her mind actually became worse, and it never occurred to her to request prayer for herself. However, one Sunday morning a year later while she knelt at the altar rail for communion, "the clouds in my mind parted for a moment, and on that beam of light a voice said within me, 'Go to Hollis Colwell and ask him to pray for you.'"[110] Out of obedience, she made an appointment to see him the next day. By the time she arrived at his office, the fear and depression had become overwhelming. She writes, "If he had not prayed at all but had merely tried counseling, whether directive or nondirective, I would not be here now. I am not imagining this."[111] Due to her mental state, she did not even know what he said or prayed. However, the result was immediate. She exclaims, "All heaven broke loose upon me and within me! Great waves of joy flooded my mind!"[112] She sang and shouted in the car during the entire drive back home.

As Agnes left, Hollis invited her to return for prayer again if needed. His offer was fortuitous, for although she found some instantaneous and profound relief, it was not complete or permanent. After a few days, "the waves of joy receded, and the darkness began to creep around the corners of my mind."[113] He prayed for her again, and again she experienced immediate relief. However, she could now carry on more of a conversation, so he asked her what activity brought her joy. When she mentioned how she used to enjoy writing, he ordered her to begin writing for at least two hours each morning; she protested that she did not have the time because of her family duties and responsibilities, but he insisted.[114] The healing continued as she followed his instructions. Agnes went to Hollis for prayer a few more times over the next few months before he informed her she needed to begin praying in faith for her own physical and mental health as he had been praying for her. Over the next several months, she was completely healed of depression.

Agnes did not believe she could pray with the same effectiveness as Hollis, for he was ordained and she was not. Nevertheless, she felt obligated to try. She therefore began to pray for herself the way he instructed,

> making in my mind the picture of what I wanted and thanking God that it was becoming so—or better yet, that it *was* so, thinking in the ever-continuing present. So I would imagine my body strong and well, relieved of its accumulated pain and stress, and would say, "Thank You, God. Your power is working through me and I am doing this work in Your strength.[115]

Initially, she felt dishonest about thanking God for healing before it was complete. Then, she describes a Sunday morning when she felt she was becoming ill with the flu: after praying and thanking God for healing and attending the service, she "lay down on the sofa the better to have flu," and suddenly realized she was healed.[116] After that, she fully believed in healing.

Because Agnes was taught as a child that healing ceased and suffering was from God, she questioned what other Christians taught about healing. Therefore, she spent two years studying the gospels to discover what Jesus taught on prayer.[117] She then began teaching a women's Bible study in her home, which solidified her faith in healing prayer. During that time, she and Ted visited a close family friend, Rhett, in a mental hospital. Agnes desperately wanted him healed and asked Hollis to pray for him. Instead, Hollis informed her she now needed to learn to pray for others. This began her healing ministry.

Healing Ministry

Although Agnes had learned how to pray for her own healing, she recognized that Hollis had a power she did not. Desiring to learn more about healing, she asked him how she could get more power in prayer. Being strongly committed to a healthy lifestyle, he advised her "one's power depended largely on eating the right foods."[118] Although she respected his insight, she doubted his conclusion that healing power resulted from a good diet. Therefore, she started reading everything she could find on the subject, evaluating each source with the Bible, along with continually reciting her own version of the Jesus prayer throughout the day: "Lord Jesus Christ, Son of God, fill me with Thy life."[119] After a year, the women in her Bible study began to request her to pray for sick friends and family, and when she would pray for them, they recovered.

When Agnes began learning about the gifts of the Spirit, she knew she could not accept everything she heard. From the start, she rejected any teachings with "Buddha or Mohammed or the Masters of the Far East as their inspiration," recognizing they were founded on a contrary worldview.[120] She evaluated everything else according to what she found written in the Gospels. However, she still made mistakes during that time. At a Bible study in Philadelphia, she told an older Christian woman she had almost no success praying for healing from a distance. The woman replied, "that is because you are seeing them sick. . . . Unless you can learn to see them well, you only fasten the sickness upon them."[121] Agnes found this advice exceptionally helpful, and it became a core aspect of her healing model. However, the woman also told her being a channel of God's healing power required renouncing all physical (i.e., sexual) bodily desires. Agnes allowed the woman to pray for her according to this suggestion, and the result almost destroyed her marriage before she realized such a decision could only be made prior to getting married.

Another error involved attending a prayer group in Philadelphia led by a Quaker. He described a type of prayer involving communicating with departed saints. After he assured her it was not really a séance as she suspected, she agreed to attend the small meeting. After the opening prayer, the gentleman went into a trance and began to speak with different voices while a weird thin string of blue light extended from his stomach. As she felt nothing one way or the other after the meeting, she agreed to attend one more session. During that second meeting, she laid hands on one of the women for their healing. The next day, Agnes felt such depression that she could barely move, and she had a horrible taste in her mouth; the symptoms remained until she vowed never to attend another séance. She also discovered that if she prayed for anyone involved in séances or Spiritism, they not only were not healed but also usually became violently ill afterwards, sometimes even dying or committing suicide.[122] For this reason, she later excluded people from attending her SPC conferences if they had any involvement in Spiritism.

During those first three years, Agnes reported that every person she prayed for had experienced some level of healing except for one—Rhett. She eventually realized her personal feelings not only interfered with her ability to pray in faith but also prevented her from understanding God's guidance.[123] She learned to picture Jesus standing between her and the people she prayed for so she could stay emotionally detached from them. She became so accustomed to turning off her emotions during ministry that she was often "considered to be rather cold" by people in her meetings.[124] Nevertheless, she found it increased the power and effectiveness of her prayers by enabling God's love to flow through her, unhindered by her own feelings. She considered this beneficial, for she not only had an emotional nature but also was considered by many to be quite attractive.[125] Her habit enabled her to avoid unhealthy attachments, especially when she prayed with men.

After she began traveling and ministering to people, Agnes discovered she had again become pregnant. She disliked the timing of this unplanned occurrence, concerned it would interfere with her desire to continue in ministry. Therefore, she refused to allow her condition to affect her work, which had disastrous consequences. She confesses,

> I made up my mind that I would not have morning sickness or any kind of weakness, pregnant or not. I forced myself to take brisk walks and in every way to act alert and alive and would not let my body succumb to its usual ways of adjusting itself to the new life inside. God forgive me, I did not realize what I was doing. . . . I lost this baby about the middle of the third month because I had refused to let nature have its way with me.[126]

Agnes admits that although she temporarily felt relief to be free for ministry, the sorrow over this loss never left her. She eventually became convinced God wanted her to have the child, saying, "this one might have done more for God's Kingdom than I have ever done."[127] She describes this incident—and misinterpreting her emotions toward Rhett—as two major failures in judgment she committed as she was learning to walk in faith.

As Agnes became more involved in ministry, financial needs required her to begin charging for speaking engagements. World War II had begun, and Ted still made only $3000/year; therefore, she began only accepted speaking offers when they provided remuneration.[128] Possibly the most significant offer came when someone from Friend's School asked her to teach a class on healing. She writes, "Someone told a publisher about these lectures, and Eugene Exman of Harpers wrote to me and asked me to write a book for his publishing company. Thus I came to produce *The Healing Light*."[129] However, the manuscript was returned from the publisher for being too radical and direct. Submitting the manuscript to other publishers resulted in similar results, so she retired it to a bureau drawer. Two years later, she shared the manuscript with Dr. John Gaynor Banks, who agreed to publish excerpts from it in *Sharing*, his ministry's magazine.[130] Glenn Clark then read the excerpts and, after requesting a copy of the manuscript from Agnes, published *The Healing Light* himself through MacalesterPark Publishing in 1947.

Agnes and the women in her Bible study group found they could not get involved in any aspect of the war beyond interceding for the safety of their children. Praying for victory or even buying war savings stamps dulled the effectiveness of their prayers.[131] However, they could minister to soldiers who were wounded in battle. Agnes did this by volunteering once a week at the Red Cross, becoming one of the Gray Ladies, a group of women who brought recreational materials to some of the seriously wounded soldiers in the hospital.

During her time at Tilton Hospital, Agnes prayed for a young Jewish man, Harry Goldsmith, who had several bone grafts in his leg, none of which succeeded; after praying and giving him some advice on how to pray for himself, Harry was completely healed.[132] However, he later contacted her about ongoing dangerous mood swings. She prayed for healing of depression, but nothing changed. She prayed for forgiveness, but his outbursts continued. After unsuccessfully trying every type of prayer she knew, she prayed for guidance, and she believed God revealed to her that it came from his childhood traumas.[133] She then prayed for Jesus to minister to the boy through healing his memories, and Harry subsequently informed her that he was completely healed. Her inner healing ministry was birthed from this experience.

Agnes did not expect to have further books published, but she knew she had to continue writing. She considered it one of the primary parts of her identity. She explains, "How many of me are there? First, the one who prays. Second, the writer. Third, the actress. Fourth, the painter. And all of these abide in and work through a human wife and mother whose dominant concern is her husband and children."[134] She expressed her gift for acting through plays she directed at the church each Christmas, and she painted as a hobby. However, praying for the sick and writing for publication became primary aspects of her ministry as is evidenced by the numerous books she later wrote, the numbers of copies sold, and the multiple reprints of them, in English as well as other languages. Even her fictional novels and children's books describe different aspects of physical and emotional healing prayer.

Although *The Healing Light* sold slowly at first, it gradually became popular among people interested in healing. As a result, she received an increasing number of requests to speak on healing. The meetings started small but increased in size, frequency, and location until she was holding lectures around the country and overseas; around this time, Glenn Clark asked her to become one of the leaders for his Camps Farthest Out (CFO) meetings.[135] She accepted the offer, and this eventually became one of the most significant aspects of her ministry. Although the initial CFO meetings were relatively small, they quickly increased in size and became significant to the beginning Charismatic Movement. Eventually, her husband Ted began teaching with her at some of these conferences.[136] These meetings, along with her published books, likely became instrumental in her expanding impact on others involved in healing ministry and the later Charismatic Renewal.

Agnes travelled and taught much more than Ted, both at CFO meetings and at her own conferences. However, the effort became a constant drain. She recalls, "I was always and increasingly tired. One night I dreamed that I simply could not climb up to a pulpit but fell and lay exhausted there on the steps."[137] Nevertheless, she felt compelled to keep spreading the message of healing. After a trip to Tucson when the meeting was cancelled, she met with two women leaders who also felt exhausted. Since praying for strength did nothing, they prayed together for guidance and all heard God tell them to "Pray for the Holy Ghost."[138] Not understanding, they asked a Christian physician who was visiting. He told them the baptism of the Holy Spirit could change their brain physiology, enabling more power to flow into and through them. Agnes relates, "We prayed for each other with the laying on of hands . . . and the power of the Spirit fell upon us immediately."[139] She had already been ministering for several years when she received this empowering.[140] This experience was reflected in her later ministry paradigm and theology.

From her Presbyterian and Episcopal theology, Agnes knew the Holy Spirit was part of the Trinity, but she did not know about this empowerment. At that moment, they all were healed of minor physical weaknesses, imbued with a radiating sense of power, filled with a deep joy, and given supernatural answers to specific problems.[141] She later realized she not only had new strength and energy but also had received supernatural peace. She writes, "Everything that I did, either with the mind or with the body, could now be done with about half the energy that it once required, and in about half the time. I could write and not be weary, and I could cook and not faint."[142] Her life was radically changed at that time. However, her baptism in the Holy Spirit did not involve speaking in tongues, a gift she did not receive until several months later when she returned to Tucson and received prayer from friends who spoke in tongues.

From her personal experiences, Agnes not only believed the baptism of the Holy Spirit was separate from conversion but also recognized the gifts of the Spirit could be received independent of the baptism. During one CFO, a Roman Catholic priest named Francis MacNutt lamented to her how he had received the gift of tongues when some leaders prayed for him the night before, but he otherwise felt unchanged. She responded that he had already received the Holy Spirit through ordination and confirmation and just needed a release; she then prayed for the full release of the Holy Spirit's power in him, and the result was instantaneous.[143] While MacNutt claimed to receive the full empowerment after obtaining the gift of tongues, Agnes reportedly received the empowerment first—and the gift of tongues months later. She believed that the order did not matter as much as making sure that people received whatever it was they lacked.

As her ministry progressed, Agnes began to focus less on praying for others and more on teaching others how to heal the sick. Although she believed everyone should be involved in this work, she and Ted especially wanted to empower ministers with the skills needed for healing. At that point, through a grant provided by an anonymous foundation, they felt led "to start some kind of school for ministers wherein they could learn those things that the seminaries did not teach them, namely, to do the works that Jesus did, according to His commands. . . . healing of the soul, mind, and body through faith and prayer"[144] They founded the Schools of Pastoral Care (SPC) in 1955 to provide week-long teaching and training conferences for pastors and church leaders.[145] They continued to run these schools until Ted's death in 1960.

In 1965, Agnes moved to Monrovia, California, and began attending Morton Kelsey's church. She continued teaching at CFOs, SPCs, and conferences until she retired in the early 1970s. She then devoted her time to writing, completing four additional books, including her autobiography and an explanation of an incarnational theology of creation. Agnes died the Sunday before Lent, February 21, 1982. Interestingly, she seemed to know ahead of time when she was going to die. In her autobiography, Leanne Payne recounts a meeting with Agnes in the late 1970s. At the time, Agnes said to her,

> The Lord has told me His first call to take me home would be at age eighty-two, and then, as I was walking in the garden, I'm sure it was the Lord, He said, "I will extend the years to eighty-eight." I said, "Oh, no, Lord" (because I don't want to be a burden or to outlive my usefulness), "how about eighty-four?"[146]

Payne tried to convince her to accept the later age, but Agnes looked forward to her death. The day she died, she had plans to go on a glider expedition with friends. When they called beforehand to confirm her interest, she cancelled, telling them "she was going on another gliding trip."[147] She died peacefully in her home at the age of eighty-four.

Conclusion

Between her first book, *The Healing Light*, and her autobiography, *Sealed Orders*, Agnes describes her life story and develops her theology. She interpreted her mystical experiences as a child as enabling her to recognize God working with individuals in different and unique ways. Her early formation in a cultural setting other than that of her own family's ethnicity, and the traumas, fears, and depression of those early and later years gave her insight into the most effective ways to communicate to the sick and depressed. She honestly admitted to her failures in order to help others avoid making the same mistakes. Her ministry developed a strong focus on love and unity along with a high value of faith and evidence, and she avoided many of the pitfalls that affected some other healing ministries of the time, such as denying symptoms, rejecting medicine, or embracing Spiritism. Agnes desired to see the Church operating in power while being practical, and her ministry reflected that goal.

Notes

[1] Francis Burkhardt Baltz, "Agnes Sanford: A Creative Intercessor," (master's thesis, Nashotah House, 1979), 5, ProQuest (DTN 1313475). Baltz provides the most complete biographical account of Sanford available, being completed prior to her death and with her approval. It supplies valuable material not found in her autobiography. In personal correspondence from Drury to Baltz on November 28, 1976, Agnes was "very pleased" with his thesis and desired it to be "authoritative in spirit as well as in fact."

[2] Hugh Watt White, *Jesus, the Missionary: Studies in the Life of Jesus as the Master, the Model, the Proto-type for All Missionaries. On Many Scriptures, Interpretations Are Given Which Have Been Worked Out on the Mission Field* (Shanghai: Presbyterian Mission Press, 1916), 95.

[3] Francis Baltz, "Agnes Sanford," 5.

[4] Francis Baltz, "Agnes Sanford," 5.

[5] James E Bear Jr., *Volume II: The China Mission of the Presbyterian Church in the United States, 1867-1899*, vol. 2 of *The Mission Work of the Presbyterian Church in the United States in China, 1867-1899* (Richmond: Union Theological Seminary, 1963), 534.

[6] Hugh Watt White, *Jesus, the Missionary*, 98.

[7] James E Bear Jr., *Volume III: The Mid-China and the North Kiangsu Missions of the Presbyterian Church in the United States, 1899-1911*, vol. 3 of *The Mission Work of the Presbyterian Church in the United States in China, 1867-1899* (Richmond: Union Theological Seminary, 1963), 466.

[8] R. G. Tiedemann, "Baptism of Fire: China's Christians and the Boxer Uprising of 1900," *International Bulletin of Missionary Research* 24, no. 1 (January 2000): 11.

[9] Francis Baltz, "Agnes Sanford," 6. Cf. Agnes Sanford, *Sealed Orders* (South Plainfield: Bridge, 1972), 1-4.

[10] Agnes Sanford, *Sealed Orders*, 1.

[11] Agnes Sanford, *Sealed Orders*, 1.

[12] Agnes Sanford, *Sealed Orders*, 1.

[13] Agnes Sanford, *Sealed Orders*, 2, 11.

[14] Agnes Sanford, *Sealed Orders*, 5-6.

[15] Agnes Sanford, "Healing of Memories: The Forgiveness of Sins," lecture by Agnes Sanford, 28:47-28:58 (Milo: CFO Classics Library, n.d.), 1 audio cassette. Note: Bear disagrees with Sanford's description of life at a mission station in China during this time, saying, "the book is not a fair picture of a mission station—I speak from my own childhood and adult experience on the China field." See James E. Bear Jr., *Volume III*, 479. However, Bear's personal experience only qualifies as subjective opinion to contradict Sanford's own description, admittedly written in a fictionalized novel format, detailing her own childhood perspective and experiences. Realistically, they may have had significantly different experiences.

[16] Agnes Sanford, *Sealed Orders*, 63.

[17] Agnes Sanford, *Sealed Orders*, 4.

[18] Agnes Sanford, *Sealed Orders*, 4.

[19] Agnes Sanford, *Sealed Orders*, 4-5. Along with her younger brother Henry Martyn, born during their furlough in Virginia, the Whites had a girl, Junia, shortly after they returned to China.

[20] Agnes Sanford, "Our Need to Recognize Our Spiritual Self," lecture by Agnes Sanford, 1:01-5:25 (Milo: CFO Classics Library, n.d.), 1 audio cassette. Cf. Agnes Sanford, *Sealed Orders*, 5, 11.

[21] Lewis Bevans Schenck, *The Presbyterian Doctrine of Children in the Covenant; An Historical Study of the Significance of Infant Baptism in the Presbyterian Church in America* (New Haven: Yale University Press, 1940), 1.

[22] Lewis Bevans Schenck, *The Presbyterian Doctrine of Children in the Covenant*, 9, 19.

[23] Lewis Schenck, *The Presbyterian Doctrine of Children in the Covenant*, 50.

[24] Episcopal Church, "Articles of Religion XXVII. Of Baptism," in *The Book of Common Prayer: And Administration of the Sacraments and Other Rites and Ceremonies of the Church* (New York: Oxford University Press, 2007), 873.

[25] Agnes Sanford, *Sealed Orders*, 5.

[26] Agnes Sanford, *Sealed Orders*, 6.

[27] Hugh Watt White, *Jesus the Missionary*, 125.

[28] Agnes Sanford, *Sealed Orders*, 6.

[29] Agnes Sanford, *Sealed Orders*, 7.

[30] Agnes Sanford, *Sealed Orders*, 8.

[31] Agnes Sanford, *Sealed Orders*, 8.
[32] Agnes Sanford, *Sealed Orders*, 7.
[33] Agnes Sanford, *Sealed Orders*, 20; Agnes Sanford, *The Second Mrs. Wu* (Philadelphia: J. B. Lippincott, 1945), 30.
[34] Agnes Sanford, *Sealed Orders*, 9.
[35] Agnes Sanford, *Sealed Orders*, 9.
[36] Francis Baltz, "Agnes Sanford," 6.
[37] James E Bear Jr., *Volume III: The Mid-China and the North Kiangsu Missions*, 451-454.
[38] Agnes Sanford, *Sealed Orders*, 10-11. Note: Agnes does mention the hospital on page 162.
[39] Agnes Sanford, *Sealed Orders*, 11.
[40] Agnes Sanford, *Sealed Orders*, 10-11.
[41] Edward Jewitt Wheeler, Isaac Kaufman Funk, and William Seaver Woods, eds., "Polygamy and Foreign Missions," *The Literary Digest* 32, no. 24 (June 1906): 910-911. See also, William L. DeArteaga, *Agnes Sanford and Her Companions: The Assault on Cessationism and the Coming of the Charismatic Renewal* (Eugene: Wipf & Stock, 2015), 173-174.
[42] James E Bear Jr., *Volume III: The Mid-China and the North Kiangsu Missions*, 463-466.
[43] Agnes Sanford, *Sealed Orders*, 20.
[44] Agnes Sanford, *Sealed Orders*, 11-12.
[45] Agnes Sanford, *The Second Mrs. Wu*, 55-56.
[46] William L. Vaswig, *I Prayed, He Answered* (Minneapolis: Augsburg Publishing House, 1977), 28, 36-37.
[47] Agnes Sanford, *Sealed Orders*, 12.
[48] Agnes Sanford, *Sealed Orders*, 12.
[49] Agnes Sanford, *Sealed Orders*, 13.
[50] Agnes Sanford, *Sealed Orders*, 15.
[51] Agnes Sanford, *Sealed Orders*, 14. Agnes describes it as third largest in the world, but another source identifies it as "the third largest statue of the Buddha in China." See Derek Challis and Gloria Rawlinson, *The Book of Iris: A Life of Robin Hyde* (Auckland: Auckland University Press, 2002), 642.
[52] Agnes Sanford, *Sealed Orders*, 14.
[53] Agnes Sanford, *Sealed Orders*, 99-100.
[54] Agnes Sanford, *Sealed Orders*, 16.
[55] Agnes Sanford, *Sealed Orders*, 17.
[56] Agnes Sanford, *Sealed Orders*, 17. Agnes describes seeing Halley's Comet, confirming this took place in 1910 when she was twelve years old.
[57] Agnes Sanford, *Sealed Orders*, 17.
[58] Agnes Sanford, *Sealed Orders*, 18.
[59] Agnes Sanford, *Sealed Orders*, 18-19.
[60] Agnes Sanford, *The Second Mrs. Wu*, 237-240.
[61] Agnes Sanford, *The Second Mrs. Wu*, 242-243. The novel ends with their leaving Huscoufu.
[62] Agnes Sanford, *Sealed Orders*, 19.
[63] Agnes Sanford, *Sealed Orders*, 21.
[64] Francis Baltz, "Agnes Sanford," 14. Note: according to Baltz, Agnes sold her first story to the newspaper when she was ten years old, but her autobiography places this event much later. Baltz received the information from an old edition of the Worcester Telegram, and while one of his note cards shows this as taking place when Sanford was ten years old, a more detailed note card, describing the contents of the article, states it took place when she was thirteen years old; the later age fits her autobiography. There-

fore, the statement provided in Baltz's published dissertation was likely an unintentional transcription error.

[65] Agnes Sanford, *Sealed Orders*, 22. Agnes no longer remembered the pseudonym she had used for the publication of the stories, and she gives no other details about them, so there seems to be no way to obtain copies of the stories.

[66] Agnes Sanford, *Sealed Orders*, 23.

[67] Agnes Sanford, *Sealed Orders*, 23.

[68] Although he related demonism to psychological disorders, he believed Satan was a real entity who had authority over a number of subordinate spirits. See Hugh Watt White, *Demonism Verified and Analyzed* (Shanghai, China: Presbyterian Mission Press, 1922): 112-115.

[69] Agnes Sanford, *Sealed Orders*, 25.

[70] Agnes Sanford, *Sealed Orders*, 27.

[71] Agnes Sanford, *Sealed Orders*, 27.

[72] Agnes Sanford, *Sealed Orders*, 28.

[73] Agnes Sanford, *Sealed Orders*, 28-29.

[74] Agnes Sanford, *Sealed Orders*, 269, 276. The lump disappeared with prayer but later returned after she continued to push herself, and she required surgery and x-ray therapy the second time because it did not respond to prayer; similarly, the cough persisted and only disappeared after four days of rest in an oxygen tent in a hospital.

[75] Agnes Sanford, *Sealed Orders*, 29.

[76] Agnes Sanford, *Sealed Orders*, 30.

[77] Agnes Sanford, *Sealed Orders*, 32.:

[78] Agnes Sanford, *Sealed Orders*, 31-34.

[79] Agnes Sanford, *Sealed Orders*, 44.

[80] Agnes Sanford, *Sealed Orders*, 36.

[81] Agnes Sanford, *Sealed Orders*, 36.

[82] In an article examining several major healing ministries, Henry Knight categorized Agnes' theology as stressing God's faithfulness over His sovereignty; see Henry H. Knight III., "God's Faithfulness and God's Freedom: A Comparison of Contemporary Theologies of Healing," *Journal of Pentecostal Theology* 1, no. 2 (April 2003): 65-89. However, this author does not believe that his interpretation fully recognizes the potential of her theology in this respect; see Martin L. Dignard, "God's Faithful Freedom: Healing as an Outflow of God's Presence," *Journal of Pentecostal Theology* 23, no. 1 (Spring 2014): 68-84.

[83] At the time of her attendance, the school was actually called Peace Institute. See www.peace.edu/about_wpu/history

[84] Agnes Sanford, *Sealed Orders*, 43.

[85] Agnes Sanford, *Sealed Orders*, 43.

[86] Agnes Sanford, *Sealed Orders*, 45.

[87] Agnes Sanford, *Sealed Orders*, 48.

[88] Agnes Sanford, *Sealed Orders*, 53.

[89] Agnes Sanford, *Sealed Orders*, 57.

[90] Agnes Sanford, *Sealed Orders*, 70. Beginning from this incident, the frequency and duration of periods of depression seemed to increase with Agnes until she was eventually healed.

[91] Agnes Sanford, *Sealed Orders*, 73.

[92] Agnes Sanford, *Sealed Orders*, 70-76. Her son Ted was regularly called "Teddy" to differentiate from her husband, and her daughter Virginia was commonly called "Tookie" by both friends and family.

[93] Agnes Sanford, *Sealed Orders*, 73.

[94] Agnes Sanford, *Sealed Orders*, 75, 77.
[95] William De Arteaga, *Agnes Sanford and Her Companions*, 175.
[96] Agnes Sanford, Sealed Orders, 82.
[97] Agnes Sanford, *Sealed Orders*, 83.
[98] Agnes Sanford, *Sealed Orders*, 83-84.
[99] Agnes Sanford, *Sealed Orders*, 84-85.
[100] As will be discussed in a later chapter, Agnes believed that Christians are called to minister to all of creation, including animals, plants, and the earth itself. She also describes prayer having a tangible effect upon the atmosphere within buildings; see Agnes Sanford, *Behold Your God* (Saint Paul: Macalester Park, 1989), p. 161; also Agnes Sanford, *Sealed Orders: Her Autobiography*, p. 84. Leanne Payne, who continued Agnes' ministry, devotes much of a chapter to the spiritual cleansing of buildings; see Leanne Payne, *Restoring the Christian Soul: Overcoming Barriers to Completion in Christ through Healing Prayer* (Grand Rapids: Baker Books, 1997), 163-182.
[101] Agnes Sanford, *Sealed Orders*, 88.
[102] Agnes Sanford, *The Healing Gifts of the Spirit*, 18.
[103] Agnes Sanford, *Sealed Orders*, 93.
[104] Agnes Sanford, *Sealed Orders*, 97. Note: they regularly referred to John as "Jack."
[105] Paul Francis Egan, "The Development of, and Opposition to, Healing Ministries in the Anglican Diocese of Sydney, with Special Reference to the Healing Ministry of St Andrew's Cathedral 1960-2010" (doctoral thesis, Macquarie University, 2012), 19-20.
[106] Paul Egan, "The Development of, and Opposition to, Healing Ministries," 26.
[107] Paul Egan, "The Development of, and Opposition to, Healing Ministries," 26.
[108] Paul Egan, "The Development of, and Opposition to, Healing Ministries," 21.
[109] Paul Egan, "The Development of, and Opposition to, Healing Ministries," 21.
[110] Agnes Sanford, *Sealed Orders*, 98-99; Agnes Sanford, *The Healing Gifts of the Spirit*, 21.
[111] Agnes Sanford, *Sealed Orders*, 99.
[112] Agnes Sanford, *Sealed Orders*, 99.
[113] Agnes Sanford, *Sealed Orders*, 100.
[114] Agnes Sanford, Sealed Orders, 100.
[115] Agnes Sanford, *Sealed Orders*, 102.
[116] Agnes Sanford, *Sealed Orders*, 102.
[117] Agnes Sanford, *Sealed Orders*, 103.
[118] Agnes Sanford, *Sealed Orders*, 106.
[119] Agnes Sanford, *Sealed Orders*, 107.
[120] Agnes Sanford, *Sealed Orders*, 148.
[121] Agnes Sanford, *Sealed Orders*, 149.
[122] Agnes Sanford, *Sealed Orders*, 152-154.
[123] Agnes Sanford, *Sealed Orders*, 114.
[124] Agnes Sanford, *Sealed Orders*, 114.
[125] Agnes Sanford, *Sealed Orders*, 114.
[126] Agnes Sanford, *Sealed Orders*, 115.
[127] Agnes Sanford, *Sealed Orders*, 115.
[128] Agnes Sanford, *Sealed Orders*, 119.
[129] Agnes Sanford, *Sealed Orders*, 120.
[130] Agnes Sanford, *Sealed Orders*, 120-121. See Glenn Clark, Review of *The Healing Light*, by Agnes Sanford, "Healing Marches On." *Sharing* 15 (May 1947):10. Although Clark had written books on healing, he admitted, "For those who would learn how to heal the sick this is the best text ever written."
[131] Agnes Sanford, *Sealed Orders*, 176.

[132] Agnes Sanford, *Sealed Orders*, 182-183; Agnes Sanford, *The Healing Light: On the Art and Method of Spiritual Healing from the Christian Viewpoint and in the Christian Tradition*, 2nd ed. (St. Paul: Macalester Park, 1947), 34-36. Note: Agnes does not identify the soldier's real name in her books; however, he later allowed her to mention his name in public and gave interviews on the healing he experienced through her prayers. See William L. De Arteaga, *Agnes Sanford and Her Companions*, 205ff.

[133] Agnes Sanford, *Sealed Orders*, 195-196.

[134] Agnes Sanford, *Sealed Orders*, 121.

[135] Agnes Sanford, *Sealed Orders*, 141.

[136] Agnes rarely provides dates in her autobiography or other books, making it almost impossible to give a completely accurate timetable of these later events. De Arteaga compares this with books about Corrie Ten Boom. See William L. De Arteaga, *Agnes Sanford and Her Companions*, 184, n. 33.

[137] Agnes Sanford, *Sealed Orders*, 216.

[138] Agnes Sanford, *Sealed Orders*, 217.

[139] Agnes Sanford, *Sealed Orders*, 218.

[140] Agnes does not identify the year when she received this experience of receiving the Holy Spirit, nor does she specify the time when she later received tongues; however, Baltz indicates that this initial infilling took place sometime in the "early 1950s" with her receiving the gift of tongues one year later while De Arteaga identifies this first meeting in Tucson as taking place in 1953; see Francis Baltz, "Agnes Sanford," 39-40; William De Arteaga, *Agnes Sanford and Her Companions*, 222..

[141] Agnes Sanford, *Sealed Orders*, 219.

[142] Agnes Sanford, *Sealed Orders*, 219.

[143] Agnes Sanford, *Sealed Orders*, 225-226; "Interview – Francis & Judith MacNutt," by David Kyle Foster, *Masteringlife.org*, September 1, 2008, http://masteringlife.org/index.php/mastering-life/articles/miscellaneous/item/35-interview-francis-judith-macnutt; note: article no longer available on the website as of March 22, 2018.

[144] Agnes Sanford, *Sealed Orders*, 238, 247.

[145] Francis Baltz, "Agnes Sanford," 49.

[146] Leanne Payne, *Heaven's Calling*, 256.

[147] Leanne Payne, *Heaven's Calling*, 261.

CHAPTER 3

PRINCIPAL INFLUENCES ON HER THEOLOGY

Agnes wrote *The Healing Light* in 1947, and it became a foundational source for the developing Charismatic Movement. However, her theology did not form in a vacuum. Her Presbyterian upbringing instilled in her several orthodox Christian beliefs, based on the *Westminster Confession of Faith* and *The Shorter and Longer Catechisms*. She later joined the Episcopal Church where *The Book of Common Prayer* informed her theology and practice. Before her ministry began, she was impacted through the teachings of Hollis Colwell, an advocate of New Thought, and she eventually accepted many aspects of the Unity School of Christianity while dismissing the radical views of Christian Science, the movement's two largest offshoots. Agnes believed science revealed truths about God, and she often relied on scientific principles in her works, including strongly promoting the scientific method in her first book, *The Healing Light*. She also incorporated specific aspects of Jungian Psychology into her anthropology. However, she consistently rejected Spiritist and Occultic approaches. An examination of her works along with secondary sources will reveal the philosophies, theologies, and ideologies that influenced her worldview.

The Presbyterian Church

Agnes grew up on a Presbyterian mission field in China. Her parents taught her the denomination's official teachings, which stemmed from Calvin's *Institutes of the Christian Religion*. Those teachings framed their theology, doctrines, and practices. As members of the Southern Presbyterian Church in the United States, they held a strongly Fundamentalist interpretation of their founding documents: *The Westminster Confession of Faith* and *The Larger and Shorter Catechisms*.[1] Agnes studied the *Shorter Catechism* as a child until she became proficient in its teachings, which informed her understanding of Christian orthodoxy. The Presbyterian doctrines of the supremacy of Scripture, the divinity of Christ, and the cessation of the *charismata* especially affected her theology.

The Presbyterian Church of the United States viewed Scripture as final authority for doctrine and practice. According to the *Westminster Confession of Faith*, "The whole counsel of God concerning all things necessary for His own glory, man's salvation, faith and life, is either expressly set down in Scripture, or by good and necessary consequence may be deduced from Scripture."[2] In essence, the Bible provides everything necessary for life and faith. Similarly, the *Shorter Catechism* declares, "the Scriptures principally teach, what man is to believe concerning God, and what duty God requires of man."[3] The Bible, specified as the 66 books of the Protestant canon, identifies everything appropriate for theology and practice. More than a third of the *Shorter Catechism* (and a quarter of the *Larger Catechism*) describes the meaning and application of the Ten Commandments as the foundation for morality and ethics.[4] Both the *Westminster Confession of Faith* and the *Shorter and Longer Catechisms* promote Scripture for evaluating theology and practice.

Agnes relied upon Scripture for evaluating truth in her ministry. When she first began to learn about healing, she used the Bible as her primary guide: "So with the Bible as my textbook, I set myself to learn these ways."[5] If she could not find some type of scriptural support for a claim she read, heard, or saw, she would dismiss it or put it aside for later consideration. Agnes stressed different parts of the Bible at different points in her ministry. When she first sought to understand how faith related to healing, she relied exclusively on the words of Jesus in the Gospels; however, when she began to evaluate various approaches to healing prayer, she used the Ten Commandments as a litmus test.[6] Her choices reflect her early Presbyterian education. She clearly relied on many of the basics of the *Shorter Catechism* to identify the best vehicle for judging spiritual practices and theological truth.

On at least one occasion, Agnes's Presbyterian upbringing prevented her from accepting teachings contrary to Christian orthodoxy. The Apostle's and Nicene Creeds clearly identify redemption as provided only through Jesus Christ, the only-begotten Son of God, of One essence with the Father, incarnate of a virgin; both *The Westminster Confession of Faith* and *The Shorter Catechism* affirm this position as indispensable for the Christian faith.[7] The early creeds clarified this doctrine in reaction to early Gnostic teachings, some of which found their way into New Thought philosophy. As Agnes began studying some concepts in New Thought, she briefly considered Adoptionism, the belief Jesus was only a man who received the Christ Spirit at baptism. She writes,

> There was a time when I tried to believe thus: that He was one of the Great Masters, not a unique Being divinely conceived and miraculously born. But a sadness would come upon me as I thought thus, and at times I would feel like Mary at the tomb: "They have taken away the Lord."[8]

She explains that her prayer power was dimmed until she reaffirmed the orthodox perspective on the divinity and redemptive role of Christ. She admits some people may see results without believing in the incarnation and the virgin birth, but they eventually recognize something is missing: "They are believing only one-third of those Christian mysteries that they need to believe in order that the signs may follow (Mark 16:17-18)."[9] She felt a loss of both peace and joy while she considered adoptionism, and the feeling remained until she rejected the erroneous doctrine.

In her autobiography, Agnes repeatedly associates cessationism with her own disillusionment toward Christianity. She did not understand how Scripture could be read literally in every way except when it came to miracles. Recalling the missionary woman in China who committed suicide, Agnes wondered if she could have prayed for her:

> Perhaps the reader is thinking, "Well, of course!" But in those days it was not, "Of course." We were fundamentalists. That meant that we believed implicitly in every word in the Bible, yet we did not believe in healing through prayer. We were supposed to obey Jesus in every word that He said. Yet when He said, "The works that I do shall ye do also," we didn't obey Him, and indeed considered it a heresy that anyone should try to do His works. I do not blame these good people, including my parents, for this strange contradiction, for so they had been taught. The real heresy had taken place centuries ago.[10]

Combatting cessationism became a driving force for Agnes in her healing ministry, and she devoted her life to returning a belief in the miraculous to the mainline denominations.

The Presbyterian Church of the early twentieth century affirmed cessationism. Benjamin Breckenridge Warfield, professor of Didactic and Polemical Theology at Princeton Seminary and chief editor of the *Presbyterian and Reformed Review* journal, published *Counterfeit Miracles* as a polemic for cessationism and against Pentecostalism. According to De Arteaga, the text "to this day is still used by many cessationists as a prime resource."[11] Other scholars also recognize Warfield as a major contributor to and proponent for this doctrine. Jon Ruthven states,

> The cessationist doctrine found its classic expression in post-reformation era Calvinism.... The doctrine that revelatory and miraculous spiritual gifts passed away with the apostolic age may best be approached by examining the central premises of the most prominent and representative modern expression of cessationism, Benjamin B. Warfield's *Counterfeit Miracles*.[12]

The very first chapter of Warfield's book is titled "The Cessation of the Charismata." Concerning the use of the gifts of the Spirit, Warfield says, "It was the characterizing peculiarity of specifically the Apostolic Church, and it belonged therefore exclusively to the Apostolic age," and "[the gifts] were part of the credentials of the Apostles as the authoritative agents of God in founding the church. Their function thus confined them to be distinctively the Apostolic

Church, and they necessarily passed away with it."[13] Although *The Westminster Confession of Faith* does not specifically mention the cessation of the gifts, it had become a recognized Presbyterian doctrine.

As a child on the mission field, Agnes was taught the theology of the Presbyterian Church. Their positions on the supremacy of Scripture and the divinity and redemptive work of Christ undergirded her later theology and ministry. However, the denomination had also promoted cessationism, which she initially accepted as true. Even when she became an Episcopalian, she did not reconsider the validity of that doctrine. However, when her youngest son was healed of his recurring ear infection through prayer, she realized not only that miracles had not ceased but also that not every denominational doctrine was correct. She began to study the Bible to identify errors in her theology and developed a habit of evaluating teachings according to Scripture instead of accepting or rejecting whatever a group or a person taught. In this instance, both truth and error in Presbyterian theology led her to discover correct aspects of Christian orthodoxy.

The Episcopal Church

Agnes became Episcopalian when she married Edgar (Ted) Sanford, who not only taught at the Episcopal boys school in China but was a priest in the same denomination. The Episcopal Church originated as the United States branch of the worldwide Anglican Communion. It became a separate entity in 1789, shortly after the American Revolution, in reaction to a requirement within the Church of England for all clergy to swear allegiance to the king of England.[14] Until the late twentieth century, the denomination maintained a conservative position on the interpretation of Scripture and the operation of its founding document, *The Book of Common Prayer*. Although both the Episcopal and Presbyterian Churches originating from the Church of England resulted in numerous similarities in their catechisms, they differ in a few significant doctrines and practices. The liturgy and sacramental theology of the Episcopal Church—especially in relation to the confession of sin, the Lord's Supper, and the laying on of hands—directly influenced Agnes's theology and the prayer model commonly used in her ministry.

Unlike many Protestant denominations, the Episcopal Church believes sacraments mediate God's power to believers. According to the denomination's Articles of Religion,

> Sacraments ordained of Christ be not only badges or tokens of Christian men's profession, but rather they be certain sure witnesses, and effectual signs of grace, and God's good will towards us, by the which he doth work invisibly in us, and doth not only quicken, but also strengthen and confirm our Faith in him.[15]

The words *effectual*, *work*, and *quicken* in their eighteenth-century definition confirms an understanding beyond a memorial or commemorative act. According to their Catechism, "The sacraments are outward and visible signs of inward and spiritual grace, given by Christ as sure and certain means by which we receive that grace."[16] Although described initially as signs, the remainder of the definition indicates sacraments should be viewed as vehicles through which God's grace is received by the participant. The described results of the sacraments suggest "grace" imparts supernatural power to the recipients.

In most Protestant churches, forgiveness does not require confession of sins to another person. For instance, in the *Westminster Confession*, "every man is bound to make private confession of his sins to God, praying for the pardon thereof," and any public confession is normally "to those that are offended."[17] However, in addition to Baptism and the Lord's Supper, the Catechism of the Episcopal Church affirms five other sacraments, including Reconciliation, "the rite in which those who repent of their sins may confess them to God in the presence of a priest, and receive the assurance of pardon and the grace of absolution" while the duty of the priest was to "declare pardon in the name of God."[18] Although confession before a priest is not required, it is recommended when confessing to God alone fails to bring sufficient peace or awareness of forgiveness.

The Episcopal Church views the Eucharist as more than a commemoration or memorial service. According to the Articles of Religion for the denomination, the Lord's Supper involves "partaking of the Body of Christ ... [and] the Blood of Christ."[19] The full definition denies any change in the actual substance of the bread and the wine, which excludes transubstantiation as an interpretation. The Catechism associates clear benefits for those participating in the sacrament: "The benefits we receive are the forgiveness of our sins, the strengthening of our union with Christ and one another, and the foretaste of the heavenly banquet which is our nourishment in eternal life."[20] Just as confession of sins to a priest provided a mediated grace for forgiveness, participation in the Eucharist mediated the forgiveness of sins, the presence of the Lord, and strength for a life of faith.

Similar to the Presbyterian Church, the Episcopal Church recognizes two major sacraments as being specifically commanded by Jesus in the gospels: Baptism and The Lord's Supper. However, the Episcopal denomination also describes five additional minor sacraments. Of the minor sacraments, three specifically incorporate the laying on of hands: Ordination, Confirmation, and Unction for the sick. In all three cases, the laying on of hands provided for the impartation and empowerment of the Holy Spirit. Ordination and Confirmation referenced the baptism of the Holy Spirit while Unction for the sick intended to provide both forgiveness and physical healing to those in need.

The Catechism defines Ordination as "the rite in which God gives authority and the grace of the Holy Spirit to those being made bishops, priests, and deacons, through prayer and the laying on of hands by bishops."[21] This sacrament was intended to include an impartation of and empowerment by the Holy Spirit. In the Ordination service for a priest, the bishop recites a prayer referencing Pentecost as the time Christ "poured his gifts abundantly upon [His] people," lays hands on the person, and prays that God will "give [His] Holy Spirit . . . with grace and power" to the person.[22] In the context of the service, the sacrament intimates the baptism of the Holy Spirit and the receiving of the charismatic gifts for the purpose of ministering to the people.

Confirmation likewise incorporates the laying on of hands in order to impart the presence and power of the Holy Spirit to a believer. According to their Catechism, it is "the rite in which we express a mature commitment to Christ, and receive strength from the Holy Spirit through prayer and the laying on of hands by a bishop."[23] The "strength from the Holy Spirit" includes supernatural empowerment. The Confirmation service repeatedly references itself as a fulfillment of the Baptismal Covenant, including a prayer for God to "fill them with [His] holy and life-giving Spirit."[24] The service itself describes an impartation of power. In the actual service, the bishop prays for God to "send them forth in the power of that Spirit" and lays hands upon each believer, asking God to "strengthen [the individual] with your Holy Spirit [and] empower [the person] for service."[25] The Baptismal and Confirmation sacraments describe a two-step process in which believers receive the Holy Spirit and are empowered. Although neither service mentions the word "gifts," they describe the person receiving power for service.

The sacrament of Unction for the sick involves elders in the church laying hands on people to impart forgiveness and physical healing. The Catechism for the Episcopal Church defines the rite as "anointing the sick with oil, or the laying on of hands, by which God's grace is given for the healing of spirit, mind, and body."[26] Although laying hands on the person appears optional in the definition, it forms an expected part of the entire healing service. After reading several scripture passages about healing, including James 5:14-16, the priest lays hands on the sick person, praying "to drive away all sickness of body and spirit" and "restore [the person] to wholeness and strength"; when the rite includes anointing the person, the priest first prays over the oil, praying that God will "Send [His] Holy Spirit to sanctify this oil; that, as your holy apostles anointed many that were sick and healed them, so may those who in faith and repentance receive this holy unction be made whole."[27] The healing service may also include Holy Communion.

Agnes understood confession as a sacrament of healing, and she herself received healing through it. After years of ministry, she felt empty and emotionally drained. A friend told her "the confessional is the church's way of passing on power," and after she tried it, she called it "the most effective way I have found so far," describing a sense of power flooding her and feeling "for the first time that Jesus loved me. Something touched my heart. A stream of tenderness was released within me. And I knew that this was the forgiveness of Jesus Christ— His life, given for me."[28] She learned that confession could not only bring forgiveness for sins committed by the person but also minister healing to sins committed against the person by others. In her book on depression, she explains,

> The truth is that any wound to the soul so deep that it is not healed by our own self-searching and prayers is inevitably connected with a subconscious awareness of sin, either our own sins or our grievous reactions to the sins of others. The therapy that heals these deep wounds could be called the forgiveness of sins or it could be called the healing of the memories. Whatever one calls it, there are in many of us wounds so deep that only the mediation of someone else to whom we may "bare our grief" can heal us. . . . And the act of going to him for help was called the Confessional or the Sacrament of Penance.[29]

The concept that people could mediate healing power to others became a core aspect of Agnes's healing model, and she believed confession of sin—including not only those actions committed against others but also the person's own harmful, negative, or unloving reactions to offenses committed by others—was a significant vehicle of healing.

Agnes fully recognized a supernatural healing power in Communion, above and beyond forgiveness of sin. In her autobiography, she describes kneeling at the altar to receive the bread and wine, a common manner in the Episcopal Church, when God told her to get prayer from Hollis Colwell; however, she links this to a possible act of faith by another person in church, releasing power into the sacrament: "Maybe someone there had made a special effort to forgive and thus prepare the soul for the receiving of the life of Christ through the Communion."[30] Agnes did not make this statement lightly, for she taught people to see the Lord's Supper as a source of healing. She laments a time when the Church forgot the power in the sacraments: "There came an age so dark that even the last resort of the sick, the sacrament of Holy Communion, was looked upon as a forerunner of death . . . never dreaming that it would restore them to life."[31] She considered the Communion elements of bread and wine as sacraments of healing.

Agnes considered the Communion service one of three sacraments especially effective for receiving healing. She writes, "The sacraments, especially baptism, confirmation and the Holy Communion—let us consider them as channels of healing."[32] However, she also understood The Lord's Supper as a way to minister healing to others by partaking of the elements in an intercessory fashion. Agnes mentions using the Communion service as part of intercessory healing prayer in *The Healing Light* but describes it more fully in her first novel, *The Lost Shepherd*.[33] However, the approach advocated in the novel dangerously approaches substitution, carrying the burdens of others over an extended period of time. Over time, she found it less harmful and more effective to dedicate her involvement in the service to the person's healing. She recalls, "we prayed for healing for certain individuals, often sharing our projects beforehand and sometimes making them our special intention for the Communion and receiving for them with prayer and fasting. . . . And it worked."[34] The sacrament of Communion could not only provide healing and forgiveness for the person taking the elements but also become a vehicle for ministering healing to others who were not present at the service.

The laying on of hands for the impartation of the Holy Spirit became a component of Agnes's ministry. Although she and Ted did not ordain ministers, she believed in the intention of the Ordination and Confirmation services. When Francis MacNutt attended his first CFO meeting and received prayer for the baptism of the Holy Spirit, he felt disappointed, having "no interior experience of the Spirit" from the prayer; he recalls,

> I felt awful about it. Later that day, Agnes Sanford came up and asked me what my experience had been. So I explained my confusion. She said, "Well, I did not want to say anything to detour you, but I felt the way they would probably pray, as if you didn't have the Spirit already, was probably not right. I could see in your face and everything you already had the Spirit, and I felt that the way they should've prayed was that the Spirit that was in you through baptism, ordination, and confirmation be released." So the next evening, she prayed with me, and I was filled with overwhelming joy and laughter.[35]

Her statement reflects her own experience of receiving the empowerment of the Holy Spirit when she prayed with two women in Tucson with the laying on of hands.

The first time Agnes attended a Confirmation service after her own experience, she connected the rite to the intention. She explains, "Some months later . . . I attended a confirmation service. And for the first time, I saw what it was! 'Why, the bishop is doing what we three people did in the desert!' I thought with unbounded surprise. 'He's praying for the Holy Spirit!'"[36] She recognized that an impartation of power was meant to follow prayer with the laying on of hands—when accompanied with faith and expectation. This practice became part of the closing services for the Schools of Pastoral Care:

> Two or three leaders lay hands on everyone who comes to the altar rail and pray that the gifts and power of the Spirit, already implanted in him through his ordination, will increase within him and set him on fire with holy love and power.[37]

She believed a person could receive the Spirit and power through the laying on of hands.

Agnes certainly promoted the laying on of hands for healing. Through her first book on healing, *The Healing Light*, she repeatedly relates incidents of healing through the laying on of hands. At one point, describing ways to receive healing, she writes,

> The most powerful healing method of all, we have not yet tried: the method of healing by the faith of someone else who acts as a receiving and transmitting center for the life of God. This is the oldest of all methods of healing, and it is the simplest. It is the method Jesus used, and that He taught His disciples to use. . . . Jesus in His loving kindness lent God not only His spirit and His mind but also His body. . . . And He gave His followers a training course in this type of healing and sent them out on missions to preach and to teach and to lay their

hands upon the sick and heal them.[38]

Agnes describes the importance and use of laying hands on the sick for healing not only in this passage but throughout the rest of the chapter. When she first sought to learn about healing, she "studied the four Gospels and did exactly what Our Lord commanded."[39] A significant number of healings in the Gospels involve physical touch, so her emphasizing the practice of laying hands on the sick for healing is not surprising.

The sacramental theology of the Episcopal Church directly affected Agnes's ministry. From an early age, she had an active imagination, seeing God's power in nature, so she could easily imagine the power of God channeled through the sacraments. Confession and the Lord's Supper became significant vehicles for forgiveness and healing. The belief that Baptism could bring an impartation of the Holy Spirit logically extended from her childhood Presbyterian catechism, which taught that baptism incorporated an infant into the Christian Church. Confirmation and Ordination completed the work of Baptism and brought empowerment through the Spirit. The sacrament of Unction simply reflected the examples she found in the Gospels. The Episcopal Church profoundly affected Agnes's ministry and theology.

New Thought, Unity Christianity, and Christian Science

New Thought is a metaphysical ideology that elevates mind and thought to the level of divinity and ultimate reality. Although New Thought rejects many fundamental premises of the Christian orthodox faith, it extensively uses the Bible, reinterpreted in alternative ways, and describes Jesus as the perfect example of an enlightened human being. Christian Science and The Unity School of Christianity, also called Unity Christianity or Unity, both developed out of New Thought. During the early years of the twentieth century, both New Thought and Unity Christianity influenced many leaders in Christian healing ministries, including Agnes.

New Thought ideologies began long before the early twentieth century. In *New Thought, Ancient Wisdom*, Glenn Mosley traces the preliminary foundations of New Thought to the early seventeenth century although Phineas P. Quimby is considered the actual founder.[40] He incorporated prior works and concepts into an actual movement. Mary Baker Eddy, the founder of Christian Science, had a significant health recovery under Quimby's direct care and became his student; Eddy later denied his influence, but both her terminology and concepts reflect his teachings.[41] Unity Christianity developed independent of the Christian Science movement. Unity was founded at the end of the nineteenth century by Charles and Myrtle Fillmore as New Thought's "most prominent group."[42] Although Christian Science and Unity Christianity have no direct affiliation to each other, both can be traced directly to the teachings and ideology of New Thought.

Unity Christianity incorporated numerous New Thought terms and concepts into a Christian framework, providing new meanings and rejecting several conventional and historical doctrines. According to both Raymond Cunningham and Joseph Williams, many early Pentecostals and Christians interested in healing accepted New Thought concepts on healing while simultaneously rejecting Christian Science because the former neither rejected the existence of a material world nor required commitment to a specific church as the latter did.[43] In other words, Unity made New Thought teachings more palatable to believers while Christian Science became anathema. Because of this distinction, almost all metaphysical approaches to healing in the early twentieth century were identified under the New Thought label—except Christian Science.[44] Although Unity Christianity held questionable concepts, Eddy's approach was largely considered too extreme.

As the name suggests, New Thought focuses heavily upon a person's thoughts. Williams explains that God is described as the "Divine Mind" and "Infinite Intelligence," controlling and shaping reality.[45] Defining God in terms of thought became popular with groups stressing the healing power of the mind. Along with other metaphysical types of healing, New Thought

> (1) deemphasized personal conceptions of the divine; (2) stressed the correspondence between supernatural and natural realms governed by discernible laws, collapsing stark distinctions between the two; and (3) by extension underscored the manipulative ability of spiritual power by adepts for personal—and often quite tangible—ends (such as healing).[46]

In other words, New Thought does not reject the idea of "God" as much as redefines God as an impersonal force and associates that force with the mind.

New Thought also incorporates psychological terms and concepts. In his book on E. W. Kenyon, Dale Simmons describes New Thought in largely psychological terms. According to this movement, each person has a spirit—often described in terms of the subconscious—connected to the universe, and perfection comes by freeing oneself of the limitations of self.[47] Reminiscent of Rene Descartes, the proponents of the ideology often equate the "self" to the person's mind and thoughts. As well as everyone having a "universal spirit," each person also has two minds:

> New Thought discovered what it refers to as the subjective (subconscious) and the objective (conscious) mind. The objective mind is able to reason inductively and thus draws conclusions on the basis of the massing of evidence that may then be put to the test of experimental proof. The subjective mind, on the other hand, can only reason deductively, as indicated by the fact that it accepts uncritically whatever suggestion may be impressed upon it, and it works out in great fidelity whatever may logically follow from the suggestion. It is the storehouse of all past experiences. . . . Because the subjective mind is so undiscriminating,

and since all of the *thoughts* that reside there will ultimately become *things*, it is up to the objective mind to act as guardian gatekeeper.[48]

Using the objective mind to join with the universal spirit was necessary because thoughts of the subjective mind would eventually affect a person's physical reality.

Mosley explains that the Unity School was founded by Charles Fillmore upon the idea that "it was possible for all men and women to achieve the same level of consciousness attained by Jesus."[49] Instead of considering Jesus as God incarnate, God became incarnate in Jesus through his mind. Both New thought and Unity Christianity distinguish between Jesus the historical human being and the Christ. He became Jesus the Christ by learning to transcend his ordinary human consciousness, which He did by understanding the principles of Divine Mind:

> The only difference between you and Jesus is that He had absolute faith that the Father principle would respond to His word . . . those who hold this Jesus Christ ideal constantly before them, and affirm both silently and audibly that what He manifested can be manifested by all, thereby become themselves the Helper.[50]

New Thought here exceeds adoptionism, suggesting people can become equal not only to Jesus but perhaps even the Holy Spirit through faith and knowledge. Mosley, defining prayer as silent thoughts and audible confessions, states, "Prayer *is* the vehicle for identifying with Infinite Mind," a common name in both Unity and New Thought for God.[51] Therefore, prayer becomes the act of using thoughts and words to shape reality by tapping into cosmic forces.

Unity affirmed good in all religious belief systems, similar to New Thought, yet its proponents strongly promoted the Bible for containing truth. However, the truth they found in Scripture vastly differs from the teachings commonly accepted by the orthodox Christian Church; instead, they referenced precepts they consider to be hidden within biblical verses. Mosley describes the truly enlightened as those who "had grown beyond the creeds, doctrines, and dogmas of denominationalism" and had identified the laws that could shape reality.[52] Unity considers Jesus the primary example of a human being who understood these truths and transcended natural limitations. His teachings remain the primary focus of meditation and personal revelation, recognizing that "not all of the Bible can be accepted literally and that it must be interpreted practically and inspirationally."[53] For example, in relation to Jesus telling the disciples they would receive when they pray in faith and believe, "Unity placed special emphasis on the word *believe*. A person needs to conceive him- or herself to be the expression or *pressing out* of God; the student was instructed to believe with the man, Jesus, 'I and my Father are one.'" [Italics are from the original source].[54] The obvious meanings of many of Jesus' statements were ignored in favor of nuanced meanings of the individual words, the thoughts they entailed, and the act of speaking the words correctly.

The compilation *New Thought Classics* by Emma Curtis Hopkins and Thomas Troward contains more examples of statements by Jesus, reinterpreted according to New Thought. In His dialogue with the rich young ruler, Jesus says, "Why do you call Me good? No one is good except God alone" (Mark 10:18, NASB). Hopkins provides a very esoteric interpretation of this passage. She explains, "The first name of God is Good, and the first name of the Good is God. . . . [therefore] The Good I am seeking is my God."[55] Of course, Christian orthodoxy rejects equating "God is Good" with "Good is God" as New Thought does. Nevertheless, Hopkins explains that whatever the person identifies as the Good they are seeking is the person's God.

In another example of New Thought wisdom, Hopkins analyzes the common use of the words "Omnipresent" or "Omnipotent" for God. She points out that "OM" was a name for God used in meditation by ancient peoples of Asia, and the syllable "Ni" is located between "God" and the Present (OM-Ni-Present) reality of a person's Potential (OM-Ni-Potent), so understanding what "Ni" means will help people recognize what prevents God (i.e., their Good) from their Present reality; she then states that "Ni" stands for "nothing" in Latin, which indicates that "nothing" separates people from their Good in their Present reality.[56] In her discussion, she explains that people must identify the "nothing" in their life, but the commonest meanings are doubt—a faith in nothing—and incorrect or missing confessions—a doing of nothing. New Thought thus often elevates specific words far above their original or obvious meanings.

Although Christians rejected many of the metaphysical premises of New Thought, several core ideologies and concepts found noticeable approval. In *Spirit Cure*, Joseph Williams points out that New Thought had a noticeable effect on many Pentecostals during the early years of the Pentecostal movement, especially in relation to healing. He writes, "Pentecostal healing increasingly converged with a powerful current in U.S. religion rooted in the late-nineteenth-century New Thought tradition . . . [when] believers were thrilled to learn that they could speak positive realities into existence, provided that their desires matched the desires of God."[57] Many early Pentecostals, like their forefathers in the nineteenth century Divine Healing Movement, denounced orthodox physicians, medicine, and medical treatment. Some went so far as describing physicians as servants of the devil.[58] However, they did not always reject natural approaches to health, such as nutrition, homeopathy, and herbal remedies. Williams explains that although many Pentecostals denounced healing through the mind along with psychology and medical care, they incorporated many aspects of New Thought into their healing practices and theology.[59] Nevertheless, they quickly ruled out beliefs they considered inconsistent with major Christian orthodoxy and doctrines.

In summary, most early Pentecostals rejected New Thought's description of God as a cosmic "Divine Mind," holding His Personhood inviolate. They believed Jesus reflected the perfect example of how a person should live, but they knew He was God from beginning to end; they found the concept of Him being a man who attained to Christ-hood through enlightenment anathema. Still, many Christians incorporated other parts of New Thought into their healing theology. Believing God created the universe according to specific spiritual laws perfectly fit with a God who spoke the world into existence and provided humanity with laws for their good. Believers accepted that some laws could be so comprehensive that even scientists and believers of other religions might discover them. The belief that people's thoughts and words affected their life had enough biblical verses for support to be accepted by many believers. Many Christians disliked the idea of a conscious and subconscious mind, being wary of psychology, but they recognized times when conscious beliefs differed from internal feelings, making the concept of different levels of thought and awareness seem valid. Therefore, certain aspects of New Thought and Unity Christianity were readily accepted into an orthodox Christian worldview.

Agnes incorporated many metaphysical beliefs into her paradigm. She admits, "Most people think that one cannot be both a metaphysician and a sacramentalist. But I have found that one can, and that knowing both methods gives a widely varying approach to different minds.... I have learned to combine the sacramental with the metaphysical approach."[60] However, many Christians objected to metaphysical concepts, and in later editions of her book, the first two sentences of the above quote are omitted, and the word "meditative" replaces the word "metaphysical" in the last sentence. Still, Williams describes a "growing acceptance of metaphysical-style forms of healing" in these groups:

> In mimicking metaphysical models, many of the faithful blurred the boundaries separating natural and supernatural healing in ways that freed them to draw confidently on the healing insights of modern science without relinquishing their vision of the world as drenched in the presence of the Spirit.... [displaying an] ever-increasing willingness over the course of the twentieth and early twenty-first centuries to borrow and appropriate rival metaphysical practices.[61]

The metaphysical ideas accepted by Agnes differ from many common interpretations. In the introduction to *The Healing Light*, Glenn Clark exclaims, "Never have I met one who combined the metaphysical and the sacramental approach as she does. I have never met anyone more Christ-centered nor anyone more church-centered."[62] De Arteaga takes care to differentiate the term's original meaning from its current usage. He explains,

> This jars the contemporary Christian reader, as the term "metaphysical" now connotes New Age, tarot cards, crystals, etc. We must understand that what Agnes meant as "metaphysical" was New Thought, Unity Christianity, and Prof. Clark's Christian New Perspective.[63]

Although she affirmed numerous metaphysical concepts into her healing model and theology, she rejected aspects that clearly disagreed with Christian orthodox teachings.

New Thought obviously influenced Agnes, for she makes several statements to that effect. Her first major introduction to healing occurred when Hollis Colwell prayed for her son's ears. Describing the incident, she writes,

> He did not argue, preach, or in any way try to convince me of the reality of spiritual healing. If he had done so, I would have stiffened in my refusal, for I was not prepared to hear this iconoclastic "new thought."[64]

She put "new thought" in quotation marks, indicating a term synonymous with the name of the movement. She also speaks positively of at least one New Thought text. While referencing the period in her life when she was first learning about healing, she says,

> Then someone gave me a copy of Emmett Fox's *The Sermon on the Mount*, and although the language of this book was not that to which I was accustomed, speaking of "treating" and "demonstrating" when I would have said "praying" and "receiving answers to prayer," still it thrilled my soul because it made clear to me the reality of the spiritual body that interpenetrates the physical body, and of the spiritual world in which we really live.[65]

At the time she desired to understand how healing took place, Fox's book offered some of the answers through an analysis of the primary collection of Jesus's teachings. She also mentions *What Seek Ye?* by H. B. Jeffrey but does not indicate any personal opinion about the book.[66] Both Fox and Jeffrey are recognized New Thought authors.

As well as referencing New Thought in her works, she incorporates some of its terms and concepts. New Thought regularly impersonalizes God as a force, energy, or law—usually related to enlightened thoughts—and capitalizes words to associate a term with divinity. Although Agnes describes the Trinity not only as living and active Persons but also as personal and relational in nature, she occasionally capitalizes impersonal terms when referencing God, his actions, or certain aspects of his nature. For example, while discussing God's transcendence and immanence, she capitalizes several words:

> God is both within us and without us. He is the Source of all life; the Creator of universe behind universe; and of unimaginable depths of inter-stellar space and of light-years without end. But He is also the indwelling life of our own little selves.... "The Kingdom of God is within you," said Jesus. And it is the Indwelling Light, the secret Place of the Consciousness of the Most High that is the Kingdom of Heaven in its present manifestation on this earth. Learning to live in the Kingdom of Heaven is learning to turn on the light of God within.[67]

She also uses capitalized terms to describe the power and indwelling presence of the Holy Spirit, especially in relation to his working in the body, in the mind, and in nature. For example, concerning Paul's reference to Christians as "children of light," she writes,

> Scientists have discovered that the body is not hard, solid matter, but is made up of specks of energy.... We are therefore made not of solid and impenetrable matter, but of energy. The very chemicals contained in the body—the "dust of the earth"—live by the Breath of God, by the primal Energy, the original force that we call God.[68]

Later editions of *The Healing Light* removed capitalization from most of the impersonal terms for God, but the terminology remains. Early editions clearly reflect New Thought.

Agnes regularly makes statements reflective of New Thought influence. While describing his will, she writes, "God does nothing except by law. But He has provided enough electricity within His laws to do anything that is in accordance with His will. His will includes unlimited miracles."[69] She uses the term "electricity" as a metaphor for an invisible but present power. However, her use of metaphysical terminology becomes very apparent in her chapter on love and the need to quickly forgive others. She warns,

> Danger lurks in every form of energy. The flow of energy that we call the law of love is the rhythm for which our beings were created, the thought-vibrations in which we live and move and have our being. Every thought of anger, therefore, throws a contrary and destructive counter-vibration in to the body, and places us in danger. "Whosoever is angry with his brother—shall be in danger of the judgment." This judgment begins immediately.[70]

Both orthodox Christian doctrine and science affirms the destructive results of holding onto anger and bitterness; however, her explanation entails extremely unusual language reminiscent of New Thought, and her description would likely appeal to the portion of her audience that embraced metaphysics or avoided common Christian descriptions. In other words, her unusual wording may have appealed to her audience.

Agnes also had positive interactions with Unity Christianity, the Christianized version of New Thought. Comparing and contrasting Unity with some Christian groups that promote and practice isolation from contemporary society, she explains,

> They reach a high state of religious contemplation and there they stay. But their prayers for healing are less effective than the prayers of Unity and other modern schools of prayer, because they have not learned how to project the power of God into the being of man.[71]

In a chapter relating the importance of interacting with people, she lists Unity as more practical than some Christian movements. In an article she wrote for the *Weekly Unity* publication, she begins, "Long ago, I learned from Unity to claim by faith the life of God within me."[72] Considering Agnes only wrote two articles for magazine publications, the content of this affirmation reflects the influence Unity had on her ministry and theology.

Similar to New Thought, Agnes strongly promoted the idea of a conscious and subconscious mind. In the chapter titled "The Re-Birth of Faith: Re-Educating the Sub-Conscious," she describes the subconscious as the controlling force in a person's life:

> If the conscious mind were the only sentient force within us, the prayer outlined in the preceding chapter would probably be enough to make us well. But the part of us that reasons is only one-tenth of the consciousness. Psychologists tell us that nine-tenths of our thoughts lie below the level of consciousness. Moreover, it is this submerged part of the consciousness—this sub-conscious mind—that controls our bodies. A moment's thought shows us that this is true. In order to breathe, we do not have to think, "Now breathe in—now breathe out—now breathe in—now breathe out." The breathing is regulated by an inner control center. This inner control center is part of the spiritual body, the eternal Being. It acts under orders from God Himself until man sends into it a contrary command and throws it into confusion.[73]

This concept stems almost directly from New Thought, viewing the subconscious as the "subjective" mind, controlling the person's life. Agnes also associates the subconscious with faith. When discussing healing prayer and faith, she repeatedly describes faith as a subconscious confidence in God, connecting with God and enabling the person to receive from Him: "We must re-educate the sub-conscious mind, replacing every thought of fear with a thought of faith, every thought of illness with a thought of health, every thought of death with a thought of life. In other words, we must learn faith."[74] In other words, someone's conscious declarations of faith operated according to what the person believed subconsciously, similar to current analogies of believing with the heart and with the head.

Although Agnes incorporated terms and concepts from New Thought and Unity Christianity into her works, she evaluated those ideas according to orthodox Christian theology and biblical exegesis. Even though *The Sermon on the Mount* by Fox answered many of her questions, she did not accept everything, "setting aside a few ideas as being untenable according to my beliefs."[75] As noted, her orthodox Christian background prompted her to reject adoptionism, Spiritism, and the works of Middle Eastern masters as untenable with Christianity. Similarly, when Hollis Colwell had equated healing with a healthy diet, she dismissed his conclusion as incorrect.[76] This reflects her commitment to examine everything for potential good while using discernment to reject things that are contrary to what she believed to be orthodox. She was influenced by New Thought and Unity Christianity along with some early Pentecostal thoughts of the time, always maintaining an orthodox Christian faith.

As expected, Agnes knew about Christian Science. However, she did not accept or promote its more extreme teachings. She mentions the movement once in a relatively short paragraph concerning her attempt to read *Science and Health* by Eddy. She writes, "I tried to read it, but to me it did not make sense. It did not speak to my condition. Not that I scorn Christian Scientists. I am grateful to them, for at a time when the church had totally forgotten or denied healing, they dared to believe in it."[77] Her relatively neutral and factual comment reflects an attempt to resist disparaging a group actively promoting healing without necessarily affirming its theology. According to De Arteaga, Agnes considered them similar to non-Christians, who could still effectively pray for healing:

> Christian Scientists practitioners did indeed minister many healings, and still do today. It may bother some Christians that heretics have any spiritual power, but heresy does not negate faith expectance that God will act for the good. . . . Agnes Sanford understood this from a personal experience. In her life she had transited from Presbyterian cessationism to New Thought and finally into Pentecostalism. She reflected on her early friends in New Thought and Christian Science and believed that the reason they healed effectively was that many of them were *faith-filled monotheists* [emphasis his]. That is, that although many Christian Scientists were indeed not Christian, they did believe in one God who would answer prayer.[78]

Several times in her works, she describes instances when people became Christians either after experiencing healing through her prayer or after seeing God heal others through their own prayers. Believing God would even respond to the prayers of unbelievers became an aspect of her theology.

Although Agnes affirmed the belief in healing taught by Christian Science, she disavowed at least two major tenets of the movement: the rejection of medical care and the denial of the reality of sickness. Concerning medical care, she explains, "Nor do I see any need for refusing to cooperate with God by availing myself of any physical aids toward health that I know: rest, exercise, proper diet, and if necessary, medicine. Medicine stimulates the bodily forces, inspiring them to do the work that God made them to do. . . . Being sick, therefore, I gladly call for my best friend and advisor, the doctor."[79] She did not consider it inconsistent for God to use physical means for healing when prayer alone did not suffice. Additionally, while describing healing for a bronchial cold she caught at one time, she writes, "It would have been impossible for me to say, 'There is no such thing as a cold and therefore I am well.' My mind would not accept any such statement."[80] Agnes here dismisses the idea of denying the existence of sickness. She also counters one common perception of positive confession. She recalls,

> There was a man who said that he had to give up being a Christian Scientist because he got tired of being 'so damn happy' the whole time. The more intensely we think after one pattern the more surely we get tired of it; the more definitely we need to drop it now and then and think after a different pattern.[81]

She promoted eliminating positive confession when partaking of Confession and Holy Communion. Agnes clearly rejected the most extreme teachings of Christian Science.

New Thought and The Unity School of Christianity provided a metaphysical approach for many Christians distrustful of medicine but interested in healing during the early stages of the Pentecostal Movement. Although some core premises and concepts—such as the impersonality of God and the non-divinity of Christ—contradicted orthodox Christianity, numerous other aspects of the philosophy—such as the ability of thoughts to affect a person's life and the existence of spiritual laws governing physical reality—were accepted and assimilated by authors and leaders in healing ministries. Christian Science also developed out of New Thought, but its tenets were rejected by most Christians. Agnes incorporated many of the terms and concepts from New Thought and Unity into her theology and ministry while rejecting the more extreme aspects of Christian Science. She maintained a balance between metaphysics and orthodox Christian doctrines.

Science and the Scientific Method

In its simplest expression, the field of science incorporates logical and verifiable approaches to learning about a subject, often contrasted with faith-based paradigms. Scientists refer to the core methodology of their discipline as the scientific method.[82] However, the method does not have an absolute definition. David Stein, Physicist and president of The Center for Transcultural Foresight, describes the scientific method as "a framework for attempting to understand the universe . . . grounded in repeatable experiment and observation."[83] Proponents in other fields reference it differently. Martin Deutsch, professor of Physics at MIT, summarizes it simply as "observation, testing and measurement."[84] Clearly, no universal definition exists for the scientific method. Brian A. Woodcock, UWEC, explains that scientists regularly differ their methodology according to their specific subject of study.[85] Nevertheless, some core concepts remain constant through all the iterations: hypothesis, experimentation, observation, and repeatability for the sake of verification.

When Agnes first learned about healing, many Christians interested in healing were suspicious of science in general and medicine in particular. Nevertheless, her paradigm accepts the value of science and combines it with the prayer of faith. From her perspective, science is a field dedicated to studying the world, discovering how things work, and presenting the truth. While discussing the value of the Bible, she makes a significant statement about science. She writes, "First of all, I believe we should learn as much as we can of the sciences that concern the universe. Science is the honest attempt of honest men to arrive at truth."[86] Compared to the present day perceived conflict between science and faith, Agnes held a noticeably optimistic view of the scientific community: scientists operate with integrity to provide information about the world in the most unbiased way as possible.

Agnes developed a healing model incorporating various approaches to healing prayer, and her first book describes the model in detail, ascribing it to the scientific method. The Introduction to *The Healing Light* quotes her as saying, "The scientific attitude is the attitude of perfect open-mindedness."[87] This statement comes from her chapter "The Scientific Attitude: Choosing A Healing Prayer Objective" in the original editions of her book where she says,

> One way to understand a hitherto unexplored force of nature is to experiment with that force intelligently and with an open mind. This book suggests, for those willing to learn, a method so simple that it is childlike, as the more profound truths are apt to be. It is an experimental method. One decides upon a definite subject for prayer, prays about it and then decides whether or not the prayer-project succeeds. If it does not succeed, one seeks a better adjustment with God and tries again. This is the method of the men who have discovered and harnessed the forces of God's world—the scientists.
>
> "Blessed are the meek, for they shall inherit the earth." The scientific attitude is the attitude of perfect meekness. It consists in an unshakable faith in the laws of nature combined with perfect humility toward those laws and a patient determination to learn them at whatever cost. Through this meekness scientists have learned how to conform to the laws of nature and by so doing have achieved results. Through the same meekness those who seek God can produce results by learning to conform to His laws of faith and love.[88]

Apparently, her promotion of the scientific method raised concerns among some of her readers, for later publishers rename the chapter "Experiments in Prayer" and delete the last sentence of the first paragraph along with the term "scientific attitude" in the second sentence of the second paragraph in several editions.

Agnes believed she could best learn how to heal the sick by using a variation of the scientific method. Beginning with the hypothesis that healing was God's will, she experimented with several different approaches to prayer, observed the specific results on the sick person, and subsequently adjusted her approach accordingly. She differed from the majority of other healing ministers of her time by placing the responsibility for faith and the results of prayer largely on the person doing the praying instead of on the sick person. By considering herself the primary variable, she was able to identify some relationships between different approaches to prayer and the subsequent results. She believed a scientific method provided the best way to accomplish this goal. She therefore describes healing prayer in the scientific terms of hypothesis, experimentation, observation, and adjustment.

Agnes begins her discussion of healing by hypothesizing that healing is God's will and should be considered the norm instead of the exception. Her conviction arose from observations she made from the Bible and from science: (1) God created man and woman in His image; (2) the human body naturally tends to heal wounds and fight sickness unless the system is damaged; (3) human nature inherently resists death and sickness; (4) nature itself reflects God's eternal attributes and nature; and (5) nature itself provides numerous ingredients to cure diseases and illnesses.[89] Agnes believed these observations logically indicate that sickness is a deviation from God's intended design. Additionally, she believed healing should be expected in the Church. She says, "If one thinks of a miracle not as the breaking of God's laws but as His own using of His laws, then the world is full of miracles.... His will includes unlimited miracles."[90] For Agnes, healing occurred whenever faith and God's power were sufficiently available to overcome the sickness.

Although she recognized times when God does miracles without apparent human intercession, Agnes believed healing came mainly through prayer—from the sick person, from others, or through a combination of both. She writes, "We must learn that God is not an unreasonable and impulsive sovereign who breaks His own laws at will. As soon as we learn that God does things *through* us (not *for* us) [emphasis hers], the matter becomes as simple as breathing, as inevitable as sunrise."[91] In other words, if healing occurs irrespective of the type or amount of human participation, the results become inconsequential. Instead, she taught people to compare the results to the prayer objective so they could improve. She believed people could actually learn how to pray more effectively.

Agnes viewed prayer as an interaction between people and God according to the operation of the spiritual laws he ordained when he created the universe. She explains, "Some day we will understand the scientific principles that underlie the miracle working powers of God, and we will accept His intervention as simply and naturally as we do the radio."[92] She considered healing prayer both logical and practical, and she recommended her readers to view healing prayer as an experiment in faith. Agnes begins her chapter on the scientific attitude with an appeal to humility—to not to be afraid of failures—before she identifies her model as "an experimental method" and reminds the reader,

> Let us understand then that if our experiment fails, it is not due to a lack in God, but to a natural and understandable lack in ourselves. What scientist would be discouraged if his first experiment failed? Since we intend with His help to heal our short-comings, to repair our wiring, we need not fear to test His power by prayer.[93]

She encourages her audience to continue praying for the sick even when healing does not immediately happen. She held that if they gave up after a failure, they could not improve.

Agnes also believed developing an effective model for healing prayer required honestly evaluating success and failure. In order to do this, the prayer objective needed to be both clear and specific. In other words, the person praying for the sick needed to be able to examine the results of the prayer. She explains,

> In order to do so, we must decide on some tangible thing that we wish accomplished by that power, so that we can know without question whether our experiment succeeded or failed. . . . Let us choose one of the very simplest of prayer-experiments, remembering always that it must be tangible; that is, it must be something that we can put the finger on and say either "this has been done,"

or "this has not been done."[94]

In a somewhat bold statement, she identifies physical healing as the best option. She writes, "The simplest and most direct of all prayer-projects is the healing of the body."[95] She intended to make the process as concrete and objective as possible for her readers.

Agnes completed her scientific model by recommending the person make adjustments when healing did not occur and try again. She relates an instance of praying for a boy with an ear abscess with no success. After trying different prayer approaches, the boys condition worsened, and he developed meningitis. Unsure what to do, she contacted a friend in another city and was urged to try an option she had not considered. She tried it, and the boy was healed overnight.[96] Through that incident, Agnes was reminded of the need for perseverance. However, she did not believe in denying the existence of sickness, and she recognized that healing does not always take place:

> In certain very difficult cases there are adjustments to the laws of God that cannot be made perfectly in this lifetime. Even so, we do well to strive continually toward life in our prayers, even as we strive continually toward life in our medical care. If it is too late for the perfect healing of our bodies in this life we will at least receive enough of His power to enlighten our spirits and to relieve our pain.[97]

She therefore contended that when physical healing does not occur, healing prayer can effectively touch the person's mind and emotions, bringing comfort, peace, and growth.

Agnes incorporated the scientific method into her healing paradigm because she believed it provided the optimal approach for teaching people who desired to learn how to pray effectively for the sick. She viewed science as a discipline dedicated to discovering the truth about the world God created, and she often relates scientific discoveries in the fields of astronomy, physics, and medicine to passages of Scripture within all of her works. Her interdisciplinary view, accepting science and medicine, appealed to a large number of believers who likely viewed Pentecostal healing models, which in some cases rejected medicine, with suspicion. Although the sources are unidentified, Agnes was certainly influenced by science.

Jungian Psychology

Though some of her views related to the mind and the subconscious originated with New Thought and the Unity School of Christianity, Agnes also relied on concepts in the field of psychology to describe many of the principles of faith and healing. She believed psychology explained the way spirit, mind, and body worked together to promote or prevent healing and wholeness. Her discussion of the subconscious becomes especially pronounced in her writings on inner healing, which she describes as healing of the memories. Although she rarely identifies her sources, as will be shown, she was influenced by the teachings of C. G. Jung, at least as far as it was communicated to her. Notable similarities exist between Jungian psychology and New Thought, making some of his concepts easily integrated into her paradigm.

Carl Jung became prominent during the early and middle twentieth century for his theories on personality and the unconscious. He studied medicine at Basel University, Switzerland, but during his fourth year and immediately prior to taking his qualifying exams, he switched to psychiatry.[98] He found it a better fit than becoming a medical doctor. He began working with Freud, but their friendship ended when he abandoned Freud's theories to pursue his own views on personality and symbolism.[99] Both agreed on the existence of the subconscious but held different beliefs concerning its operation and relationship to mental illness. The occult had interested Jung since childhood, with much of his psychology informed by Spiritism, Alchemy, and Parapsychology.[100]

Jung believed people are born with whole personalities that may become damaged by negative life circumstances. His view contradicted the popular view in the field, including Freud's, which maintained that "personality is acquired part by part, and that only later, if at all, does any sort of coherent organized unity appear."[101] Instead, he considered personality an inherent whole, which became affected by life circumstances. According to Hall and Nordby, Jung claimed that people had to strive to remain whole beings and avoid becoming internally disconnected or conflicted through traumatic circumstances—and work for connection when internal conflicts occurred:

> Man does not strive for wholeness; he already has it, he is born with it. What he must do throughout his life span . . . is to develop this inherent wholeness to the greatest degree of differentiation, coherence, and harmony possible, and to guard against it breaking up into separate, autonomous, and conflicting systems.[102]

Similar to the body containing multiple organs that ideally work together in unity, the personality contains numerous parts designed to operate harmoniously. Although the whole included multiple systems, he differentiated between three main components:

> In Jungian psychology the personality as a whole is called the *psyche*. . . . The psyche is composed of numerous diversified but interacting systems and levels. Three levels in the psyche can be distinguished. These are *consciousness*, the *personal unconscious*, and the *collective unconscious*. Consciousness is the only part of the mind that is known directly by the individual.[103]

Therefore, people have direct access to only one of three levels of their thoughts and emotions.

Jung also maintained a different view of the unconscious than other psychiatrists. While Freud believed negative experiences formed the unconscious, Jung considered it an intrinsic aspect of the originating personality.[104] Additionally, he delineates between individual (personal) and corporate (collective) aspects. The personal unconscious contains a full record of the person's experiences while the collective unconscious maintains primordial images and memories tracing back to pre-human ancestry.[105] In other words, people not only have memories of events in their lives but also are affected by instinctual recollections of their race, species, and evolutionary ancestors. Jung called these evolutionary and racial images "archetypes" and considered them universal for all humans; the four major archetypes consist of the Persona, the Anima and Animus, the Shadow, and the Self.[106] The archetypes individually and collectively influence the psyche. Therefore, people are not only influenced by their own experiences but also by the memories and beliefs of their genetic ancestors.

Jungian psychology seems to have certainly influenced Agnes through her associations with Jungian psychologists and analysts. When she moved to California after her husband Ted's death, Morton Kelsey became her pastor. She eventually invited him to co-lead some of the Schools of Pastoral Care with her, and she even lived with him and his wife for a period of time.[107] Kelsey not only studied Jungian psychology at the Jung Institute but also became a Jungian analyst and is recognized as one of the strongest advocates of Jungian Psychology within the Christian Church. In *Healing & Christianity*, he recalls,

> Through Agnes Sanford and the Schools of Pastoral Care I came to know many of the leaders of the charismatic movement within the Baptist, Congregational, Methodist, Presbyterian, and Lutheran churches.... About the same time I became involved in Jungian analysis and studied at the Jung Institute in Switzerland.[108]

Kelsey began promoting many of Jung's concepts in the schools. Payne devotes most of a chapter in her autobiography to concerns related to Kelsey's promotion of Jungian Psychology in the Schools of Pastoral Care.[109] His teachings affected some of the material being taught in the conferences. Even before meeting Kelsey, however, Agnes had familiarity with Jungian psychology through her youngest son Jack, who had become a Jungian psychologist.[110] Although her understanding of the conscious and subconscious began with New Thought, Jung's teachings likely built on those metaphysical concepts. Agnes and Ted actually planned on taking courses in psychology at one time, but believed that God prevented them from proceeding.[111] She describes it as the one time God may have used sickness to prevent them from making a mistake when they neglected to seek Him.

Jungian psychology almost certainly influenced some of Agnes's works. Her main book discussing healing for depression, *The Healing Gifts of the Spirit*, references numerous terms and concepts from Jung. In the introduction, she uses the Jungian terms "ego" and "self" as well as mentioning the "psyche" in quotation marks; additionally, she describes concepts often related to Jung, such as the effect of the collective unconscious and parts of the personality.[112] The entire book discusses healing from a psychological perspective in conjunction with the spiritual impact of unhealed memories and the need for forgiveness of sins. She also makes references that are undeniably related to Jung. For example, in a chapter dealing with the seriousness of praying for people with mental illness, she writes, "What then of the shadow side that, as my son said, everyone has within him? Shall there be no shadow—nothing to dim the light of the ever-burning spirit within us?"[113] Here, Agnes uses Jung's term for the animal nature within people, but she reinterprets and redefines it to describe a need for a balance between spiritual experience and normal human life; in other words, she explains that people burn out from attempting to maintain an elevated level of spirituality when normal daily activities—such as doing laundry, washing dishes, working in a garden, or cleaning the house—are disdained.

Agnes referenced Jungian terms and concepts beyond his personality theory. For her, the subconscious played a large role in healing. In *Behold Your God*, she describes the subconscious in a way that is similar not only to Jungian psychology but also to New Thought. She writes,

> The subconscious, though it responds to suggestion, is very slow in changing its ways. It is a childlike mind, tending to be both obstinate and timid. And this tendency is aggravated by the fact that the subconscious mind exists not only in the present but also in the past. In other words, the subconscious remembers everything that you have ever experienced or thought or studied or felt. It is one of the functions of the subconscious thus to tend the memories. Everything that we have ever known or thought is stored away there, that it may be incorporated into our experience of life or recalled for our use.[114]

Her description of the subconscious here matches Jung's own definition of the Personal Unconscious.

Agnes goes even further into Jungian theory while discussing the healing of the memories. In another of her books, she specifically mentions the collective unconscious:

> For now we know that we have within us another mind than the conscious, and that this unconscious mind is not disconnected from life but is connected with the mind of the race: the collective unconscious. Therefore we can "pick up" thoughts and impressions from another or from life outside ourselves or from the memories of the race. Now into this collective unconscious, into these race memories, Jesus Christ entered, and there He lived during the days that we rightly call Passion Week. He made a rapport in the Garden of Gethsemane not merely with one person as you and I do when we intercede for another, but with all people who ever lived or ever will live upon the face of the earth; for He is from everlasting to everlasting and with Him a thousand years are as one day.[115]

She uses the collective unconscious in the same way as Jung describes it, even using the term "unconscious" instead of "subconscious" and referencing "race memories" in the passage. Although she does not specifically mention Jung, her use of the terminology along with an identical definition indicates a practical knowledge of his works.

At another point in the same book, Agnes actually mentions Jung. In a chapter on exorcism, she discusses the dangers related to bitterness and unforgiveness, saying,

> However, this thing can go one step farther: according to Carl Jung, there are actually outside entities or thought currents of evil, and it is possible that one of them will enter and live in this house of anger that we have built, so that in truth we are troubled—or, as people say, "possessed" by an evil spirit.[116]

She obviously had some knowledge of Jung and his psychology at this point, even if it might be considered just a popular understanding. In his book, De Arteaga argues that Agnes did not accept Jung's teachings but simply adopted some of his vocabulary from people who discussed his works.[117] However, her not only using his terms but also mentioning him by name suggests that she believed and affirmed some of his basic philosophy and concepts. Although she clearly did not accept everything he taught, she likely had at least a rudimentary knowledge of Jung, and his teachings certainly influenced her theology.

Conclusion

Agnes's theological development began with her Presbyterian upbringing and her study of the *Westminster Confession of Faith* and *The Shorter and Longer Catechisms*. These instilled in her a reliance on Scripture, especially the gospels and the Ten Commandments. At the same time, she accepted the Presbyterian teaching on cessationism and believed healing and miracles no longer took place. When she joined the Episcopal Church, she was introduced to the *Book of Common Prayer* and gained a new understanding of sacraments and the liturgy. She eventually promoted Confession, Communion, and Unction as significant avenues for healing. After she saw her son healed and received healing from depression, she discovered the principles of New Thought and Unity Christianity. She believed many of their metaphysical concepts, which profoundly affected her theology and healing model. Simultaneously, she rejected Christian Science and Spiritism as incompatible with orthodox Christianity. Agnes also developed a profound respect for science, believing it explained how the world worked. In *The Healing Light*, she describes healing in terms of the scientific method. She gained some knowledge of Jungian Psychology, at least from her pastor Morton Kelsey and her son John Sanford, but she often reinterpreted the terms and concepts to fit her Christian theology. All of these sources had some influence on Agnes and affected the development of her healing theology and paradigm.

Notes

[1] The Southern branch of the Presbyterian Church of the United States later became more liberal in its theology, but at the time of her membership, it was distinctly fundamentalist. To avoid redundancy, future mentions of her background may simply reference "Presbyterian" without specifying the branch.

[2] "The Westminster Confession of Faith" in *The Westminster Confession of Faith and The Westminster Shorter Catechism* (New York: Krill Press, 2015), 1.6.

[3] "The Westminster Shorter Catechism" in *The Westminster Confession of Faith and the Westminster Shorter Catechism* (New York: Krill Press, 2015), Q&A.3.

[4] *Shorter Catechism*, Q&A.40-82. The *Larger Catechism* devotes 50 questions to the same topic.

[5] Agnes Sanford, *Sealed Orders*, 107.

[6] Agnes Sanford, *Sealed Orders*, 103, 148.

[7] *Westminster Confession of Faith*, 8.1-8; *Shorter Catechism*, Q&A.21-22.

[8] Agnes Sanford, *Behold Your God*, 71-72.

[9] Agnes Sanford, *Behold Your God*, 72.

[10] Agnes Sanford, *Sealed Orders*, 49. See also Agnes Sanford, *Behold Your God*, 2.

[11] N. V. Hope, "Warfield, Benjamin Breckenridge" in *Who's Who in Christian History*, edited by J. D. Douglas, Philip W. Comfort, and Donald Mitchell (Wheaton: Tyndale House, 1992), 704-705; William De Arteaga, *Agnes Sanford and Her Companions*, 77.

[12] Jon Ruthven, "On the Cessation of the Charismata: The Protestant Polemic of Benjamin B. Warfield," *Pneuma* 24, no. 1 (Spring 1990), 15.

[13] Benjamin Breckenridge Warfield, *Miracles: Yesterday and Today; True and False* (Grand Rapids: Wm. B. Eerdmans, 1953), 5-6. Text was originally published in 1918 as *Counterfeit Miracles*.

[14] The Episcopal Church, "Preface" in *The Book of Common Prayer*, 9-11.

[15] The Episcopal Church, "XXV. Of the Sacraments" in *The Book of Common Prayer*, 872.

[16] The Episcopal Church, "The Sacraments" in *The Book of Common Prayer*, 857.

[17] *Westminster Confession of Faith*, 15.6.

[18] The Episcopal Church, "The Ministry" and "Other Sacramental Rites" in *The Book of Common Prayer*, 856, 861.

[19] The Episcopal Church, "XXVIII. Of the Lord's Supper" in *The Book of Common Prayer*, 873.

[20] The Episcopal Church, "The Holy Eucharist" in *The Book of Common Prayer*, 859-860.

[21] The Episcopal Church, "Other Sacramental Rites" in *The Book of Common Prayer*, 860-861.

[22] The Episcopal Church, "The Consecration of the Priest" in *The Book of Common Prayer*, 533.

[23] The Episcopal Church, "Other Sacramental Rites" in *The Book of Common Prayer*, 860.

[24] The Episcopal Church, "Holy Baptism" in *The book of Common Prayer*, 305.

[25] The Episcopal Church, "Confirmation" in *The Book of Common Prayer*, 418. See also "Baptism" in *The book of Common Prayer*, 309.

[26] The Episcopal Church, "Other Sacramental Rites" in *The Book of Common Prayer*, 861.

[27] The Episcopal Church, "Ministration to the Sick" in *The Book of Common Prayer*,

454-455.

[28] Agnes Sanford, 2nd ed., 121-126.

[29] Agnes Sanford, *The Healing Gifts of the Spirit*, 126-127.

[30] Agnes Sanford, *Sealed Orders*, 98.

[31] Agnes Sanford, *The Healing Light*, 2nd ed., 54.

[32] Agnes Sanford, *Behold Your God*, 161.

[33] Agnes Sanford, *The Lost Shephard: A Moving Novel of Life in the Spirit*. (New York: J. B. Lippincott, 1953).

[34] Agnes Sanford, *The Healing Gifts of the Spirit*, 69.

[35] "Interview – Francis & Judith MacNutt," by David Kyle Foster, *Masteringlife.org*. Note: numerous grammatical corrections have been made to the quotation.

[36] Agnes Sanford, *Sealed Orders*, 220.

[37] Agnes Sanford, *Sealed Orders*, 248-249.

[38] Agnes Sanford, *The Healing Light*, 2nd ed., 90-91, ff.

[39] Agnes Sanford, *Sealed Orders*, 103.

[40] Glenn R. Mosley, *New Thought, Ancient Wisdom: The History and Future of the New Thought Movement* (Philadelphia: Templeton Foundation, 2006), 45.

[41] Raymond J. Cunningham, "Ministry of Healing: The Origins of the Psychotherapeutic Role of the American Churches" (doctoral dissertation, John Hopkins University, 1965), 46-48, ProQuest (DTN 6510270). See also William De Arteaga, *Agnes Sanford and Her Companions*, 83-87.

[42] William De Arteaga, *Agnes Sanford and Her Companions*, 81; Glenn R. Mosley, *New Thought, Ancient Wisdom*, 3-10; cf. Joseph W. Williams, *Spirit Cure: A History of Pentecostal Healing* (New York: Oxford University Press, 2013), 116.

[43] Raymond Cunningham, "Ministry of Healing," 114; Joseph Williams, *Spirit Cure*, 17-18, 41, 76-80.

[44] Raymond Cunningham, "Ministry of Healing," 113.

[45] Joseph Williams, *Spirit Cure*, 16.

[46] Joseph Williams, *Spirit Cure*, 15. Williams often identifies these ideologies as "mind-cure."

[47] Dale H. Simmons, *E. W. Kenyon and the Postbellum Pursuit of Peace, Power, and Plenty* (Lanham: The Scarecrow Press, 1997), 80.

[48] Dale Simmons, *E. W. Kenyon*, 81.

[49] Glenn Mosley, *New Thought, Ancient Wisdom*, xiii.

[50] Glenn Mosley, *New Thought, Ancient Wisdom*, 15.

[51] Glenn Mosley, *New Thought, Ancient Wisdom*, 20.

[52] Glenn Mosley, *New Thought, Ancient Wisdom*, 10.

[53] Glenn Mosley, *New Thought, Ancient Wisdom*, 23.

[54] Glenn Mosley, *New Thought, Ancient Wisdom*, 16-17.

[55] Emma Curtis Hopkins, "Scientific Christian Mental Practice" in Emma Curtis Hopkins and Thomas Troward, *New Thought Classics* (Lexington: CreateSpace Independent, 2013), 10, 15.

[56] Emma Curtis Hopkins, "Scientific Christian Mental Practice" in *New Thought Classics*, 15-25.

[57] Joseph Williams, *Spirit Cure*, 76.

[58] Kimberly Ervin Alexander, *Pentecostal Healing: Models in Theology and Practice* (Blandform Forum: DEO, 2006), 61.

[59] Joseph Williams, *Spirit Cure*, 76-80.

[60] Agnes Sanford, *The Healing Light*, 2nd ed., 131, 167. It is not clear whether the editors forced the changes in the book or whether Agnes herself revised the wording to

make the book more acceptable to a larger audience.

[61] Joseph Williams, *Spirit Cure*, 10, 21, 23. Williams uses "metaphysical" for religions that impersonalize God, stress laws allowing supernatural forces to affect nature, and advise people how to gain spiritual power; however, he recognizes that Christians rejected the first aspect. *Spirit Cure*, 15, 180n52.

[62] Agnes Sanford, *The Healing Light*, 2nd ed, 10.

[63] William De Arteaga, *Agnes Sanford and Her Companions*, 196-197.

[64] Agnes Sanford, *Sealed Orders*, 97.

[65] Agnes Sanford, *Sealed Orders*, 103.

[66] Agnes Sanford, *Sealed Orders*, 190.

[67] Agnes Sanford, *The Healing Light*, 2nd ed., 19.

[68] Agnes Sanford, *The Healing Light*, 2nd ed., 30.

[69] Agnes Sanford, *The Healing Light*, 2nd ed., 20.

[70] Agnes Sanford, *The Healing Light*, 2nd ed., 56.

[71] Agnes Sanford, *The Healing Light*, 2nd ed., 144.

[72] Agnes Sanford, "Thy Kingdom Come" *Weekly Unity* 63 no. 9 (June 1971), 1.

[73] Agnes Sanford, *The Healing Light*, 2nd ed, 42.

[74] Agnes Sanford, *The Healing Light*, 2nd ed., 44.

[75] Agnes Sanford, *Sealed Orders*, 189. Additionally, in personal correspondence from Drury to Baltz on December 31, 1977, Agnes says she "has always liked Unity, and had no change in her attitude toward them, while realizing a certain lack in their understanding of Christ. She was always Christ-centered herself, was 'grown up' in that area, but she needed development in the area of doing the works of Jesus, which is where Unity helped her enormously. Her gratitude to Unity is because they directed her thinking in the area where she was in need of growth and did not, of course, disturb her essential centeredness of Christ."

[76] Agnes Sanford, *Sealed Orders*, 107. Colwell promoted *The Life Abundant* Movement, initiated by Dr. Robert Bell's book, *The Life Abundant*. Sanford believed in eating healthy but was otherwise not influenced by the movement. See William De Arteaga, *Agnes Sanford and Her Companions*, 180-184.

[77] Agnes Sanford, *Sealed Orders*, 103.

[78] William De Arteaga, *Agnes Sanford and Her Companions*, 87.

[79] Agnes Sanford, *The Healing Light*, 2nd ed., 84.

[80] Agnes Sanford, *The Healing Light*, 2nd ed., 89.

[81] Agnes Sanford, *The Healing Light*, 2nd ed., 137.

[82] The author previously presented portions of this section in an unpublished conference paper on Agnes Sanford. See Martin L. Dignard, "The Scientific Method in the Healing Paradigm of Agnes Sanford" (paper presented at The Holy Spirit, Science, and Theological Education Conference, Virginia Beach, March 2016).

[83] David E. Stein, "The Scientific Method after Next," *World Future Review* 4, no. 1 (Spring 2012): 34.

[84] W. Stanford Reid, "The Christian and the Scientific Method," *The Westminster Theological Journal* 24, no. 1 (November 1961): 4.

[85] Brian A. Woodcock, "'The Scientific Method' as Myth and Ideal," *Science & Education* 23, no. 10 (May 2014): 2073-4.

[86] Agnes Sanford, *The Healing Power of the Bible* (San Francisco: Harper & Row, 1969), 8.

[87] Agnes Sanford, *The Healing Light*, 2nd ed., 9.

[88] Agnes Sanford, *The Healing Light*, 2nd ed., 21.

[89] Agnes does not present these observations in one location, but they permeate the

entire book. For examples of each, see Agnes Sanford, *The Healing Light*, 2nd ed., 19, 24, 27-28, 34, 43, 84-85.

[90] Agnes Sanford, *The Healing Light*, 2nd ed., 20.
[91] Agnes Sanford, *The Healing Light*, 2nd ed., 19.
[92] Agnes Sanford, *The Healing Light*, 2nd ed., 20.
[93] Agnes Sanford, *The Healing Light*, 2nd ed., 21, 23.
[94] Agnes Sanford, *The Healing Light*, 2nd ed., 22-23.
[95] Agnes Sanford, *The Healing Light*, 2nd ed., 24.
[96] Agnes Sanford, *The Healing Light*, 2nd ed., 25-27.
[97] Agnes Sanford, *The Healing Light*, 2nd ed., 25.
[98] Calvin S. Hall and Vernon J. Nordby, *A Primer of Jungian Psychology* (New York: Penguin Putnam, 1999), 21.
[99] Calvin S. Hall and Vernon J. Nordby, *A Primer of Jungian Psychology*, 24.
[100] Calvin S. Hall and Vernon J. Nordby, *A Primer of Jungian Psychology*, 21, 25.
[101] Calvin S. Hall and Vernon J. Nordby, *A Primer of Jungian Psychology*, 32.
[102] Calvin S. Hall and Vernon J. Nordby, *A Primer of Jungian Psychology*, 33.
[103] Calvin S. Hall and Vernon J. Nordby, *A Primer of Jungian Psychology*, 33.
[104] Calvin S. Hall and Vernon J. Nordby, *A Primer of Jungian Psychology*, 38.
[105] Calvin S. Hall and Vernon J. Nordby, *A Primer of Jungian Psychology*, 35-43.
[106] Calvin S. Hall and Vernon J. Nordby, *A Primer of Jungian Psychology*, 42-53.
[107] Agnes Sanford, *Sealed Orders*, 271, 276, 298.
[108] Morton Kelsey, *Healing & Christianity* (Minneapolis: Augsburg, 1995), 194.
[109] Leanne Payne, *Heaven's Calling: A Memoir of One Soul's Steep Ascent*, 237-248.
[110] John A. Sanford, *Healing Body and Soul: The Meaning of Illness in the New Testament and in Psychotherapy* (Louisville: Westminster/John Knox, 1992).
[111] Agnes Sanford, *Sealed Orders*, 145-146.
[112] Agnes Sanford, *The Healing Gifts of the Spirit*, 9-10.
[113] Agnes Sanford, *The Healing Gifts of the Spirit*, 153.
[114] Agnes Sanford, *Behold Your God*, 60.
[115] Agnes Sanford, *The Healing Gifts of the Spirit*, 136.
[116] Agnes Sanford, *The Healing Gifts of the Spirit*, 194-195.
[117] William De Arteaga, *Agnes Sanford and Her Companions*, 218.

CHAPTER 4

UNDERSTANDING HER HEALING PRAYER MODEL

Agnes wrote *The Healing Light* in 1947 to describe a simple and direct way for people to pray for the sick. Her model vastly differed from most of the other approaches practiced in the Christian church at the time. She saw healing as the natural result of God's presence interacting with His creation, redeeming it from corruption. As such, his willingness was a pre-established factor. Healing prayer no longer consisted of requesting God to act but instead involved mediating his power to the sick. She relied heavily on the scientific method and an understanding of psychology for the framework of her approach. Her model focuses on four basic steps: connecting with God, receiving power from him, believing the power has an effect, and observing the results. The steps could be used by the person needing healing or by someone else on behalf of the sick. Agnes developed a model that addresses many concerns raised by healing ministries in the Church today.[1] Her model provides notable opportunities for resolving conflicts and avoiding mistakes.

Foundational Premises

Agnes based her healing prayer model on several ideological premises. From a theological position, she considered healing to be intrinsically related to God's nature and character. Healing naturally took place whenever God's presence impacted the fallen world. Psychologically, she believed the subconscious played an integral role in both faith and health. Healing prayer heavily relied on belief in the heart. Agnes also believed science explained the truth about the world. She considered the scientific method the most honest and humble approach to knowledge. These ideologies formed her paradigm.

God's willingness to heal forms a fundamental aspect of most healing theologies. Healing ministries often describe his willingness as the way his omnipotence relates to his benevolence. In other words, God's power and goodness form two primary factors in numerous discussions on healing, reflected in multiple theodicies to explain the existence of suffering and evil, especially in relation to sickness, disease, and death. The occasional discrepancy between scriptural promises and personal experiences suggests some type of conflict between God's power and goodness. As Agnes states, "we doubt the *willingness* or the *ability* [emphasis hers] of God to actually produce within our lives and bodies the results that we desire."[2] She equates God's willingness with goodness and his ability with power.

In the context of healing prayer, the incongruity between biblical promises and human experiences results in a perceived tension between God's willingness and His ability. For example, Knight employs a continuum between God's sovereignty and His faithfulness to evaluate various healing paradigms, making the two concepts appear as polar extremes.[3] Problematically, his dualistic perspective results in an apparent conflict between God's supremacy and integrity. On a linear scale, as one aspect of God's nature is emphasized, the other aspect is necessarily diminished. Knight's methodology works for identifying many strengths and weaknesses in the most common approaches to healing, but his premise implies an inherent and ongoing tension within the Godhead—at least temporarily. If healing is understood as the result of God's sovereignty balanced with his faithfulness, it suggests either a conflict between His omnipotence and his benevolence or a necessary redefinition or contextualization of those concepts. In other words, either God wants to heal but cannot, or God can heal but does not want to do so. Healing ministries have often refuted one or both conclusions either by contextualizing God's ability by interjecting free will or by contextualizing God's goodness by placing it on its own continuum in which some goods outweigh and conflict with others. However, both adjustments suggest additional inherent conflicts and limitations.

Agnes developed a healing model based on a theology that provides an alternative to the dichotomy between God's omnipotence and benevolence. Knight references Agnes in his article but evaluates her on the same continuum and with the same methodology instead of recognizing her unique perspective. In his opinion, she "attempt[s] to guarantee faithfulness by circumscribing God's freedom."[4] However, her understanding of healing differs drastically from the other ministries he describes. Agnes considers healing not as an act of God but as a result of his presence. Most healing paradigms understand prayer for the sick as an attempt to elicit an affirmative response from God. As Robinson states, "For most Christian believers prayer for healing had the same rationale as for any other petition. Any positive outcome was seen as an act of special providence."[5] Healing takes place when God responds favorably to prayer and actively changes the situation. In his discussion of healing models throughout Church history, Ronald A. N. Kydd similarly defines healing as "restoration of health through the direct intervention of God."[6] In most healing paradigms, prayer involves petitioning God to respond by granting the healing.

As discussed, Agnes regularly describes God's power in terms of energy or light. She considered this an accurate analogy of the way His Presence fills and sustains the universe: just as heat and light continually radiate from the sun, God's power constantly emanates in creation. She describes the energy as invisible, ongoing, and active, writing.

> There is a kind of light that cannot be seen but which has within it the principle of creativity. Perhaps it is the original creation—a moving, vibrating radiation that came into being when God said, "Let there be light," and there was light (Gen. 1:3)! By the interposition of will *plus* faith [emphasis hers], man can introduce into a situation an increased flow of God's creative energy. For there is in the universe a vibration like the vibration of light, and its tendency is to create life. It may well have been the first creation of all, and out of it all worlds may have evolved.[7]

Agnes believed the same power that created the world also restores it. The creative power constantly proceeds forth from God: "There is a river, a stream, a flow of a life-giving element. And we can make contact with this Life that flows from God."[8] Since God does not change, the power proceeding from him remains constant, reflecting his perfect nature. Healing results when his creative power interacts with his creation. However, an affective interaction requires a medium, such as prayer, faith, and the sacraments. Agnes understands healing prayer not as requesting God to act but as the opening of a channel through which God's power becomes available to his creation. Just as sunlight causes warmth, God's power naturally restores his creation from corruption. Her paradigm thus abrogates any conflict between God's willingness (goodness) and ability (power).

Psychology had a major impact on Agnes's healing model, especially her view of the mind. The subconscious mind not only keeps a record of the experiences and actions of the person's life but also manages most of the natural operations of the body:

> Our little crafts go forth upon the sea of life under the general orders of our Head: to cross the deep waters of this life and land safely upon the other side. There is a hidden engineer within our bodies, placed there by God to see that we do this. The sub-conscious engineer acts under a blanket order from God, who is love and life and who gives us His love and bids us live. There is also a captain in our heads: the conscious mind, which enables us to cooperate with God in a reasonable way.[9]

Agnes believed the conscious mind involves our logical facilities and cognizant thoughts while the subconscious regulates all other physical processes. In her perspective, the subconscious formed part of the person made in God's image. She writes, "This inner control center is part of the spiritual body, the eternal Being. It acts under orders from God Himself until man sends into it a contrary command and throw it into confusion."[10] Her explanation suggests she associated the subconscious with the conscience and the law of God written on every person's heart (Romans 2:15). However, the person could intentionally disregard and act counter to an inborn moral code.

Agnes viewed sin as a barrier to healing prayer. In her paradigm, God did not limit the flow of healing power as much as the person's subconscious did. In other words, if unforgiveness, bitterness, or sin remained unresolved, the person's conscience would not believe itself worthy of receiving and channeling God's healing power. She writes,

> We must believe not only that God is a Creator, but also that he is righteous, and that when we ask of Him wholeness of body He asks of us wholeness of soul. God is good. That does not mean that He is indulgent—complacent—easy-going. Goodness includes severity, for only by severity can real goodness be maintained (Rom. 11:22). God is good, and since He has breathed the breath of life into us, there is something in us that demands goodness.... Thus we find that part of prayer for healing is a sincere and strenuous attempt to keep God's laws of goodness.[11]

In her paradigm, people are created in God's image, and the human spirit has an inherent recognition that a holy God requires people to pursue righteousness in their lives.

She describes instances when healing prayer became pointless until the person addressed sin. For example, when a woman's heart condition returned, she responded,

> "What's the matter with you, Anne?" I asked. "There must be something the matter, or your heart wouldn't act up again after it got well."
>
> "Well, the real trouble with me is that I hate my mother-in-law," said Anne, stating a fact that a year ago she had not recognized. "My mother-in-law lives with me, and, honestly, she's the meanest woman I ever saw. I do everything for her and she has the best of everything in the house, but still..."
>
> "Well, then, there's no use praying for you to get well, is there? We will have to pray for you to like your mother-in-law."[12]

When they met a year later, Anne had not only been healed but looked so young and healthy that Agnes did not recognize her. Concerning the relapse, she explains,

> God in His grace healed Anne's heart without waiting for Anne to become perfect ... but God's Holy Spirit entering Anne to give her wholeness, moved inevitably in her spirit as well as her body, and made her aware of her unworthiness. Becoming aware of her hatred toward her mother-in-law, her own spirit demanded that she must try to give forgiveness while she asked more of God's forgiving and healing love.[13]

In her perspective, known sin can prevent a person from receiving from God. She writes,

> Now let us look once more at the mechanics of our beings and try to understand this matter. We are three in one: conscious mind, subconscious mind and an

inner divine intelligence that we may call spirit. Anne's conscious mind wanted to get well and she had prayed for years, "Oh Lord, please heal my heart." But her subconscious mind did not open itself to God's power because it did not believe.

> ... For here is the truth, and no evasion or denial of the truth can prevent it from being so: sin separates us from God and dims the power of our prayers.[14]

A person cannot be completely open to God while simultaneously harboring sin.

Although Agnes affirmed that sin could prevent a person from receiving healing from God, she put more emphasis on the lifestyle of the person praying for others. After accidently backing into a telephone truck and leaving the scene, she could not forget it:

> In due time I went home and tried to say my usual prayers. No use. I could feel them fall dead at my feet. "It's that telephone truck," I thought, with a justifiable annoyance that the truck should have been standing there anyway. Then the reason (or the enemy) made one final attempt. "I'm sure those trucks are insured," said I to myself, "and probably the insurance comes off the telephone bill. And I pay my telephone bills, so it's all right." But as the hours passed, I became more and more depressed and the power of prayer flowed away from me into thin air. I had promised to make a sick call that afternoon, but I cancelled it, saying that I was not in the right mood and so my prayers would do not good. Finally, I called the Bell Telephone Company and confessed my sin against the fender. "Oh, I'm so glad you called," said the voice on the phone. "That would cost three dollars, and the driver would have had to pay the cost if you had not called." I wrote a check for three dollars and with it brought such relief that I wondered whether the angels in heaven were singing with joy over one sinner who repented. So you see there is something else that we need to do besides continuing with prayer. We need also from time to time, and especially if the spirit telegraphs to us a message of discomfort, to pray the prayer of guidance, saying, "Lord, what is wrong in me?" There are times, in other words, when we should reverse our method of thinking. We should focus our attention not on those things that are good and beautiful but on the dust on the window-panes of our souls, so that we can wipe away that dust and increase our receptivity to the light of God's love.[15]

Agnes equated the subconscious with the conscience, and sin in a person's life would also hinder the flow of God's healing power in prayer for other people.

Agnes regularly described faith in terms of a subconscious confidence in God. In her paradigm, mental (conscious) faith operates in conjunction with faith in the heart, and a person has to cultivate new internal thought habits in order to learn faith. She explains,

> The sub-conscious mind, psychologists tell us, keeps everything that we have ever stored within it. By the time we are middle-aged most of us have accumulated in the sub-conscious all manner of thought-suggestions of fear, illness, limitation and lack, every one of which is in direct contradiction to the voice of

God. From this store-room of memories there floats into the conscious mind a continual stream of doubts, fears and negations. . . . We must also gently and patiently teach ourselves a new thought-habit. We must re-educate the sub-conscious mind, replacing every thought of fear with a thought of faith, every thought of illness with a thought of health, every thought of death with a thought of life. In other words, we must learn faith.[16]

Agnes understood the subconscious to be a fundamental component in faith. Although conscious statements, decisions, and thoughts certainly had an impact on a person's life, prayer was most effective when faith became internalized in the heart. She emphasizes, "If the inner being is clogged by negative thoughts of doubt, those thoughts make a barrier so that God's healing power cannot work through a man, as Jesus said to His disciples when they failed to heal the demoniac boy (Mark 9;19)."[17] If the person had internalized doubts, they would block at least some of the flow of God's healing power.

As discussed, Agnes considered science to be a discipline devoted to discovering the truth about the world. She considered medicine and biology to be instances where people discovered aspects of God's work and provision in His creation. She remarks,

> In the middle ages, many a child died of smallpox because science had not yet discovered the smallpox vaccine. Yet the vaccine was here all the time awaiting discovery. And many a person dies because humanity has not discovered *His* [emphasis hers] healing power as it operates through the being of men. Yet that power is here, awaiting our adjustment to it. . . . The sulpha drugs, for instance, are a source of power implanted in nature for man's use, just as electricity is a source of power implanted in nature for man's use. . . . [Eventually] the light of God will shine so radiantly through all mankind that there will be no need of other forms of healing. But if we contract appendicitis or typhoid in the meantime, we had best be grateful for the physician. To insist upon getting well by our own efforts in such a case might be a gesture of faith, but it is equally likely to be a gesture of spiritual pride. Moreover, it is hardly kind to the family who must look after us nor to the doctor who must pick up the pieces if we fail.[18]

Agnes did not view science and faith as contradictory. She obviously believed in healing prayer, but she also considered medical care acceptable when prayer did not result in healing. For example, she advised a woman with a tumor to seek medical help when it did not respond to prayer even though the woman wanted to rely solely on faith:

> "There's nothing wrong with my peach tree," I told her. "It's not bringing forth fruit yet, but it's growing. Your faith is younger than my peach tree, and it's growing too. But maybe the thing you want it to bring forth is too big for it. If I wait two or three years, my tree will bear peaches. But in the meantime, if I want peaches I'll buy them at the A. and P. If you wait two or three years, maybe your faith will be big enough to heal a growth like this. But in the meantime, if you want healing, you'd better get the doctors to help you."[19]

In her paradigm, God provided doctors and medicine for healing when prayer by itself did not result in wholeness. She understood science to be a discipline devoted to honesty and humility, trying to learn the truth about God's creation and uncovering truths about God in the process—even if not all scientists accepted or realized it in the process.

Agnes based her healing prayer model on the scientific method. As mentioned, she believed "the scientific attitude is the attitude of perfect meekness. It consists in an unshakable faith in the laws of nature combined with perfect humility toward those laws and a patient determination to learn them at whatever cost."[20] She regularly described her model in terms of an experiment, and she advised her readers to have a clear and specific goal in conjunction with an honest evaluation of the results of the prayer. She recognized observation and verification to be core aspects of a scientific approach to knowledge and adapted those concepts to prayer. Because power was continually flowing from God, healing prayer could subsequently be evaluated according to its effectiveness on a specific condition, and the type of prayer could be revised according to the situation. Although inner healing was more subjective in nature, relying upon emotional results, physical healing was more objective and could be verified and confirmed. She considered the scientific method as the perfect foundation for her healing model.

Agnes had three major premises to her healing prayer model. Theologically, she did not view healing as an act that God did in response to prayer. Instead, she believed power continually flowed from God as part of his nature, and healing was the natural result of his redemptive and restorative energy interacting with his fallen creation. As such, God's willingness no longer became a variable in healing prayer. Psychologically, Agnes considered the subconscious mind an integral aspect of healing prayer. While the conscious mind involved cognizant thoughts and actions, the subconscious oversaw the natural operations of the body as well as maintained a record of all personal experiences. She equated the subconscious mind with the conscience, inborn with a general concept of God's laws and further informed by the person's spirit, especially for Christians. In her healing paradigm, the ability to receive or channel healing power required faith within the subconscious, which entailed not only learning new thought processes but also sincerely attempting to live a holy lifestyle; unresolved sin often resulted in a sense of internal unworthiness, blocking the flow of God's healing power. Scientifically, Agnes believed discoveries about the material world revealed truths about God and His creation. In her perspective, science was a field devoted to honesty and humility, attempting to learn how the world works. She incorporated the scientific method into her healing model, believing it offered the perfect approach to understanding how to pray for the sick both effectively and honestly. Using these premises, Agnes developed a four-step healing prayer model.

Step One: Contacting God

The first step in Agnes's healing prayer model involves contacting God. In her view, seeking anything from God first requires a conscious act of connecting with him. Although prayer becomes the primary vehicle for making this connection, it has to be interactive; in other words, it is more dialogue than petition, more cooperation than concession, and more empowerment than request. In her model, prayer involves the person receiving power from God to accomplish the intended objective. She viewed healing prayer in terms of participation instead of just as supplication and observation.

As previously discussed, Agnes believed God's power continually flows from him, similar to the way light radiates from the sun. People who believe in him and submit to His commands can become physical channels of that power to others. The dust jacket of her primary work summarizes her belief succinctly:

> Beginning with the principle that only the amount of electricity that flows through an iron will heat it for us, and hence only the amount of God's creative power that flows through us will heal us, Agnes Sanford writes in a most stimulating manner about how to get this infinity of God's creative power to flow through us. It isn't a question of YOU healing anyone, even yourself, it is a matter of placing yourself in such a way that God uses YOU as a channel for His healing power. God heals, but He must work through people.[21]

For Agnes, healing prayer was not requesting God to act sovereignly and then waiting to see if anything happened; instead, it was a conscious act of mediating his presence to the sick. Her definition of "contacting God" in this first step, therefore, must be understood as different from a prayer of supplication or petition, hoping to elicit a desirable response. Instead, she wanted her readers to realize that God seeks physical and participatory channels through whom he can provide the answers for their needs.

Agnes recognized a clear distinction between prayer as a solicitation directed *to* God and as an invitation connecting *with* God: the former relies on convincing God to act sovereignly while the latter focuses on receiving power being offered cooperatively. She believed supplicatory prayer could become an activity that potentially ignored both logic and sensibility. Using the analogy of a faulty iron, she writes,

> If we try turning on an electric iron and it does not work, we look to the wiring of the iron, the cord, or the house. We do not stand in dismay before the iron and cry, "Oh, electricity, *please* come into my iron and make it work!" We realize that while the whole world is full of that mysterious power we call electricity, only the amount that flows through the wiring of the iron will make the iron work for us. The same principle is true of the creative energy of God.[22]

She clearly presents an image of the futility of asking God for a miracle while remaining ignorant of the human side of the process. The assumption that nothing can interfere with prayers being answered leads to fatalism and results in a faulty view of God:

> We have tried often to make this creative power flow through us, saying, "Oh, God, please do this or that!" And He has not done this or that, so we have concluded that there is no use in prayer, because God, if there is such a Being, will do as He likes regardless of our wishes. In other words, we doubt the *willingness* or the *ability* of God to actually produce within our lives and bodies the results that we desire. We do not doubt our own ability to come into His presence and fill ourselves with Him, but His willingness to come into us and fill us with Himself.[23]

Recognizing human imperfection, she taught people to take responsibility for their spiritual life and relationship with God. She considered this as an attitude of humility. For her, accepting personal limitations is necessary for learning how to pray effectively.

Agnes describes "contacting God" as the first step of her prayer model, but she did not consider it simply to mean asking him to do a miracle. The connection needed to be much more participatory than simply making a prayer of supplication. Relating the incident when her son was healed of an ear infection through a minister's prayer, she explains, "God's water of life could rush through him, for the pipe-line between his spirit and God's spirit was intact. He was in harmony with God."[24] She uses "harmony" here to describe a person operating from a place of communion with God. In her opinion, those who desire to pray for the sick effectively need to take time to focus on him before they make their requests. She states, "Therefore we begin our prayer not by clamoring for this and that before we have even reached His presence, but by thinking about Him in the way that makes Him most real to us."[25] This position reflects her premise that healing prayer involves mediating God's healing power to the sick. She states this in *Behold Your God*:

> Now in order to ask anything of any person we must draw near to him. And so we must first of all draw near to this Almighty God.... And in the prayer of faith it is absolutely necessary to make this contact in order to establish a channel through which the actual energy of God's healing power can flow.[26]

In her view, healing power flows through people as they connect with God through faith.

Meditating on God's holiness functions as one possible way a person can initiate communion with God. Referencing the first sentence in the Lord's Prayer, Agnes writes,

> "Hallowed by Thy name." Thus begins the model prayer of all ages. This is the most practical of all possible beginnings, because thinking about His holiness connects us with Him. Few of us would begin shouting to a friend whom we wish to visit while still six blocks down the street. Few of us would begin speaking

to someone on the telephone before the operator had given us the connection. Yet many of us begin begging for all kinds of little human things before we have realized the one great divine thing which is His own holiness.[27]

For her, connecting with God begins by making God the center of a person's attention. Her descriptions also portray this step as necessary for meaningful communication with God. She describes the importance of this whether praying to receive a personal healing, praying for the healing of others, or praying as a step of forgiveness. In non-theological language, she declares, "We find indeed that all forms of prayer fuse into a high consciousness of God."[28] When it came to healing prayer, however, she stressed this aspect of personal responsibility primarily in the context of the one doing the praying instead of the one receiving prayer.

Along with focusing a person's attention on God, the first step of Agnes's healing model also aims to remove anxiety; her use of the word "harmony" suggests a state of peace. In her books, she often describes fear and worry as inhibitors and blocks to faith and power. When she begins to discuss the first step of her healing model, she quotes the verse "Be still and know that I am God" (Psalm 46:10) immediately before she says,

> Let us then lay aside our worries and cares, quiet our minds and concentrate upon the reality of God. We may not know who God is or what God is, but we know that there is something that sustains this universe, and that something is not ourselves. So the first step is to relax and to remind ourselves that there *is* [emphasis hers] a source of life outside of ourselves.[29]

She sought to lead people into an experience of prayer marked by quietness, confidence, and positive expectation. Indeed, she considered peace so important that she even lists physical steps to minimizing stress prior to prayer, such as sitting in a comfortable position, breathing deeply, and clearing the mind of nervous and anxious thoughts.[30] Because she viewed faith as a confident expectation that proceeds from the subconscious mind, she recognized the importance of minimizing agitation, distress, and tension. As people focus their thoughts on God, it fosters an atmosphere conducive to healing prayer and promotes communion with him.

The first step in Agnes' healing prayer model involves contacting God. She believed that effective healing prayer requires taking the time to make a connection with God before requesting anything from him. This contact facilitates a person entering into a state of communion with God, which allows the person to receive healing or to become a channel of God's healing power for the sick. Additionally, meditating on his character and nature, even briefly, aids in reducing fear, anxiety, and stress that inhibit an attitude of faith. She viewed this first step as a practical and necessary part of praying for the sick.

Step Two: Turning on the Power

Agnes describes the next step in her healing model as turning on the power. As discussed, connecting with God requires a deliberate act; similarly, after making contact with God, a person needs to actively become a channel through which power flows for healing the sick. She did not believe power for healing automatically flows from God to a sick person any more than electricity automatically flows through an iron or a lamp irrespective of it being plugged in and turned on at the time; although unexplained miracles happen, effective healing prayer takes place when a person chooses to be the conduit through which power reaches those who need it. The flow of power usually follows a prayer of intention, vocal or silent; a mental image, picturing and affirming the intended effect; or an intentional act, such as laying hands on the sick. The person needs to begin by doing something appropriate to the situation.

As discussed previously, Agnes believed power continually emanates from God, sustaining all of creation; however, the mediation of healing to others normally requires a willing participant. As might be expected, she considered prayer to be the primary way a person initiates an active flow of divine healing energy. She explains, "The second step is to turn it on, by some such prayer as this[:] 'Heavenly Father, please increase in me at this time Your life-giving power.'"[31] Whether a person desires to receive power for a personal healing or to be a channel of healing for another, receiving from God happens first. To a certain extent, she believed connecting with God almost certainly led to receiving power from Him. She writes,

> The very chemicals contained in the body—the "dust of the earth"—live by the Breath of God ... This being so, it is not strange at all that when we establish a closer connection with God in prayer, we should receive more abundant life—an increased flow of energy. The creative force that sustains us is increased within our bodies.[32]

In this respect, the second step of her healing model proceeds seamlessly from the first, building upon an improved relationship and increased level of communion with God.

Receiving from God constitutes only the first part of the step, however, for the flow of healing power must be directed to a specific need in order to affect a change. Agnes stressed that the prayer should be clearly directed toward a defined need; in her model, the person aims for specificity and avoids general, vague, or uncertain language: "Being connected we then give and receive a clear message and speak toward a definite end, that the purpose of the call may be accomplished."[33] Because this step releases power directly for the identified need, the prayer should be spoken with a confidence and expectation of the intended result. Her model operates on the premise that God wants to perform the healing, requiring the person to pray in faith that the desired result will follow. As she explains, "For while love is the wiring that connects our souls with

His, faith is the switch that turns on the power," and "By the interposition of will *plus* faith [emphasis hers], man can introduce into a situation an increased flow of God's creative energy."[34] For her, faith means that the person prays for a specific result and expects a positive outcome—although the result might not be immediate or complete.

The third chapter of *The Healing Light* specifically discusses turning on the flow of healing power to the sick. Although Agnes mentions "the prayer of faith" in several places, her definition differs from many contemporary sources. Relating her prayer for a young child, she writes,

> I went to see a little girl who had been in a cast for five months following infantile paralysis. One day I placed my hands above the rigid knee . . . and I asked that the light of God might shine through me into the small, stiff knee and make it well.
>
> "Oh, take your hands away!" cried the little girl. "It's hot."
>
> "That's God's power working in your knee, Sally," I replied. "It's like electricity working in your lamp. I guess it has to be hot, so as to make the knee come back to life. So you just stand it now for a few minutes, while I tell you about Peter Rabbit."
>
> By the time the erring Peter had returned home without his shoes and his new red jacket and had been put to bed with castor oil, the pulsation of energy in my hands had died away.
>
> "Now crawl out to the edge of the bed, Sally, and see if that leg will bend," I directed the child.
>
> She pulled herself to the edge of the bed and sat up. And the leg that had been rigid, bent at an angle of forty-five degrees. Within two weeks she was walking.[35]

In this instance, praying in faith did not indicate belief in an instantaneous healing but a conviction that power was flowing through her to the child to restore her leg. The full healing took longer, but a noticeable change occurred immediately following the prayer.

Silent prayer works equally well when appropriate. Agnes describes an incident when a mother asked how to pray for her daughter to be healed of depression, anxiety, and a lack of love. She advised the mother to "stand beside her when she's asleep and lay your hands on her . . . [and] say to yourself, 'By faith I see my child loving and happy and open-hearted and well, as God made her and wants her to be. And in the name of Jesus Christ, I say that this shall be.'"[36] In this instance, she instructed the mother to pray silently instead of out loud, presumably so she would not awaken her daughter in the process. She subsequently records the prayer as having been successful. In another case, Agnes describes praying for a woman who appeared to be depressed. She recalls,

> On one of my most joyful and therefore one of my most powerful days, I entered the elevator of a tall city building and an employee entered after me. She stood with her back to me, but I knew by every sagging line in her body that she was depressed.

"How you doing, sister?" asked the elevator boy.

"Oh-h-h—tired before I begin."

"I bless you in the name of the Lord," I thought. "I see you as a child of God, strong and refreshed and joyful, for through my prayers His strength is entering into you." The girl's bent shoulders lifted immediately. "I dunno!" she cried to the elevator boy in quite a different voice. "Maybe life's not so bad, after all. I got a hunch today's going to be a good day." The elevator door opened and she tripped down the corridor lightly, head held high. She had come to life more rapidly than any plant can come to life when water is poured upon it!³⁷[37]

In both cases along with others she recounts, the prayer was thought instead of spoken. She believed a person could also release a flow of power through a silent prayer as long as faith was involved.

Additionally, Agnes taught people to use the imagination to release a flow of healing power. She describes this practice in conjunction with prayer, and she sometimes stressed it more than the prayer itself. She states,

> When we ask for the indwelling of God's Holy Spirit in the body, let us think of that part of the body that most needs His life. Let us imagine His light and life glowing there like a fire, shining there like a light. Then through the rest of the day let us continually give thanks that His life is at work within us accomplishing His perfect will and recreating us after His image and likeness, which is perfection.[38]

For her, the ability to imagine health and healing activates the faith of the person. When she explained to a soldier how to receive healing for his leg, which had received multiple unsuccessful bone grafts, she advised him to do the following:

> "Well then, ask that Something to come into you. Just say 'Whoever you are or whatever you are, come into me now and help nature in my body to mend this bone, and do it quick. Thanks. I believe you're doing it.' Then make a picture in your mind of the leg well. Shut your eyes and see it that way. See the bone all built in and the flesh strong and perfect around it. And play like you see a kind of light shining in it—a sort of a blue light, like one of these Neon signs, shining and burning and flowing all up and down the leg."
>
> "Why do I do that?"
>
> "Because that's the way you make it happen. No matter what you want to make, you first have to see it in your mind, don't you? Could you make a table if you didn't first see in your mind the kind of table you're going to make?"
>
> "I get you."
>
> "Good! Then after you see the leg well, give a pep talk to all the healing forces of your body. Say, 'Look here, I'm boss inside of me and what I say goes. Now get busy and men that leg.' And then congratulate them and tell them they're doing a good job, because they won't work for you unless you encourage them. And after this, forget them and think of the life outside of you again, and say "Thank You, God. I believe it's going to be O.K."'[39]

Even though he did not know God, his daily prayer in conjunction with using his own imagination resulted in his leg being completely restored without any further surgery.

Agnes believed the imagination bridges the conscious and subconscious minds. As mentioned, she believed "will *plus* faith" results in effective prayer. While the conscious mind prays as the person chooses, the subconscious reveals actual beliefs. In her view, the subconscious significantly influences a person's life, including the ability to receive healing power. In a chapter dedicated to the topic, she writes,

> If the conscious mind were the only sentient force within us, the prayer outlined in the preceding chapter would probably be enough to make us well. But the part of us that reasons is only one-tenth of the consciousness. Psychologists tell us that nine-tenths of our thoughts lie below the level of consciousness. Moreover, it is this submerged part of the consciousness—this sub-conscious mind—that controls our bodies. . . . This inner control center is part of the spiritual body, the eternal Being. It acts under orders from God Himself until man sends into it a contrary command and throws it into confusion.[40]

Contrary commands—such as negative thoughts, fears, and doubts—hinder people from receiving all the life and power available, whether through prayer or the natural healing processes of the human body; however, using the imagination to reinforce a prayer of faith could counter those hindrances and release a flow of healing power.

At times, healing power operates through touch without any specific prayer. Agnes relates two such instances. In the first, she prayed repeatedly for a child with an ear infection, but instead of getting better, he became significantly worse. Struggling with her own faith, she called a friend for advice. She writes,

> I began to wonder whether it was God's will for him to die. Upon my knees I wrestled with this problem, knowing that if I were to accept God's will for a little child as blindness, agony and death, my experiments in healing were over. . . . But I cut myself away from this convenient excuse for failure as a ship going out to sea drops its shore-lines. I telephoned to an older and more experienced prayer-worker from a neighboring city . . . [who] directed me to go to the little boy at a certain time and place my hands upon him. "But don't try to do anything, dearie," she advised me. "You've been trying too hard, and it's upset you. Just be still and *know* [emphasis from source]; He is God and His power is flowing into you through me." I followed her directions. The child was by this time unconscious. He did not rouse as I stood beside him in the dark, my hands on his brow. Yet I was so conscious of a heavenly presence with us that I returned home giving thanks.[41]

Within two days, the child had recovered. In this situation, she placed her hands upon the child with the intention of being a channel of healing power without any mention of prayer or imagination. In the second instance, she prayed for a child with pneumonia:

> I knelt beside her little crib in silence, laid one hand upon the small, congested chest and slipped the other one beneath her back. Soon the waxy frame of the baby was filled with a visible inrushing of new life. Even the hands and feet vibrated, as if an electric current were entering into her. A look of tension on the tiny face was smoothed away and she passed from a semi-conscious condition into a natural sleep. Two hours later her doctor came into the room. . . . and he beheld his small patient, bright-eyed and cheerful, sitting up in bed.[42]

Agnes does not mention praying or imagining anything in this account. She simply placed her hands upon the child for healing, and the girl completely recovered.

The second step of Agnes' healing model involves turning on the flow of healing power. Once a person has made contact with God, the second step provides a channel for his presence to physically affect the situation. Whether a person seeks a personal healing or healing for someone else, there must be some type of activation by faith. A flow of power often follows a prayer of faith, confidently declaring the specific desired result, and it can be either audible or silent. Additionally, picturing the intended result and laying hands on the sick person usually accompany the prayer. However, the imagination or physical touch sometimes suffices without any prayer. A conscious act, intended to release a flow of power for healing, forms the fundamental essence of her second step.

Step Three: Believing the Power is Flowing

After a person has made a connection with God and prayed to turn on a flow of healing power, the next step involves believing that the power is actually flowing. In other words, the person who prayed must believe that the prayer has made a difference. While the second step focuses on acting in faith, the third step centers on maintaining an attitude of faith in the subconscious. Part of this attitude of faith involves the person thanking God that power is physically flowing and healing has started to happen. Agnes did not teach that people should claim that a healing already happened or had been completed if they were still sick; however, she did believe that they should accept the healing process as having begun, whether they saw an immediate difference or not. Thanking God, therefore, was part of the step that affirmed their faith as well as placed their focus on him instead of on the circumstances.

As mentioned, the third step in Agnes' healing prayer model involves accepting that power has begun flowing from God to the identified need. She writes, "The third step is to believe that this power is coming into use and to accept it by faith. No matter how much we ask for something it becomes ours only as we accept it and give thanks for it."[43] Although she first presents the step in terms of someone praying for a personal healing, it operates the same when praying for someone else: the person must believe that the prayer of faith has released healing power to the sick and that the flow of healing will continue until the person becomes well. In her ministry model, healing often takes place as a process over time as God's presence acts upon a person's body to restore it. She did not believe that healings always happen instantaneously. As she explains it,

> If we have sought God for a simple thing such as healing of a cold in the head, we may find that healing perfected in a few minutes. If we have sought Him for the rebuilding of bones or nerves or sinuses, the complete healing may take time and patience.[44]

She knew some healings require people to continue believing during the ongoing process.

Agnes did not consider it inappropriate for a person to pray for a healing multiple times. In fact, she often advised people to make prayer a regular habit until the healing was completed. However, she did distinguish between an initial prayer and subsequent prayers. Continuing from the last passage, she writes,

> In which case, while we seek daily to reconnect our spirit with the Spirit of God in prayer, we need not repeat any request for healing that we have once made. We need only give thanks that *it is being accomplished* [emphasis hers]. Never say, "please," more than once. Say, "Thank you." "Thank you," that it is well when it isn't? Not necessarily. There is no virtue in forcing a statement of faith that the inner doubt denies. But one can always say, "Thank You that Your life is entering into me at this time, rebuilding everything toward health." One can always use his creative imagination, make a picture in his mind of that perfection that he hopes will be his and look steadily upon that picture until it is accomplished. Thus, by harnessing the imagination and training the will one can arouse and build his faith.[45]

Because step three involves believing power began flowing when a prayer is first prayed, any behavior contradicting that belief would interfere with the process. Nevertheless, she recognized that healing often requires ongoing prayer. When a soldier asked how often he should pray for his leg to be healed, she replied, "Once a day at least, three times a day if it doesn't get tiresome. And always at the same time every day, because then you get in the habit of thinking like that at that time and it helps a lot."[46] She advocated for continued prayers for healing, but she stipulated that they should reaffirm prior prayers.

Because Agnes viewed faith as originating in the subconscious, she believed a person's thoughts were vital to any ability to receive or impart power. Therefore, she stressed the importance of developing a way of thinking that creates an atmosphere conducive to healing. She explains,

> So we learn faith by trying to understand that we are children of light and then correcting every thought that denies our glorious heritage of life and love. This daily practice will gradually fill the subconsciousness with the new thought-habit of faith, so that one day it will overflow into our lives, as a well daily filled

with water one day overflows its banks. When that day comes we will not need to correct our thoughts any more, for faith and peace and joy will be our instinctive and natural reaction to every situation.[47]

While she did not advocate that people should claim to be well when they were still sick, she did discourage language affirming sickness or infirmity. For her, negative or fatalistic words undermine faith within the subconscious. She writes,

> The sub-conscious mind does not respond to reason, but only to suggestion. Every time we think, "Oh dear, I'm afraid I'm catching cold," the sub-conscious mind picks up the suggestion, "Catch a cold." God has equipped the body with white corpuscles whose express purpose is to destroy enemy cold germs and so preserve the body in God's image and likeness of perfection. But the thought, "I'm afraid I'm catching a cold," sends a contrary order to the inner control center . . . [and] the natural resistive forces of the body are thrown into confusion, because they are acting under two conflicting orders. Their efficacy is weakened, and the body is much more likely to catch a cold.[48]

Agnes recommended that people intentionally make a habit of having their thoughts and words reinforce the idea that their prayers are working and power is flowing to the sick.

Thanking God for healing forms a significant aspect of the third step of Agnes' healing prayer model. She believed thankfulness not only reflects faith but also promotes an atmosphere of receptivity. She states, "No matter how much we ask for something it becomes ours only as we accept it and give thanks for it."[49] In her view, being thankful enables a person to receive from God. She considered this a vital step in the process. She writes,

> We give thanks for [His gifts] because we believe that we are receiving them. Therefore we do receive them. For our joyful thanksgiving testifies to our faith, and through the doorway of our faith He enters in. How many Christians down through the ages have failed to receive the answers to their prayers by failing to take this last step—the step of giving thanks! God is standing before us with the answer in His hands. But unless we reach out our hands and take it by giving thanks for it, we are not apt to receive it. For while love is the wiring that connects our souls with His, faith is the switch that turns on the power. . . . Just believing a set of facts about God does not necessarily turn on the power in a single one of our prayer-objectives. In order to do that, we must believe that we are receiving the thing that we desire. If we really believe this, we will naturally rejoice and give thanks for it. And when our belief is weak, the act of rejoicing and giving thanks will awaken our faith.[50]

Agnes believed thankfulness undergirded a positive attitude toward God and promoted healing. In her sequel on healing prayer, she even describes a lack of thankfulness, gratitude, and generosity as a major hindrance to receiving from God.[51] She taught that thanking God for healing helped continue the process.

Agnes describes the third step of her prayer model as developing and releasing faith toward God. The person should maintain a belief that power is flowing from God and thank him that the power is having an effect. During the process, the person should adjust both thoughts and words to reinforce faith without claiming any result the person's subconscious would consider dishonest. Thankfulness toward God is a core aspect of her model because it makes the person receptive to God's power and keeps the focus on him.

Step Four: Observing the Results

The fourth step in Agnes' prayer model involves observing the results of prayer and evaluating whether a different approach is necessary. She affirmed the scientific method and believed people should adjust how they pray to become as effective as possible. In order to judge the effectiveness, she recommends making prayer objectives as specific and tangible as possible; in her view, vague or general requests usually signify hesitancy instead of faith. She held a very practical and pragmatic attitude toward healing prayer, considering failure a pathway to success by helping people recognize where their prayer process needs improvement. She often describes prayer in terms of scientific experimentation and suggests that perseverance along with faith, commitment, and honesty can enable anyone to become more effective in praying for the sick.

Agnes defines the final step of her prayer model in terms of choosing a tangible and specific objective and then observing the result. She writes,

> And the fourth step is to observe the operations of that light and life. In order to do so, we must decide on some tangible thing that we wish accomplished by that power, so that we can know without question whether our experiment succeeded or failed. Many Christians are afraid to do this.[52]

She advises people to pray with specific language and goals to optimize learning and growth. By viewing healing prayer as an experiment, failure actually becomes an opportunity for improvement: "What scientist would be discouraged if his first experiment failed? Since we intend with his help to heal our shortcomings, to repair our wiring, we need not fear to test His power by prayer."[53] Her prayer model regarded God's willingness to be an accepted premise, leaving human interactions as the remaining variable. As such, she intended her model to help people become better at praying for the sick by identifying when certain types of prayer work and when they do not. She declares,

> This book suggests, for those willing to learn, a method so simple that it is childlike, as the more profound truths are apt to be. It is an experimental method. One decides upon a definite subject for prayer, prays about it and then decides whether or not the prayer-project succeeds. If it does not succeed, one seeks a better adjustment with God and tries again. This is the method of the men who

have discovered and harnessed the forces of God's world—the scientists.⁵⁴

She believed prayer needs to be approached with an allowance for human improvement instead of assuming that every negative outcome is necessarily God's will.

Although Agnes believed that praying in faith means maintaining confidence that power continues to flow after an initial prayer, she also recognized that adjustments should be made if healing does not happen. Concerning the boy with an ear infection that continued to get worse, she writes,

> I was once asked to pray for a little boy with abscessed ears. The child improved for twenty-four hours, then relapsed. I prayed with him again and the same thing happened again, more than once. Each relapse was worse than the last and he was finally taken to a hospital and operated upon for mastoid. Even the cooperation of prayer and science did not save him. The poison began to eat into the bones of the head. He was on the verge of spinal meningitis. Feeling sure that since Jesus never failed to heal a little boy brought to Him by faithful parents and so we should never fail, I sought more power in prayer. My methods were perhaps childlike. But through them I learned, as children learn. I went to see the little boy in the company of a minister, and again with two or three friends, hoping by just the right combination of minds to provide God with the right kind of a wire for the inflowing of His power. The boy's condition grew steadily worse.⁵⁵

After making every adjustment she knew, she began to struggle with her faith in God's willingness to heal the boy; instead of acquiescing to her doubts, however, she called a prayer partner for advice, attempted an entirely different approach, and saw the boy healed. She believed that her refusal to give up not only kept the boy from dying but also resulted in his getting well.

Agnes instructed people to treat healing prayer like a scientific experiment in which they persevered until the objective succeeded. She often described it in terms of attempting to prove a hypothesis. Using the example of Thomas Edison, she says,

> When Edison had tried some hundreds of times to find a wire that could transmit a continuous flow of electricity, and had failed some hundreds of times, he did not say, "It is not the will of electricity to shine continuously in my wire." He tried again. He believed that it *was* [emphasis hers] in the will, that is, in the nature, of electricity to produce this steady light. He concluded, therefore, that there was some adjustment to the laws of electricity that he had not yet made, and he determined to make that adjustment. For more than six thousand times he tried again. And he succeeded in making electricity shine continuously in a wire. That is faith.⁵⁶

She viewed perseverance as a sign of humility and faith. However, she did not consider medicine contrary to faith, especially if a person had a serious condition. When a woman lamented to her that a prayer of faith did not remove a stomach growth, she replied, "Maybe the thing you want it to bring forth is too big for it.... If you wait two or three years, maybe your faith will be big enough to heal a growth like this. But in the meantime, if you want healing, you'd better get the doctors to help you."[57] She advised people not to put themselves at risk needlessly. When the woman persisted in requesting prayer, she agreed—under the condition that the woman would get medical help if the growth did not disappear; when it persisted, she directed the woman to have surgery.[58] Although she believed that healing was God's will, she viewed medicine and medical care another vehicle through which He provided healing and health. For her, science and faith held no contradiction.

As discussed, the second step of Agnes' prayer model flows seamlessly from the first and into the third; similarly, the first three steps lead to the fourth. A person connects with God in order to receive power to tangibly affect a specific situation. She repeatedly uses the analogy of electricity to describe her first step and frames it with a clear result:

> And just as a whole world full of electricity will not light a house unless the house itself is prepared to receive that electricity, so the infinite and eternal life of God cannot help us unless we are prepared to receive that life within ourselves. *Only the amount of God that we can get in us will work for us* [emphasis hers].[59]

Her language clearly describes connecting with God in order to receive power for a specific result. The second step also operates in relation to tangible results. Having contacted God, the person prays "toward a definite end, that the purpose of the [prayer] may be accomplished."[60] She considered vague prayers insufficient for this process because the results would be too general to identify actual success or failure. Likewise, step three involved specifically thanking God for a concrete change along with using the imagination to picture the definite goal. She writes,

> [Let us] *create in our minds* [emphasis hers] the picture of that person well. Thus, we set in motion our powers of spiritual creativity. Those things that we see in our minds tend to become so. This is a lawa s certain as the law of gravity, and to this law we shall return again and again. Let us draw the image in our minds. Let us make the blueprint. Let us dwell at the time of prayer and at all other times, whenever the person comes to mind, on the picture of that one well.[61]

In her view, a person can only evaluate the effectiveness of prayer and the ability to be a channel of healing power by objectively recognizing whether or not the prayer goal was achieved. Therefore, the objective needed to be concrete, specific, and tangible.

The fourth step in Agnes' healing prayer model involved observing the effects of the prayer of faith and making adjustments according to the results. She believed healing prayer could be approached like an experiment so the person could objectively evaluate the effectiveness of various methods. Additionally, she taught people to persevere when a healing did not take place instead of concluding that the healing was not God's will. For her, healing was a process that often took time, and people could improve in their faith as well as their ability to be a channel for healing power to the sick. However, she considered medical treatment as an acceptable option when prayer alone did not result in complete healing. Her fourth step merged the prayer of faith with the scientific method.

Conclusion

Agnes based her healing prayer model on several theological and scientific premises. She believed healing was God's will because it reflects his intrinsic nature as well as physical observations in nature. Instead of viewing healing prayer as supplication for a sovereign act, she believed it involves a person being a vehicle through which God's presence affects and restores someone to health. Using the scientific method as a framework, she developed a four-step model of contacting God, turning on the flow of power, believing the power was flowing, and observing the results of the prayer. Because she believed perseverance results in improvement, she advised people to view healing prayer as an experiment in learning how to receive and release power to the sick. Her model significantly joined a respect for science with a devotion to faith.

Notes

[1] Some parts of this chapter were previously discussed in the author's published article *God's Faithful Freedom* as well as an unpublished presentation on Agnes' use of the scientific method.
[2] Agnes Sanford, *The Healing Light*, 2nd ed., 17.
[3] Henry H. Knight III, "God's Faithfulness and God's Freedom," 65-89.
[4] Henry H. Knight III, "God's Faithfulness and God's Freedom," 70-74, 78.
[5] James Robinson, *Divine Healing: The Formative Years, 1830-1890*, 3.
[6] Ronald A. N. Kydd, *Healing through the Centuries: Models for Understanding* (Peabody: Hendrickson, 1998), xv.
[7] Agnes Sanford, *Behold Your God*, 16.
[8] Agnes Sanford, *Behold Your God*, 16.
[9] Agnes Sanford, *The Healing Light*, 2nd ed., 42-43.
[10] Agnes Sanford, *The Healing Light*, 2nd ed., 42.
[11] Agnes Sanford, *Behold Your God*, 42.
[12] Agnes Sanford, *Behold Your God*, 43.
[13] Agnes Sanford, *Behold Your God*, 44.
[14] Agnes Sanford, *Behold Your God*, 45-46.
[15] Agnes Sanford, *Behold Your God*, 47.
[16] Agnes Sanford, *The Healing Light*, 2nd ed., 43.
[17] Agnes Sanford, *Behold Your God*, 35.
[18] Agnes Sanford, *The Healing Light*, 2nd ed., 27-28.
[19] Agnes Sanford, *The Healing Light*, 2nd ed., 85.

20. Agnes Sanford, *The Healing Light*, 2nd ed., 21.
21. Agnes Sanford, *The Healing Light*, 2nd ed., dusk jacket.
22. Agnes Sanford, *The Healing Light*, 2nd ed., 17.
23. Agnes Sanford, *The Healing Light*, 2nd ed., 21.
24. Agnes Sanford, *The Healing Light*, 2nd ed., 18.
25. Agnes Sanford, *The Healing Light*, 2nd ed., 39.
26. Agnes Sanford, *Behold Your God*, 14-15.
27. Agnes Sanford, *The Healing Light*, 2nd ed., 39.
28. Agnes Sanford, *The Healing Light*, 2nd ed., 71.
29. Agnes Sanford, *The Healing Light*, 2nd ed., 21-22.
30. Agnes Sanford, *The Healing Light*, 2nd ed., 37-38; *Behold Your God*, 16-17.
31. Agnes Sanford, *The Healing Light*, 2nd ed., 22. Colon added within quote for clarity.
32. Agnes Sanford, *The Healing Light*, 2nd ed., 31.
33. Agnes Sanford, *Behold Your God*, 22.
34. Agnes Sanford, *The Healing Light*, 2nd ed., 40; *Behold Your God*, 16.
35. Agnes Sanford, *The Healing Light*, 2nd ed., 31.
36. Agnes Sanford, *The Healing Light*, 2nd ed., 67.
37. Agnes Sanford, *The Healing Light*, 2nd ed., 68-69.
38. Agnes Sanford, *The Healing Light*, 2nd ed., 28.
39. Agnes Sanford, *The Healing Light*, 2nd ed., 34.
40. Agnes Sanford, *The Healing Light*, 2nd ed., 42.
41. Agnes Sanford, *The Healing Light*, 2nd ed., 26-27.
42. Agnes Sanford, *The Healing Light*, 2nd ed., 33.
43. Agnes Sanford, *The Healing Light*, 2nd ed., 22.
44. Agnes Sanford, *The Healing Light*, 2nd ed., 28.
45. Agnes Sanford, *The Healing Light*, 2nd ed., 28.
46. Agnes Sanford, *The Healing Light*, 2nd ed., 36.
47. Agnes Sanford, *The Healing Light*, 2nd ed., 45.
48. Agnes Sanford, *The Healing Light*, 2nd ed., 43.
49. Agnes Sanford, *The Healing Light*, 2nd ed., 22.
50. Agnes Sanford, *The Healing Light*, 2nd ed., 40.
51. Agnes Sanford, *Behold Your God*, 54-57.
52. Agnes Sanford, *The Healing Light*, 2nd ed., 22.
53. Agnes Sanford, *The Healing Light*, 2nd ed., 23.
54. Agnes Sanford, *The Healing Light*, 2nd ed., 21.
55. Agnes Sanford, *The Healing Light*, 2nd ed., 26.
56. Agnes Sanford, *The Healing Light*, 2nd ed., 25.
57. Agnes Sanford, *The Healing Light*, 2nd ed., 85.
58. Agnes Sanford, *The Healing Light*, 2nd ed., 86.
59. Agnes Sanford, *The Healing Light*, 2nd ed., 19.
60. Agnes Sanford, *Behold Your God*, 22.
61. Agnes Sanford, *Behold Your God*, 34.

CHAPTER 5

A Decidedly Christian Theology

Agnes uses unusual terminology and concepts in her works, leading some to doubt her Christian faith. Nevertheless, she promotes a solidly Christian worldview. She describes her theology in depth in *Behold Your God*, her sequel to *The Healing Light*. She bases her beliefs about God and salvation on her Presbyterian and Episcopal background, and her views conform with Christian orthodoxy. Along with many Christians interested in healing in the early twentieth century, she embraced metaphysical concepts but interpreted them in light of a worldview formed by her childhood in China, developing a relationship with God more experiential than intellectual. Additionally, she embraced some doctrines and beliefs that defy easy categorization but qualify as nonessentials. Agnes makes numerous statements and describes experiences considered questionable by many Protestants and Evangelicals, but none of her deviations from the normal Christian paradigm qualify as heresy, and her theology affirms her Christian faith.

Christian Orthodoxy

As discussed, Agnes clearly embraced some New Thought and Unity School of Christianity concepts, terminology, and stylistic effects (capitalization) in her writing. However, she maintained an orthodox Christian perspective on the Trinity as three relational persons—Father, Son, and Holy Spirit. She clearly incorporated traces of Jungian psychology into her anthropology, including the concept of the collective unconscious and the shadow. Nevertheless, she rejected any Spiritist, atheistic, or occultic influences from his works, using the Ten Commandments as a guide and retaining the biblical foundation of the redemptive work of Jesus Christ as the only way to God. The foundation of her Presbyterian and Episcopal heritage undergirded her Eastern-Western Modern worldview, and her commitment to Christian Scripture, along with respect for the *Westminster Confession of Faith*, the *Shorter and Longer Catechism*, and the *Book of Common Prayer*, grounded her theology.

The Trinity

Although New Thought and Jungian psychology clearly influenced Agnes, her understanding of God developed primarily from her Presbyterian and Episcopal theology. The prominence of unusual language and uncommon descriptors for God result not from heretical and errant views of God but from an attempt to introduce healing and faith to people unfamiliar with the Christian view on the topic. Early editions of *The Healing Light* include a noteworthy subtitle: *On the Art and Method of Spiritual Healing from the Christian Viewpoint and in the Christian Tradition*; later editions either shorten the subtitle to *The Art and Method of Spiritual Healing* or omit it entirely.[1] At least to some extent, she wrote the book to include people outside the Christian tradition. Agnes meant her works to be missional, so she incorporated the language of her target audience.

New Thought describes God as a cosmic force instead of a relational Person and often uses impersonal terminology, such as "Divine Mind" or "Infinite Intelligence" as a descriptor. Although Agnes embraced some metaphysical concepts, she rejected any depersonalization of God. In her primary theological work, she affirms his personhood:

> Now in order to ask anything of any person we must draw near to him. And so we must first of all draw near to this Almighty God. In one sense, of course, we are already near to Him.... in Him we live and move and have our being.... Yet some people today tend to minimize this tremendous fact from which all other facts evolve. "God is Divine Mind," they say, "and we have Divine Mind within us." "God is the creative principle, and we have and can use the creative principle." There is a shred of truth in this, of course. But this is only a small part of the whole great truth.... As the Presbyterian Shorter Catechism expresses it, "God is a Spirit, infinite, eternal and unchangeable, in His Being, Wisdom, Power, Holiness, Justice, Goodness and Truth." God is more than Divine Mind or Divine Wisdom. God is more than a current of power that heals. God is love, but God is more than love. God works according to truth, but God is more than merely a certain principle of thinking that one might call "truth." GOD IS. God is the Father Almighty, and man can make contact with Him and know Him.[2]

Agnes certainly allows for a more metaphysical approach than many Christians might consider beneficial. Nevertheless, she clearly describes God as a relational Person and rejects any attempt to depersonalize Him as a cosmic force or philosophical principle.

In the same passage, Agnes declares God created the world from himself. She strongly believed God had infused his creation with himself, being present through it. Some readers have therefore identified her as a pantheist. However, she refutes any concept of equating God with the universe. While describing his nature, she also writes,

> He sent forth His word and life evolved from the Creator Himself. Thus in Him we live and move and have our being. He is in the world about us, so that those who see God in trees and stones and running brooks are glimpsing a bit of the truth. But God is not limited to the one aspect of His eternal glory that formed the inanimate creation. God is more than His creation.... God did not cease to be, in giving [people] souls. He still IS, existing outside of them as well as inside of them! This is a simple, obvious, primary.... God is not only in us or the sun or the rocks or the trees. God IS. Before all worlds, God IS. When all worlds shall be rolled up as a garment and shall disappear, still God IS. If there were no living being to know Him, still God IS. As the Presbyterian Shorter Catechism expresses it, "God is a Spirit, infinite, eternal and unchangeable, in His Being, Wisdom, Power, Holiness, Justice, Goodness and Truth." God is more than Divine Mind or Divine Wisdom. God is more than a current of power that heals. God is love, but God is more than love. God works according to truth, but God is more than merely a certain principle of thinking that one might call "truth." GOD IS.[3]

Although she describes God as immanent in creation, she does so without negating his transcendence and completeness apart from that creation. She rejected pantheism.

Agnes maintained an entirely orthodox position on the person of Jesus Christ as the Son of God. She admits to considering adoptionism for a time but rejected it as untenable.[4] For her, the doctrine of the incarnation was absolute and essential. She states, "So God is a loving father and He means to help us and He will. He is so eager to help us that He came to us, long ago, in a new way, entering this world through gates of birth, and incarnating His love in the Son of Man, Jesus Christ" and "God forbid that I should for a moment dare to believe that Jesus Christ was not conceived by the Holy Ghost, born of the Virgin Mary."[5] In line with New Thought as well as much of Western Christian thinking, Agnes believed Jesus presents a perfect example of human potential; however, she understands he does so only because of his unique status as God incarnate in the flesh—not an enlightened master.

Agnes also held an orthodox Christian view of the third person of the Trinity. She discusses the Spirit in a chapter titled "The Holy Spirit and His Power." She begins the chapter by briefly referencing Jesus' promise to send the disciples power from Heaven and subsequently fulfilling it on the day of Pentecost. She then asks,

> What do we mean when we speak of the Holy Ghost or the Holy Spirit? Do we refer to the Christ spirit within us ... the breath of God that fills the universe . . . or the voice of God guiding our thoughts and actions? These three phrases express quite different concepts. Let us try, therefore, to clarify our thinking concerning the Holy Spirit. [The ellipses are from the original source].[6]

Considering that she wrote this book prior to the beginning of the Charismatic Movement, she poses valid and logical questions. After discussing some mystical experiences related to the various gifts, she cautions her readers to seek the giver directly instead of the gifts:

> But if we seek God and his Holy Spirit, all these lesser things are added unto us. For the Holy Spirit is by His very nature and being the giver of all super-sensory gifts. The Holy Spirit is moreover that aspect of the God-head sent into the world for the express purpose of giving life to our spirits. As the love of God was incarnated in Jesus Christ for the redemption of our subconscious minds, so the light and fire and power of God is released through the Holy Spirit for the redemption of our spirits. There is in all of us an uncomprehended longing for a third person of the Trinity.[7]

Her admonition reflects cautions still expressed within Charismatic, Pentecostal, and Renewal branches of the Church today.[8]

After discussing the appropriate attitude toward the Holy Spirit and the gifts of the Spirit, Agnes relates her own experience of operating in the healing ministry. Prior to receiving the baptism of the Holy Spirit, she felt continually drained and exhausted from everything she was doing, but after Spirit baptism, she experienced joy and power that made the work significantly easier—and she even remarks that she could often get more accomplished in less time.[9] Before closing with recommendations on how a person can receive the baptism of the Spirit, she makes a declaration of who the Holy Spirit is:

> Yes, there is a third Person of the Trinity: God, the One God, manifesting Himself through a third divine Personality. Even as Jesus always IS ("Before Abraham was, I AM") so also the Holy Spirit always IS. In the very beginning, the Spirit of God moved upon the face of the waters (Gen. 1:2). As the ever-existing Being of the Son leaped into time upon earth on the first Christmas Eve, so the ever-existing Holy Spirit was projected forth from God through Christ and leaped into time upon our earth on the day of Pentecost.[10]

Agnes understood the Holy Spirit to be the Third Person of the Trinity, fully God and always existing—not an impersonal cosmic force or some type of universal principle.

Agnes often uses metaphysical and psychological terminology in her chapter on the Spirit, but her explanation reflects an orthodox view of the Holy Spirit. As if to confirm the importance of believing the Spirit is a person, she says,

> How is He received? He, the third Person of the Trinity, the Spirit of truth? By invitation and by faith; an invitation to *Him* [emphasis hers], not to a vague something that we call the Christ within or Divine Mind or even the Universal Spirit. That is good, but it is not good enough. It is a step *toward* Him [emphasis hers], but a step not long enough to actually reach Him. We need to ask Him, the divine Personality perfected through Christ's work on earth and sent to us

through the ascended spirit of Jesus Christ, to come into us and set on fire the spiritual parts of us.[11]

Although Agnes often incorporates unusual terminology and concepts for God, she unequivocally declares her orthodox beliefs in the Trinity as Father, Son, and Holy Spirit, three persons in One, and not some vague force or universal concept.

Agnes's understanding of the role and nature of the Holy Spirit seemed to change between the time she wrote her first book and its sequel. As discussed, she had been involved in healing ministry for several years before she had her own experience of baptism in the Holy Spirit, which profoundly affected her. She did have a successful healing ministry prior to that time, but it involved teaching and ministering not from a sense of joy but from obedience. She writes,

> I was always and increasingly tired.... Yet I continued to go from city to city in the United States and in Canada, to proclaim the truth: that Jesus lives and heals today. In this one way I know that I really love the Lord. It is not in my nature to feel the joy of a gushing emotion toward Him, though I wish that were so. But insofar as I know what He requires of me, that I try to do, for His sake.[12]

In other words, she was exhausted by the work she was doing, but she did it because she knew God wanted her to do it. However, following the baptism in the Spirit, she received "First of all, the gift of joy; we were swept with a joy transcending any that we had ever known before. This heavenly rapture came, not from the mind, but from the heart—from within, like a well of water springing up unto everlasting life, even as Jesus told the woman at the well in Samaria."[13] In her autobiography, Agnes seems to suggest that the baptism of the Holy Spirit is a pivotal step in Christians becoming something different than they otherwise would be. She explains, "Some churches are now awakening into this glory of the Lord, this coming of His Holy Spirit, this actual mutation of human beings into the sons of God."[14] The baptism enables the Christian to become something more.

The evolution in her theology becomes apparent when *The Healing Light* is compared to *Behold Your God*. In her first book, she focuses primarily on the laws of God and the practical steps of faith. The entire book uses metaphysical and scientific language to describe healing prayer, and even the sacraments are explained from that perspective. Most significantly, none of the fifteen chapters are devoted to the person or power of the Holy Spirit.[15] As she writes in her autobiography, she knew He was part of the Trinity, but she was unaware of any active role He had in healing ministry. Describing her understanding prior to her own baptism in the Holy Spirit, she explains,

> A voice spoke within all three of us saying, "Pray for the Holy Ghost." This amazed us. We had not the least idea what it meant. We were not apt to speak of the Holy Ghost anyway, but addressed the Third Person of the Trinity as the

Holy Spirit. We assumed, as most good Christians do, that we had this evanescent sense of Christian brotherhood or whatever it was that these words meant.[16]

Prior to her experience, she believed in the Holy Spirit, but her understanding was somewhat unclear and non-specific.

Agnes wrote *Behold Your God*, her sequel on healing, after her experience of Spirit baptism, and the change in her theology is evident. She includes the chapter "The Holy Spirit and His Power" to discuss his Person and the infilling in detail.[17] Compared to her prior time in ministry, she now considered the baptism in the Holy Spirit to be vital for living a complete Christian life. She explains, "What happens when the spirit of man is thus infused with the life of the Holy Spirit? Man's spirit is then given such life that, body and mind being yielded to it and put under its control, it can interpenetrate and illumine both conscious and subconscious minds."[18] In other words, the infilling of the Spirit actively changes the believer. She did not believe that the baptism in the Holy Spirit was necessary for salvation, clearly seeing the forgiveness of Jesus Christ as sufficient; however, she then writes, "But this is not the final state of the sons of God! Those who go farther in the Christian life make room for the Holy Spirit by the cleansing of the subconscious being and then fill that inner chamber with the light and holiness of the Spirit, so that the impulse of sin dies within one and the new creature in Christ Jesus is born (Rom. 8:1-11)."[19] She considered the baptism in the Holy Spirit a necessary experience for complete change. The very next chapter, "The New Creature in Christ Jesus," is largely a continuation of this chapter, describing how the Holy Spirit changes the believer from the inside out following the infilling.[20] Clearly, her own experience significantly changed her perspective not only on ministry but also on how Christians are to live their lives. For her, the baptism in the Holy Spirit enabled a believer to be changed and become something entirely new.

Soteriology

Although Agnes discusses salvation throughout all her works, she devotes two entire chapters in *Behold Your God* to describing the redemptive work of Christ on Calvary along with another chapter to His bodily resurrection, ascension, and abiding presence. She states unequivocally at the beginning, "Jesus was forthright and explicit in stating that no man came to the Father but by Him (Matt. 22:34-40). And the essence of Christianity is a belief in Jesus Christ—not merely in His teachings, but in Himself as the open door to God."[21] Agnes affirms this basic tenet of the Christian faith: Jesus is the only way to the Father. While New Thought focuses on his teachings as life and a representation of truth, she directs her readers to him: "History is full of prophets and masters who taught truth. Even the great law of love was not His invention. . . . But Christianity is not founded on this law but on Jesus Himself who alone can help us keep this law."[22] Although she often gives examples of unbelievers benefiting from following biblical principles, she clearly states her own commitment to orthodox Christology and the redemptive work of Christ.

Agnes rejected both universalism and pluralism. Her personal commitment to the Christian faith as the only avenue to salvation becomes clear when she writes, "True, in the above chapters I have outlined some principles of faith. But as we try to practice them, we come to a block in our own unredeemed natures, and without Jesus we can go no further."[23] She knew and taught that redemption comes only through Jesus Christ even though other religions may contain some truth gained from general revelation. She compares and contrasts general revelation with the words of Jesus, saying,

> Jesus did not invent a straight and narrow way of life in order to make things difficult for us. He only made plain to us the original creative principles through which God works. These principles are built into our spirits, our minds and our bodies, and neither Jesus nor anyone else can evade nor avoid them. They had been seen more or less dimly by religious thinkers of all ages. Jesus Christ restated them, however, with much greater force; outlining not only acts that we cannot do without danger to ourselves, but also thoughts that we cannot think without harm to ourselves.[24]

Her words do not indicate salvation is possible through other faiths as much as it suggests the existence of an inherent moral or ethical impulse built into the human nature, similar to Paul's description of God's law written into all human hearts (Romans 2:12-15).

Agnes clearly indicates salvation requires the person to make an act of faith, and the object of that faith must be a relationship with Jesus Christ. She explains, "First of all, we can receive this redeeming life of God by asking Jesus Christ to come into us."[25] Her phraseology clearly matches evangelistic language. She devotes the rest of the chapter to describing how her readers can receive Him, including those raised in churches, saying,

> Yes, I am talking about receiving Jesus. But we have done this long ago, we think, or our parents have done it for us in baptism! . . . But there is one trouble with being born and brought up in the church, and that is that we may not know whether we ever *of our own volition* [emphasis hers] accepted Christ or not. And if we do not really with the whole heart long for His indwelling, then, even though baptized, there are still closed doors within our subconscious minds.[26]

She does not describe the gospel in terms of escaping the threat of eternal damnation, but she clearly presents faith in Jesus as the only avenue to complete forgiveness of sin.

Agnes ascribes salvation solely to the work of Christ at Calvary. Nevertheless, she believed non-Christians could effectively pray for the sick and even receive healing. In her opinion, God's loving nature means He provides for any who seek Him earnestly in faith just as He provides sun and rain to those who do not believe.[27] In other words, healing and miracles are not solely for Christians but are for any who seek God in truth. De Arteaga equates this with the position of many of the people in the Old Testament; they were not Christians, but they could still pray to God and receive answers, including both Jewish and Gentile races. He writes,

> We should note that Jesus credited certain semi-pagans with greater faith than the children of Israel, as for instance the Syrophoenician woman of Matthew 15:21-28 and the centurian with the sick servant (Matt. 8:10). Agnes Sanford understood this from a personal experience. In her life she had transited from Presbyterian cessationism to New Thought and finally into Pentecostalism. She reflected on her early friends in New Thought and Christian Science and believed that the reason they healed effectively was that many of them were *faith-filled monotheists* [emphasis his]. That is, that although many Christian scientists were indeed not Christian, they did believe in one God who would answer prayer. They thus had the same access to answered prayer as an Old Testament Jew.[28]

Although Agnes believed non-Christians could receive miracles from God—similar to the numerous healings and miracles described in the Old Testament and in the Gospels—she did not accept a view of universalism or pluralism: faith in Christ was the only source of salvation.

The Resurrection is a core aspect of the Christian faith. According to Paul, the forgiveness of sins depends upon a literal bodily resurrection (1 Corinthians 15:12-17). Agnes wholeheartedly affirmed this basic doctrine of the Christian faith. Continuing her discussion of the redemptive work of Christ, she writes, "And finally, He raised His own body from the tomb and transformed it into the new order of being promised to all of us: the resurrection body."[29] She did not consider the resurrection an analogy, a metaphor, or a myth; it was a literal event. In her discussion of the process, she even ponders how it may have taken place:

> The body of Christ in the tomb not only had to be resurrected cell by cell, as the body of Lazarus was resurrected, but also presumably the process of making blood had to be tremendously speeded up, so that as nature replenishes the blood for one who has given a blood transfusion, so nature should replenish His blood stream—after the blood transfusion that He gave to humanity.[30]

For Agnes, each step in the redemptive work had a very specific and practical effect, all of which related directly to the fallen human condition. Although her entire chapter on the resurrection incorporates metaphysical concepts, it presents solid orthodox theology.

In her chapter on the Holy Spirit, Agnes crafts a passage not only summarizing the internal relationship of the Trinity but also their relationship to human beings. Within one paragraph, she expresses the oneness of the Godhead in three persons, the nature and work of each member of the Trinity, the need for and the result of the redemptive work of Christ on the whole person, and the promise of the Holy Spirit given on the day of Pentecost. She writes,

> Anyone of any tribe or nation or language who in any sincere way turns to a Great Spirit, calling Him God or Allah or Life or whatever else he will, opens a door that God may enter his conscious mind and answer his prayers according to his faith. One may turn to Channel One only and the overflowing love of God will do for him whatever is possible through one channel alone. But this power cannot reach to the depths of the subconscious mind. If we want the cleansing power that frees the subconscious, which we call forgiveness, we need to tune to Channel Two of this God, the channel adapted to that very purpose: Jesus Christ, the second Person of the Trinity. And finally, if we need still more light to dispel the darkness of the world and to guide us into the way of peace, we can turn to Channel Three, the Holy Spirit, the Comforter, the Light-giver, whom the Father sent to us in the Son's name (John 14:26) that we should have new light in our spirits.[31]

Within this passage, Agnes clearly confirms the biblical nature of her understanding of the Godhead as well as the redemptive work of Christ. Notwithstanding her favored use of metaphysical terminology and concepts, her theology and soteriology are orthodox.

Scripture

Agnes uses Scripture prodigiously throughout all of her works. During her childhood, she devoted an hour each morning to studying the Bible, and she admits to being required to memorize large portions of Scripture. In *Behold Your God*, she provides biblical references or paraphrases scriptural passages in almost every paragraph except when telling a story or explaining a concept. In the first chapter, for example, she provides thirty-three Bible verse citations in eleven pages—not including quotations, paraphrases, and references without citations—and one of the citations identifies multiple passages from seventeen books in the Old and New Testaments.[32] Clearly, the Bible formed the foundation of her theology, and she relied upon it heavily. Although she never actually declares a specific hermeneutical method, she makes statements suggesting a moderate approach.

In keeping with New Thought, Agnes stressed the transformative benefits of obeying the commands of Jesus. On the one hand she believed anybody seeking the truth with sincerity and integrity could connect with God in prayer and benefit from following His commandments. On the other hand, and contrary to New Thought, she considered the Bible to be fully authoritative concerning the nature of the Trinity and the redemptive work of Christ as the only means of salvation. In respect to these views, she holds a position somewhere between what may be viewed as conservative and liberal interpretations of Scripture. Agnes believed the Bible was factual in respect to the occurrence of miracles, including the crucifixion, death, and bodily resurrection of Jesus Christ. However, she also makes statements in her writing that indicate she did not always hold to a literal interpretation of Scripture.

Agnes viewed science as a discipline devoted to discovering the truth about the world, and she had high regard for scientific principles. As mentioned, she refers to science as "the honest attempt of honest men to arrive at truth."[33] She believed that true scientific discoveries would not contradict Scripture but instead could be relied upon to provide insights for interpreting and explaining parts of it. In the Foreword to *The Healing Power of the Bible*, she elucidates her position on the way science and the Bible work together. She explains,

> Having memorized this Bible daily from early childhood (not always of my own volition), I have it still there deep in the mind, an abiding foundation of faith. . . . As one grows toward maturity, disturbing doubts nevertheless cast shadows upon this "book about God." How can He have made the world in six days, when the evidence of science suggests a growing period of billions of years? How can a flood have covered the whole earth? How could Elijah go up to heaven in a chariot of fire? Did Jesus really turn water into wine, and feed five thousand people with five loaves of bread? The rationalist of the present day says No: these things are only ancient myths. But many of us cannot be content with this dismissal of the Holy Book. . . . We find our answers not in evading doubts but in seriously looking for answers to them. Where then shall we look? First of all, I believe we should learn as much as we can of the sciences that concern the universe. . . . endeavoring to see how science and the Bible fit together, and how the one helps us to understand the other.[34]

Agnes obviously did not dismiss biblical accounts of miracles, for she stresses them in all of her works. However, she often relies on science to explain how they occurred.

Agnes believed the events in the Bible did happen, but she accepts they may not have happened exactly the way the Bible describes. For example, she affirms the Genesis account of creation but trusts science to explain how it took place. Repeatedly using the phrase, "so the Bible says and so science says," she declares, "the Creator caused life to evolve upon the earth."[35] She presents a faithful account of Theistic evolution. However, she rejects an entirely evolutionary view, saying, "God made man in His image, after His likeness" but "those living beings, when they were fully created, did not evolve according to plan. The Creator took a long chance when He made them—when He breathed the breath of life, His spirit, into creatures of flesh."[36] Her phrases "fully created" and "did not evolve according to plan" suggest an incomplete process. She confirms this later when she writes, "The spirit of man was in the beginning an offshoot of God's spirit—God breathed His own life into man when He distinguished him from the beasts of the field and caused him to become a living soul (II Cor. 5:17)."[37] Man and woman may have begun like other animals, but they became something different. Agnes often presents a similarly moderated perspective on Scripture.

Experiential Theology

Agnes clearly adopted numerous metaphysical terms and concepts from her limited involvement with New Thought and Unity School of Christianity. However, she kept a fully orthodox Christian belief system as the foundation of her theology and ministry. She perceived God's presence as being incarnate in the world around her, both filling and sustaining all things. Additionally, she believed healing and forgiveness proceed forth from God, being inherently related to his nature instead of exclusively volitional acts of his will. In these respects, her theology is more reflective of the experiential nature of sacramental and liturgical denominations than the dogmatic and intellectual character of many fundamentalist Protestant churches. Agnes may present experiences, concepts, and terminology profoundly uncommon for Christians in Western society, but her upbringing in China seemingly had a significant impact on the formation of her worldview. Her writings are best be viewed in the context of experiential Christianity.

Agnes viewed the entire universe in light of the incarnation. In the same way God became flesh within Mary's womb, so he created the entire universe by his Spirit. Referencing Genesis 1:2, she writes, "In the beginning, remember, the earth was without form and void and there was nothing except God Himself. Therefore, He sent forth His word and life evolved from the Creator Himself."[38] She rejected pantheism but endorsed a position related to Christian sacramentalism—God within creation. In language reminiscent of Psalm 104:30, she says, "God is both within us and without us. He is the Source of all life; the Creator of universe behind universe; and of unimaginable depths of inter-stellar space and of light-years without end. But He is also the indwelling life of our own little selves," and "the very chemicals contained in the body—the 'dust of the earth'—live by the Breath of God."[39] God did not just create life by the power of the Spirit but also continues to sustain it by His Presence (Colossians 1:17; Hebrews 1:3).

Agnes's view here does not conflict with Christian theology. In almost identical language, Gregory of Nazianzus states, "He spoke and taking some of the newly minted earth his immortal hands made an image into which he imparted some of his own life. He sent his spirit, a beam from the invisible divinity"; similarly, Basil of Caesarea says, "The Spirit is the essence of life"; and according to Theophilus of Antioch, "If he withdrew his breath, the whole would utterly fail. It is by him that you speak, O man. His is the breath you breathe."[40] Her position not only aligns with historic Christian doctrine but also predates contemporary Pentecostal theology. Amos Yong also describes the Spirit as the breath of God, who created and sustains creation.[41] However, the concept of incarnation does not necessarily apply only to people. Using the word "enchanted" in this context, James K. A. Smith writes, "nature, then, is always more than 'the natural.' It is suffused with something more; there is always more than meets the naturalizing eye," and declares "all of creation . . . is charged with the presence of the Spirit."[42] Though perhaps not fully developed, Agnes's incarnational view of creation may be said to not only mirror Church history but also to anticipate contemporary Pentecostal theology.

Had Agnes written about her incarnational view of creation simply as an intellectual doctrine, she might have avoided being labeled a pantheist. However, she describes numerous instances of not only seeing but also experiencing God in and through creation. As a child, she twice experienced "indescribably dreamy bliss" and "ecstasy that was not entirely of this world" through nature, and once as a teenager, she felt herself "beyond the swing of time or place" as she lay on a ship's deck and gazed at the stars.[43] Because of her disillusionment with Christianity during her early years, she did not associate the experiences with the possibility that God was revealing Himself to her through His creation. After her deliverance from depression, however, she began to suspect as much. In *Creation Waits*, she describes a profound experience of God touching her through nature, and the experience impacted her to such an extent she later compares it with her baptism in the Holy Spirit and her subsequent receiving of the gift of tongues:

> One bright, cold October morning I rowed across the lake, dragged the boat up on a pebbly beach, and climbed out of. I lay down on the pine needles beneath some trees and sunbathed. Lying there entirely alone, for the lake was deserted in the fall, I prayed that God's light would come into me through the sun. I imagined that light entering into the whole of my being, and so it did. The experience was unlike anything that ever happened to me before or since. I *felt* the light, like an intense heat shining into me, and I was filled with a sudden bliss that was so great I could hardly stand it. It was frightening, yet I didn't want it to stop. But stop it did, just as I was crying out in my mind, "Lord, if this doesn't stop soon, I'll die!" It ceased, leaving me shaken to the depths. . . . [but] the peace of the Lord, which seemed to be the aftermath of the light, remained with me.[44]

For Agnes, God's presence somehow incarnates creation, allowing nature to become a sacramental channel of his grace and power. Her view foreshadows Yong and Smiths' description of nature being infused and sustained by the Presence of the Holy Spirit.

When first learning about healing, Agnes read the Gospels repeatedly to see how Jesus healed the sick. According to the Gospel writers, Jesus came to a sinful world, full of people who did not know Him (John 1:10), and healed many who did not initially profess any faith in Him—or who did so only after receiving a healing (Luke 17:12-19). As already discussed, Agnes believed God provides healing for any who honestly seek Him. She relates healing to the incarnation, declaring, "As I believe that He did in a literal sense precipitate the full being of God into human woman, I can then believe that He can precipitate His personal healing power into my own human being."[45] Because she viewed the entire creation in terms of the incarnation, being sustained with God's presence, she believed even unbelievers could receive healing from God—but their experience would often lead them to God. In one of her most famous examples, she describes her interactions with a Jewish man in an Army hospital. After six months in traction, his leg was not healing. She explained to him how to receive healing:

> So I explained to Sammy that there was a healing energy in him that the doctors called "nature," that this same healing life was in the world outside of him too, and that he could receive more of it by asking for it.
> "Who'll I ask?" Sammy wondered.
>
> "Ask God. Because He is the one who made nature, and He's in nature, and He is nature."
>
> "But I don't know anything about God."
>
> "You know there's *something* outside of yourself, don't you? After all, you didn't make this world. There is some kind of life outside of you."
>
> "Oh, sure. When you're scared enough, you feel like there must be something."
>
> "Well then, ask that Something to come into you. Just say 'Whoever you are or whatever you are, come into me now and help nature in my body to mend this bone, and do it quick. Thanks. I believe you are doing it.' . . . [Then] think of the life outside of you again, and say 'Thank You, God. I believe it's going to be okay.'"[46]

Although Agnes told the soldier, "God is nature," her statement must be considered in light of her incarnational view of creation as well as her complete rejection of pantheism. Saying "God is nature" does not equate to "nature is God" just as biblical exegesis confirms that "God is love" does not mean that "love is God." It is significant, given her metaphysical tendency to occasionally capitalize impersonal terms for God, that she does not capitalize "nature" in this passage.

Agnes saw the man a month later at the hospital. He was out of traction and walking with a cane. She also noticed joy on his face. She approached him and talked with him about how his healing was progressing:

> "Do you still do what I told you to do?" I asked him.
> "Yep," he replied, "and I can walk, too, with a brace."
> "Then you'll soon walk without a brace," I told him.
> "I know it," he grinned, and a light flashed from his eyes to mine.
> I wondered, as I went on my way to the P.X., how much he knew now about God. Certainly he knew something that made him very happy![47]

Agnes's statements turned out to be more than just wishful thinking. In another book, she recounts their subsequent meeting. She writes, "I [initially] taught him only the teachings of Jesus Christ . . . I did not venture to outline for him the plan of redemption," most likely because the administration prohibited any of the staff from praying for or evangelizing the patients:

> He was finally released from the hospital, only to reappear after three months. "I broke my leg again," he explained. "And I was quite discouraged for about three days. Then I figured it out like this: *there's something else you haven't told me and that's why I'm back here* [emphasis from the original source]. Now what is it?" . . . "Yes, there is something else," I admitted. . . . [and] I gave him the New Testament and told him to read the gospel of St. John.[48]

Had the context been different, Agnes might have spoken openly about the Gospel to Sammy. As it was, she was released from service soon after when her Christian supervisor discovered that she secretly had been praying with a patient.

When Agnes saw Sammy a week after giving him the New Testament, she asked him what he thought of Jesus. His response exemplifies her own conviction in the way healing leads people to have an experience with God, similar to the way numerous people came to believe in Jesus after He healed them during His earthly ministry. She writes,

> "Well, I had to read this book three times before I got the idea," he said. "And then I read another book about him. Like him it was by a man named Matthew."
>
> "Do you believe the things that Matthew said about him?" I asked. "Do you believe that He was conceived by the Holy Ghost and born of the Virgin Mary? Do you believe He raised His body from the dead?"
>
> "Of course I do!" said the young man, looking at me in surprise. "If even I, who am nothing and know nothing, can build in two inches of my bone with God's help, why shouldn't He have been conceived by the Holy Ghost and born of the Virgin Mary? And why shouldn't He have raised His body from the dead?"[49]

Sammy believed what he read because he had seen God's healing in his own life. In her books, Agnes provides numerous similar accounts of people who were healed and subsequently developed a relationship with God. She literally believed "we can perceive His life working in us, and that is a little step toward Him."[50] She viewed healing as part of the Gospel and believed it brought people into a personal encounter with God.

Orthodox Christian doctrine declares that God is both immanent and transcendent. As already discussed, Agnes clearly refutes pantheism and maintains that God is beyond and distinct from His creation. She did not accept a view of immanence without the balancing view of His transcendence. She also refutes deism and maintains that God is active and present in and through His creation. She no longer accepted cessationism, for she saw God working supernaturally in the world. She did not accept transcendence without immanence. However, Agnes applied these doctrines to healing prayer in practical ways. She describes his immanence—being present to everyone everywhere— as being experienced through her incarnational view of creation and the sacraments, and she describes his transcendence—his being above and beyond everyone and everything—as being experienced through the healing of the memories.

Agnes regularly promoted healing prayer and the baptism in the Holy Spirit in her works and ministry. However, numerous sources identify her primarily as the originator of the inner healing movement for what she taught on the healing of memories.[51] From her understanding of psychology, she believed the subconscious recorded every memory, good and bad, and the negative ones still exerted an influence on the person even if they were submerged or forgotten. Agnes believed that the redemptive work of Christ also heals memories: "So when we need God's light to shine in the subconscious mind, we must also recognize that there is a Savior: that God through His second person . . . is able to heal our memories, or in more exact words to forgive our sins."[52] Salvation, therefore, includes healing of the soul. She connects this healing with forgiveness because "all these wounded memories come either from our own sins or from the sins of others against us, needing our forgiveness."[53] For this reason, she often recommends people suffering from depression to go to confession, for it helps them receive forgiveness and healing.

Agnes discovered this type of prayer after praying for Sammy, the soldier with the leg injury. Although he was physically healed and saved, he contacted her about major outbursts of anger he could not control. After praying different ways with no success, she prayed for guidance. She writes, "It came to me first that the trouble was not in the conscious young man but in the little boy within him who had lived in the Gestapo regime. . . . As I listened, the Lord showed me that in the heavenly kingdom, time is relative—Jesus Christ lives in all time, and therefore can go back through time and heal that which is past."[54] She prayed for Jesus to go back through time in his memories and heal the young boy. She subsequently received a letter from him that he was healed.[55] This incident confirmed to Agnes that God was transcendent even outside of time. Because all times were present and available to him, he could minister even in the past.

Agnes understood the healing of memories as forgiveness applied within the memories of the subconscious, often connecting to events of the past. However, she saw it as more than just a mental healing, for she believed God could see and access a person's whole life—past, present, and future. Because God transcended time, he can heal a past event as easily as a present one. She explains, "There is no time in heaven. In the sight of God, time is relative—time is rolled out like a carpet before Him—He can see all time at once and He can live in all time at once—therefore He must be able to go back over the years and find that little girl and heal the wounds in her mind."[56] Agnes developed a model for healing of the memories based on her understanding that God's transcendence was not only a doctrine but also an experiential reality.

Agnes often describes healing as a light or energy emanating from God. She named her first book *The Healing Light* based on this concept. She uses this metaphor both imaginatively and theologically. On the one hand, she instructs her readers, "When we ask for the indwelling of God's Holy Spirit in the body, let us think of that part of the body that most needs His life. Let us imagine

His light and life glowing there like a fire, shining there like a light."[57] For Agnes, the imagination incorporates the subconscious and provides a necessary aspect of faith, enabling the person to receive from God. However, she also views light in theological terms, believing that healing emanates from God as a type of energy just as sunlight emanates from the sun:

> St. Paul advised his friends the Ephesians to "walk as children of light": to live, that is, as if they were made of a living, moving energy like light. A few centuries ago we would have thought this just a fanciful idea. Now, thanks to the scientists, we know that it is really true.... The oldest of all stories about creation tells us that God created light before he created the sun and the earth.... Nowadays we know that light is a form of energy and that all created things are made of energy. ... God made, first of all, *light*.... We are therefore made not of solid and impenetrable matter, but of energy.... The vibration of God's light is so very real that even a child can feel it, and it was my experiments with children that showed me the action of an invisible but powerful light-vibration shining from the Father of Lights.[58]

Agnes rejected any concept of God as being an impersonal force or energy, but she did consider healing to be a force or energy emanating from him, similar to the way sunlight came from the sun. In other words, she believed healing power flows from his being.

The concept of describing an aspect of God in terms of light or energy seems foreign to Western Christianity; according to De Arteaga, however, some theologians in the Eastern Orthodox Church have done so—though not in relation to physical healing:

> Significantly, the Eastern Orthodox Church developed a theology of light dating from the Middle Ages, due in part to one of its greatest theologians, St. Gregory of Palamas (1296-1359). St Gregory called God's light "uncreated energies." His light theology and that of others in Eastern Orthodoxy concerned themselves with prayer and sanctification, which in Eastern Orthodoxy is called "deification." The use of God's light and energy was not considered for the purposes of healing prayer. An article in the premier Orthodox journal in America, *St. Vladimir's Theological Quarterly*, points to the biblical issues that Mrs. Sanford dealt with when she advocated the use of God's light and energies for healing prayer. The author of the article, David Bradshaw, shows that St. Gregory's belief in the light and energies of God is entirely consistent with the New Testament, especially the writings of Paul. All of this indicates that when Agnes Sanford wrote about the presence and use of God's light/energy *she was on firm biblical ground* [emphasis his].[59]

Even when Agnes's wording seems to go beyond discussing light or energy coming from God and suggests God is light (1 John 1:5), her theology—as De Arteaga explains—resonates with Eastern Orthodox perspectives. According to Stanley M. Burgess, Eastern Christianity has repeatedly referenced experiences of the Holy Spirit using the terminology "God is light" and "Divine Light."[60]

Essentially, Agnes uses *light, energy,* and *electricity* to describe the power of God similar to the way Pentecostals and Charismatics might use *fire, water,* and *wind* to describe the presence of the Holy Spirit.

Agnes viewed healing as an inherent effect of God's presence. Instead of viewing healing as something God does, she considered it an integral component of his nature. Christian orthodoxy maintains God does not *choose* holiness but *is* holy; he does not *choose* love but *is* love; he does not *choose* truth but *is* truth.[61] Similarly, Agnes believed God could never will something contrary to his displayed will in creation and in nature. While discussing a letter she received from loving parents, asking why their child was born with a birth defect, she responds,

> I cannot feel that it is a punishment for your sins or for the child's sins, for God loves you and your child as a father loves his children. . . . Therefore, I would continue in faith and prayer. . . . [and] look forward always to the Kingdom of Heaven, when God's will shall be done on earth as it is in heaven and tragedies like these shall be no more. This I would write in the firm belief that sorrows such as this are the result of the fall of man and thus are the work of Satan and not the will of God.[62]

Agnes viewed sickness and disease as states of imperfection, contrary to God's original intention for his creation, and the life within all living things—designed with an inherent tendency to fight illness—resulted from the supernatural breath of God within creation.

Agnes's perception reflects John Wesley's understanding of the Divine Presence in the human condition. As Kimberly Ervin Alexander points out in *Pentecostal Healing*, "for Wesley the ideas of holiness and wholeness are vitally connected. This comes from his understanding of humanity and the effects of sin and the Fall upon humanity."[63] Wesley believed redemption involves the work of the Holy Spirit counteracting some of the effects of the fall, including both sickness and death. Agnes's description of healing as an inherent result of the Holy Spirit's power and presence reflects Wesley's view of the relationship between holiness and wholeness. Wesley understood sanctification as an experiential process instead of a positional condition; in other words, the presence of the Spirit within a person facilitates a positive, transformative change in every aspect of the person.[64] Similarly, Agnes viewed healing as a normal aspect of sanctification and redemption in a person's life when God's power comes in contact with the human being.

Although Agnes maintained a biblically sound theology of God and salvation, her personal experiences often present as more mystical than orthodox. Her childhood in China may have promoted a worldview more inclined to Eastern Orthodoxy than Western Protestantism; however, her unusual experiences stem from her orthodox beliefs in the incarnation, God's nature as immanent and transcendent, his power emanating from Him as light and energy, and healing being an inherent aspect of God's nature. Though clearly not fundamentalist in her theological orientation, Agnes maintained a biblical Christian orthodox theology.

Nonessential Doctrines

Agnes maintained an orthodox view of the Trinity, of the redemptive work of Christ, and of the Bible. She applied her beliefs in God's transcendence, immanence, and nature in experiential ways, more suggestive of a sacramental orthopraxy than traditional Evangelicalism. She also held some tangential doctrines nonessential to, but also maintained by others within, Christian orthodoxy, such as her belief in Theistic evolution, the attainment of a resurrected body on earth, the Church's role in the return of Christ, a Christian's responsibility toward creation, the potential for additional forms of life in the universe, and the preexistence of the human soul. Some of her beliefs directly affected or stemmed from her theology and healing paradigm while others held little influence or impact on her worldview.

As discussed, Agnes accepted a moderate view on Theistic evolution in which God caused life to evolve on the earth. Describing her fascination with the design of the kidney bean, she writes,

> He causes these things to evolve over centuries and over milleniums and over aeons. So He works. He does not come down with a paint-brush and personally paint the kidney bean. How long it takes to evolve a kidney bean I do not know; probably not so long as to evolve the earth upon which the bean must grow—or the sun around which the earth rotates and from which it receives its life. And if you were to ask me, "Can God grow a kidney bean in one second?" I would say, "Perhaps He can but He does not." And if you were to say, "Why? Don't you believe He is Almighty?" I would reply, "Yes, but I also believe He is a Maker. And so He chooses to work according to the laws of creative action which he Himself has ordained."[65]

She did not consider evolution to be unbiblical just as she did not consider miracles to be unscientific. In her view, miracles are not exceptions to the laws of nature but are the imposition of higher laws over lower laws. She believed God ordained specific laws within creation and prefers to use them:

> We must learn that God is not an unreasonable and impulsive sovereign who breaks His own laws at will.... "But God is omnipotent!" some people say. "He can do anything He likes!" Certainly, but He has made a world that runs by law, and He does not like to break those laws. Few of us in the north would ask God to produce a full-blown rose out of doors in January. Yet He can do this very thing, if we adapt our greenhouses to His laws of heat and light, so as to provide the necessities of the rose. And he can produce a full-blown answer to prayer if we adapt our earthly tabernacles to His laws of love and faith so as to provide the necessities of answered prayer.[66]

God fashioned the universe to function according to certain specific processes, and the discoveries of science provide insight and explain how those laws operate.

Although Agnes believed God caused life to evolve on the earth, she did not view human beings as simply evolved animals. People could know God personally. She writes,

> God caused this principle of life that is in the dust of the earth to bring forth, under His orders, fish in the sea and creeping things, and then animals upon the earth, and then man. So God made man out of the dust of the earth, and breathed into him the breath of life. God's breath is God's Spirit, and His Holy Spirit coming upon Adam in whatever primal state of creation we do not know brought fourth upon the earth beings capable of knowing their Creator.[67]

As discussed previously, Agnes viewed creation itself as incarnated with God's Presence on some level. Because she regularly uses metaphysical terminology, her descriptions of God's Spirit within people and within creation sometimes sound similar. However, she affirms the existence of Adam and Eve as unique beings as well as a fall from grace:

> There is a contrary force upon our planet, which we call Satan or the devil, for so he is named in the Bible. He fell upon this earth in the very beginning.... and he tempted the newborn inhabitants of the garden of Eden to disobey the commands of God.[68]

Agnes believed God created people who could know him uniquely in a personal relationship, who were tempted by a real personality known as the devil, and who fell from a position of grace through an act of voluntary disobedience.

Agnes considered it possible for a person to be so filled with the Holy Spirit and walking in power that the body could be transformed on earth. As Alexander notes, some "Finished Work" Pentecostals, such as Carrie Judd Montgomery, also believed in the power of God to "quicken" the physical body.[69] However, Agnes differed from their position on two points: degree and process. Discussing Christ's crucifixion, she explains that even before He rose from the dead, the resurrection began:

> No wonder the graves were opened and the bodies of the saints wandered about the city and appeared to many (Matt. 27:52). The principle of resurrection took tremendous hold on men at that time, for although the resurrection had not yet taken place, the seed of immortality had been replanted in humanity.... Did those who arose from the tomb succeed at that time in achieving the kind of body in which Jesus Christ later appeared to His beloved ones? We do not know. If any of those attaining to the first resurrection (Rev. 20:6) were among us now would we perceive them? Would love draw them toward us or would fear keep them away from us?[70]

Agnes actually suggests a possibility for believers to attain a glorified body on earth. She does not here declare that anybody actually has already attained the resurrection body, and she is speaking entirely hypothetically; however, she does not rule out the possibility. Additionally, as she discusses Christ's physical resurrection, she says, "If life works fast enough in the spirit, it can overtake and transcend the death process in the body. Thus there exists the possibility, which one day shall be a probability, that the new order of being of which Christ was the first-fruits, can be achieved without the pain of death."[71] In other words, Agnes viewed the transformative power of Christ's redemption as potentially unlimited, but she also viewed it in terms of a process in which health and life overtakes sickness and death.

Agnes considered it possible for Christians to be so transformed by the indwelling power of the Holy Spirit that their bodies become like Jesus's resurrected body. However, her comments must be understood in context. After making the statement about achieving "the new order of being... without the pain of death," she lists two examples: Enoch and Elijah. Her mention of two Old Testament prophets taken to heaven provides important insight into her beliefs: neither of them remained on earth. Again resorting to a mixture of metaphysical and scientific terminology, she explains the resultant impact of someone having a resurrected body living on the fallen planet earth:

> Why did he depart? Why did he not stay on earth in his transformed and glorified body? Because that body, at the present point in the evolution of the race, cannot live comfortably on the earth, as a diver cannot remain long under water. As water is a foreign element to an earthman, so the air of this present earth is a foreign element to the resurrected man. He finds it hard to breathe this air, heavy with man's sorrow, dense with the pollution of man's sins. The resurrected body, while a real body, exists at a different rate of vibration: lives by a different kind of energy.[72]

In other words, someone with a resurrected body could not withstand existence in a world filled with sin. She believed Christians could be transformed by the presence of God and be changed, but the change would require relocating: "For there are already resurrected ones. There are those who have achieved in the spiritual kingdom that we call 'heaven' the resurrection of the body."[73] Although she discusses the possibility of obtaining a resurrected body on earth, she seems to be describing the potential for Christians to follow the example of Enoch— to walk so closely with God they are taken (Gen. 5:24).

Throughout her discussion of the redemptive work of Christ and the resurrected body, Agnes actually seems to describe the concept of *theosis*, the deification of the believer through the exchange principle. Irenaeus of Lyons, a second century theologian, states, "our Lord Jesus Christ, who did, through His transcendent love, become what we are, that He might bring us to be even what He is Himself."[74] Jesus became human so that he could elevate humanity into something more. However, Athanasius in the fourth century is best known for expounding on the concept. He writes, "He was God, and then became man, and that to deify us."[75] According to these theologians of the Early Church, Jesus became human so that He could transform human beings into something more than mere humans. De Arteaga mentions deification in conjunction with Eastern Orthodox theology and the use of "light" in the works of St. Gregory of Palamas, but he does not discuss how Agnes incorporated this into her theology of redemption.[76] Using her metaphysical terminology, she clearly describes the exchange principle of deification.

Using metaphysical terminology, Agnes describes deification as Christ's actual goal. He did not come simply to forgive humanity's sins but to change the human race into something new. She believed it began in the Garden of Gethsemane. She writes,

> For He came upon the earth to create a new order—to change the species (Eph. 4:24)—to give to those who received Him the power to become the Sons of God (John 1:12). In order to do this, He had to reach the subconscious mind, or the heart, of every human being. For the barrier between God and man was in the heart. . . . Thus Jesus Christ went into the Garden of Gethsemane and there began to accomplish this miracle that was completed on Calvary.[77]

She believed redemption began in Gethsemane. At that point, Jesus began to partake of the fear, doubt, and pain of fallen humanity. He opened himself to the subconscious grief and sorrow of the human race internally before his physical sufferings began. She says,

> He could not do this from outside of man. True, He had made Himself part of the human race by His birth upon this planet. But in order to redeem the human race it was necessary to sink deeper into humanity: to become part of the subconscious mind of every man. . . . This Jesus Christ did with every one of us in the Garden of Gethsemane. Hitherto He had turned His heart always toward God. . . . In the Garden of Gethsemane He reversed this process. He tuned His heart to the feelings of the heart of mankind. He turned away from God's light and let his spirit sink into man's darkness. Thus He lived, not in God, but for the first time, in man . . . and the sorrows of mankind rolled in upon Him.[78]

Agnes believed Jesus came to create a new order of being, setting humanity back onto the track originally intended when God created man and woman in the Garden of Eden. The first part of this redemption required Jesus to completely identify with human sinfulness, and this began in Gethsemane.

Agnes describes Christ's crucifixion and death as the next step in the redemptive process. His death alone would not suffice to atone for humanity's fallenness, for he had to experience human sinfulness:

> Whatever Jesus did, it is not a matter of transfer taking place in some other sphere of life and at some vague time in the future. It takes place here and now in us, in both our souls and our bodies. . . . The sins of mankind had become

> His. Being His, His own spirit was grieved and horrified by them, and this spiritual condemnation of evil carried to the subconscious the command toward death.... So complete was His immersion in the sins of mankind that He actually felt that God had forsaken Him.... The at-one-ment had been made with the very last soul who lived or who had lived or who was to live.[79]

She understood his death as being the direct result of His taking the sinfulness of the human race into himself. Considering His ability to heal the sick and even raise the dead, Agnes felt the scourging and crucifixion alone did not explain the speed of his death, the words he spoke on the cross, or the unnatural circumstances that followed; it was taking the sins of humanity into himself that led to His death (Romans 6:23). Once he died, the next step in the process of creating a new order of being took place. She explains,

> The spirit of Jesus Christ was satisfied. And the spirit of the Father abiding in Jesus Christ looked upon these things and was satisfied (Isa. 53:11). Thus the cloud departed from his spiritual eyes and once more He saw and knew the Father. He was free to return to the Father and to begin with joy and gladness the culminating act of His work for mankind—the resurrection and the sharing of His resurrected life with those whom He had redeemed.[80]

Based on the metaphysical and psychological components of her worldview, Agnes believed the human spirit, made in the image of God, inherently judged death as the appropriate result for sin. It was only after his death that Jesus fully satisfied the human and divine punishment for sin.

Agnes completes her description of the exchange principle in her chapter on the resurrection. While Jesus became like humanity in Gethsemane and on Calvary, the resurrection allows human beings to become like him. She explains,

> What of His resurrection?... He raised His own body from the tomb and transformed it into the new order of being promised to all of us: the resurrection body. First, this means to us that the same power that heals also resurrects: occasionally by renewing life within a corpse but usually by giving us in the heavenly kingdom a new body so that we become a new order of being, verily and triumphantly the Sons of God.... Second, the resurrection and ascension of Jesus Christ mean to us that as He shared His human-divine being with us on Calvary for the remission of our sins (which entails the healing of the subconscious mind) so now He shares His spiritual body with us for the resurrection of our souls and the enlightenment of our spirits.[81]

She describes the resurrected body as a component of the new order of being. She may not have been aware of the historical doctrine of deification, but she clearly resonates with the concept. Some aspects of transformation apply to life on earth while other parts relate to heaven. For her, the incarnation and redemption of Christ cause some aspects of eternity to infiltrate the present world, and she seems to avoid defining any limitations.

In line with her view of creation and redemption, Agnes held a post-millenialist position on the second coming of Christ. She believed the "great tribulation" has already passed, and Jesus will return after the church sufficiently prepares the world for him:

> Many Christians have given up the battle before it has even begun. They do not seriously consider the Lord's words concerning His coming again and the kingdom of heaven. They tend to fasten their eyes not on a saved and transformed earth with the glory of God shining beyond and upon it, but on the Great Tribulation, an event that is past.[82]

She considered the Roman persecution of believers to be the tribulation foretold in the book of Revelation. Instead of waiting for Jesus to rescue the Church from the world, she expected Jesus will return when the church fulfills all of his commands. She writes,

> While numbers of us are waiting for Jesus to come again in glory and make it unnecessary for us to buy a new pair of shoes, He is not likely to come because the earth itself is waiting for *us* [emphasis hers] to make it into the kind of earth whereon the Lord can abide to fulfill in it whatever is its divine destiny. When the eager longing of creation waiting for the revealing of the sons of God is satisfied, then will the Lord himself descend from heaven with a shout and with the sound of a trumpet! While we are waiting for Him, He is in fact waiting for us.[83]

She rejected a fatalistic eschatology. Though Pentecostals and Charismatics influenced by the Evangelical tradition have often maintained a premillennialist and dispensational eschatology, that view is not monolithic.[84] Interestingly, as Frank Macchia notes, Pentecostals and Charismatics often affirm an apocalyptic theology in opposition to their practices and ideology.[85] Agnes thus maintained a perspective consistent with some Renewal theology.

In many of her works, Agnes expresses a belief that healing and miracles would be more common if the Church had maintained the life and practice of the first disciples. For example, she boldly states, "We see that the lack of success in healing is not due to God's will for us but to our failure to live near enough to God so that He can accomplish His will in us."[86] Significantly, her statement focuses on those who pray for the sick and not on the sick themselves. Likewise, she considers it entirely possible that the church is largely responsible for any delay in the Lord's return. She explains, "Moreover, if we had not faltered or compromised in that battle against the forces of evil that Our Lord told us to undertake (Mark 16:15 and Luke 10:3), it is quite possible that we would have brought the day in which no child would remain or be afflicted (Rev. 21:4)."[87] She later states this concept even more directly while discussing the original creation of the world. She writes, "From time to time God's holy men have glimpsed this as the natural state, the state that will be fulfilled if there is sufficient faith among the Sons of God to bring the return of Our Lord and the establishment of the Kingdom."⁸⁸ She believed Jesus is waiting for the church to fulfill the Great Commission, which also includes the redemption of all of creation.

Agnes believed that God gave human beings authority over the earth when he created them, but she viewed the event more in terms of stewardship and responsibility than in the context of domination and subjugation. In *Creation Waits*, she describes this concept in detail, beginning the book with the words, "We have a duty to the earth on which we live.... The Lord of this great field, the earth, has ordered us to take care of it for Him until He returns. This includes not only a missionary duty to the people who live upon the earth, but also a caretaker's duty to the earth itself."⁸⁹ The cover and title page include Paul's statement that "the creation waits eagerly for the revealing of the sons of God (Romans 8:19)." Agnes considered this stewardship to be part of a Christian's calling, and her perspective on healing prayer included praying for the earth itself. She states, "We are to pray not only for sick and troubled people, but we are also to pray for the earth itself."⁹⁰ She herself took this very seriously, believing she had often seen and experienced God's presence within nature. For her, praying for the healing of the earth itself is also a command of Jesus.

According to Agnes, God loves creation and calls people to cherish and nourish it. He did not make the earth only as a life support system for human beings but as something beautiful in its own right. She declares, "His creation is the world that came into being through His breathing forth of the breath of life; it is the garden of this world planted by His love. He is delighted when He sees the many ways in which we have made the world more beautiful!" and "It is a joy to the Creator to feel His love pulsing through time, through galaxies in the far heavens and stars unknown and without number."⁹¹ Agnes took seriously the verses in Genesis that state, "God saw that it was good" (Genesis 1:10-25) and firmly believed God loves all He made. Additionally, she believed creation not only recognizes but also responds to God's love for it. Describing her love for the oceans and seas, even more than her love for flowers, she writes,

> I always feel like laughing when, from the Episcopal prayer book, I sing about whales blessing the Lord, along with all other creatures that move in the waters; yet it is joyous laughter, for I know that there is meaning and great truth therein. God's life created and supports all living creatures, and in some dim way they feel that life and rejoice in it. If even whales can praise Him, so can I!⁹²

She believed all the various parts of creation somehow worship God in their own way, and Christians are called to join in with those acts and attitudes of adoration. For her, the whole creation responds to God.

Agnes did not limit her care for creation only to plants and animals. She believed God loves the earth itself, including the rocks and ground, and He desires the healing of the entire planet. Describing this attitude in Agnes, Payne writes,

> Her faith, when released for the healing of man or of nature (whether it be a sick

child, an ailing tree, or the very rock structure struggling to right itself within the bowels of the earth), was extraordinary to behold. . . . She believed that we are commanded in the Scriptures to pray not only for the healing of mankind, but also for the healing of the earth itself. Many Christians believe that, but few seem to have the understanding of how to pray effectively for the earth. She spent her last years teaching others how to do so.[93]

When Agnes retired from most of her other teaching activities, she moved to California and purchased a home on the San Andreas Fault so she could pray for its healing. She recalls, "In due time my decision to move from New England to the West Coast was made partly because of the need of that which has become my greatest 'patient,' the San Andreas Fault."[94] She began a habit of regularly praying for the land itself to be healed of stresses, interceding for the tectonic plates to adjust themselves as smoothly as possible, not only to minimize death and destruction but also to make the land whole. She believed Jesus came to redeem the whole world so that all things could be restored to their original design, including the earth. In her opinion, creation really is waiting for the children of God to release it from its bondage to corruption (Romans 8:19-22). In her view, Christians were called to redeem the created world from destruction.

Agnes considered Jesus's command to the Church to take the gospel to all of creation a vital and necessary step toward His return. Unlike many Christians, she believed creation could also include life beyond the planet earth. Although she never declares that life actually does exist on other planets, she considered it very possible. While expressing a belief in the devil as a real being—along with angels, archangels, and the host of heaven—she uses the possibility of extraterrestrial life to support her claims:

> Is it really unscientific, then, to believe that there may be other living creatures in the universe than those upon the earth? How amazing and how amusing it is that science as it plods its way toward knowing, makes it more and more possible for us to believe what the Bible told us long ago: that there are beings who have never lived on earth! We know now that the stars are suns like ours, millions of them, among whom our sun is but one insignificant heavenly candle. . . . But recently science states that in all probability there are planets around other suns after all, as indeed why should there not be? The laws of life that produced planets around our sun are more than likely to produce the same manifestations around other suns. Moreover, now science informs us that there may be living creatures upon them![95]

While providing biblical references to angels and "sons of God," she suggests a distinct possibility of other life in the universe. She later becomes even more assertive, declaring, "If, for instance, the guess of astronomers is right that there are probably living beings on other planets than this earth, then Jesus is Lord of *all* [emphasis hers] of them."[96] She did not believe life on other worlds contradicted biblical Christianity, for she found nothing specific in the Bible that prohibited the possibility. However, it never became a focus of her theology.

At one point, Agnes even hints at the existence of fairies or leprechauns. In her autobiography, she describes a time when she and Ted stayed with a bishop and his wife. She recounts, "He was Irish by ancestry. He would read us Irish fairy tales in the evening after the lecture and would say, 'There *are* [emphasis from source] little people, you know.' Ted thought he was jesting, but I am not sure."[97] Initially, her comment seems primarily to question whether the bishop was joking or being serious about his statement. However, she later makes a related statement when she is discussing the possibility of life in the universe, suggesting she considered it a possibility; she asks,

> Does the Creator brood over His creation in such an intimate fashion that He takes note of apple trees and of the lilies of the field and of the sparrows of the air? Does He even possibly have small unseen helpers in the work of His creation? Who shall say?[98]

Agnes does not specifically declare that these other forms of life exist in nature, but she also does not rule out the possibility. Apparently, she considered it conceivable in a world full of God's majesty and undiscovered mysteries of science. However, her allowance for other life forms to exist, hypothetically, within nature or on other planets never directly or noticeably impacts her theology or affects her healing paradigm; it remained peripheral.

Finally, Agnes seems to maintain some type of belief in the preexistence of the human soul or spirit. As one of her most unusual beliefs, her comments require careful examination, especially when the actual contexts of her comments sometimes relate to entirely different topics. For example, it is while discussing the incarnation of Christ that she asks the following questions:

> Even for us it may be harder to be born than to die. Since the spirit is breathed into us from God, who knows how and in what manner that spirit may have lived before drawing near to this earth? Since there is no time with God (Psalm 90:4) and since we are heirs of immortality (Rom. 8:29), who shall say when our spirits evolved from the Godhead, speeded forth at His word—who shall say where they may have lived and in what manner they may have served Him before they were sent upon this desperate journey of life on earth? Who can tell with what dismay they may have looked on this dark earth—this small lost planet—this bit of creation taken over by the enemy? Even for us. How much more—how infinitely more difficult for Him, the Son of God . . . to be born of the Virgin Mary![99]

She does not specifically state that the human spirit preexists, but her questions certainly suggest some consideration of it. In another place, she suggests the possibility of preexistence while describing the power available to the Church as a collective body of believers. She explains how an infant, being "homesick" for God and dreading its entrance into this dark and fallen world, could be touched and comforted through the sacrament of baptism.[100] Although she is only pondering how the sacraments might work, her consideration and discussion suggest she was open to the possible existence of the infant's spirit before birth.

The clearest mention of the preexistent human spirit occurs in her autobiography. Again, the purpose of the experience she recounts concerns a healing of memories. After Ted's death, she became significantly depressed but continued in ministry. At one School of Pastoral Care, she received prayer from two people, John Sandford and a woman she never identifies. Sandford prayed for healing of the horror memory from her childhood, related to child sacrifice in Sparta, while the woman prayed for Agnes's eyes to be opened, describing a greater gift of discernment.[101] Agnes felt nothing immediately after the prayers but subsequently had a significant spiritual experience. As she recalls,

> Two days later, amazing things happened to me. Both prayers had apparently opened the door for my spirit to leap back through time. I don't know where I was in body when my spirit took this strange adventure. I am sure that I was not asleep. This was no dream. My body may have been in my study, waiting for me to come back from a meditation that became more than a meditation. But *I* [emphasis hers], myself, was somewhere very far away.[102]

As discussed, Agnes believed God transcends time and space. Therefore, all events—past, present, and future—are continually present to God. Her statement indicates her belief God showed her the historical past; she was convinced it was a real experience.

Continuing the recollection of the experience, Agnes describes being in another place, somewhere besides earth. Considering accounts provided by Daniel, Ezekiel, and John, her interpretation of her surroundings may not necessarily be literal. She writes,

> It was a deep, green valley, the surrounding folds not rocky but smooth and covered with low vegetation, something like the mountains on Oahu. There were neither flowers nor trees, only low soft bushes, none of which I recognized. This far valley was not on the planet earth, I feel sure. Nor was it "heaven" as we think of heaven. It seemed as though I was upon a new, uninhabited planet in some other solar system, around some other sun.[103]

As seen from her writings, Agnes clearly believed the universe could contain inhabitable planets. In this instance, she perceived herself somewhere neither in heaven nor on earth. Nevertheless, she is only relating an experience up to this point; she is not promoting any specific doctrine or theological significance to the event so far.

As Agnes continues relating the experience, she describes seeing Jesus in this other place. He says He is sending her to the moment in history related to the primary image that terrified her as a child; however, He assures her she will be safe. She recalls,

> I was not in a body. I saw no living thing until Jesus walked down the valley past the folded hills, and as He came, every fold filled up with light. I saw Him with the eyes of the spirit, but not in bodily form. Then He spoke to me, though not in words, only in thought. What Spirit communicated to spirit was this: that He intended to send me down to the planet earth, not in a body, but in a spirit only. He would send an angel with me for protection. And He was sending me out like a spy going into a very far country, for a specific reason.[104]

Up to this point, Agnes is relating what could be a vision or an actual event of being taken out of her body and taken up to Heaven. She continues,

> Then the scene changed instantly, as in a motion picture one scene flashes into another. I was in Sparta, Greece, and the sacrifice scene that had so often wakened me with horror was being enacted before my eyes.[105]

Apart from her preliminary statement of leaping "back through time," Agnes could be describing a vision. However, she seems to consider this to have been an actual event.

In her teaching on healing of memories, she describes God being outside of time and able to touch past memories that are present to Him. In this instance, she seems to be involved in the process where the past is a present reality to God. The context of the incident up to this point seems to focus on God's transcendence beyond time. In other words, He is showing her how all times are present and available to Him. She continues,

> The valley that I had seen was not vague, but somehow fluid, as though the life in it was not quite formed and set. But this scene in Sparta, before Christ was born—this scene was completely clear and sharp and bright. I could draw it in every detail, I could paint it: the marble temple at my right, with seven Corinthian columns and seven shallow marble steps leading down to the circular courtyard, paved with irregular stones of grey and pink and pale blue slate. People were standing in a semicircle looking at the altar. Beyond the altar, the hill dropped off sharply, and I could see past it another hill, with a marble building or two and trees that I recognized as belonging to this earth: cypress and a pale, feathery tree something like a pepper tree.[106]

She makes a clear distinction between the vagueness of the first scene and the clarity of the second scene. She considered this second description to be of an actual and historical place in time, and God was allowing her to observe it firsthand as it was actually taking place.

Agnes recalls being able to see the people with significant clarity. However, they did not see her, presumably because she was not in a physical body at the time. She says,

> The people could not see me. I could see only their backs, draped in white or pastel colors, and I could hear nothing. I stood invisible behind the group, and

> I was aware, without seeing, that an angelic presence stood beside me. Strange that I could see the people so distinctly and could not see the angel![107]

She was able to sense the angel's presence beside her, but she could only see the crowd standing around the altar. She then observes the sacrifice take place. However, she now sees it from a different perspective as if God had changed what had taken place or was showing her what had actually taken place from his perspective. She writes,

> The altar was something like a sundial. Upon the altar a boy was being sacrificed. But amazingly, as I actually looked upon this scene, the horror went away from it. I knew somehow that God had mercifully taken away the spirit of this youth, and in His own way was shielding it from a crime done in ignorance, with a vague desire to placate some sort of deity. The boy was not suffering, although his body seemed to be suffering.[108]

Her recollection of seeing the event without the horror previously associated with it precisely matches her description of the result of the healing of memories: the memory itself does not disappear, but the emotional significance of the memory changes so it no longer causes pain. In her account, she can see the event like a memory, without being seen and without experiencing the fear.

Interestingly, Payne, who was admittedly influenced by Agnes, describes a similar event when she first learned about inner healing—with one major difference. She says,

> I was on a camping trip in Oklahoma, and in the process of cleaning up the camp, I had walked out onto a huge boulder. The chore finished, I stepped back, and when I did, I stepped back in time. I saw two Indian men, and they saw me. I saw the terrain as it had been hundreds of years ago. I knew instantly that it was long before the white man had come, and that these Indian men had never before seen a white person. We were mutually astonished.[109]

While Agnes had simply observed the past event in real time, Payne actually interacted with the incident: she not only saw the two men but also states clearly they saw her. Again, these unusual experiences exemplify God's transcendence beyond time and space for both of them.

After seeing the sacrifice with new insight and without the accompanying sense of horror, Agnes finds herself back in the valley where the experience first began. At that point, Jesus again approaches and speaks with her, asking her if she is willing to be born onto such a planet. She writes,

> Then again the scene changed. I was once more in the valley and in deep grief, though it could not express itself in tears, for I was not in a body (II Cor. 12:2). Again Jesus came down the valley and spoke to me in thought, after this manner: "Now you have seen the very worst that can happen upon the planet earth. Would you then be willing to go down there, when I deem it best, and to be born

and live on that planet for the purpose of relieving suffering? If so, I must tell you that it will be a hard life."[110]

Agnes recounts her memory of the conversation as best as she could, making clear that they were thoughts and impressions—not actual words. The wording certainly suggests a belief in the preexistence of the human spirit, but the point of the entire experience was not to expound a new doctrine but to bring forth a significant healing. Agnes had not only been carrying grief and sorrow from Ted's death but also bitterness and resentment over the hardships in her childhood. This experience permanently changed that. She writes,

> I do not remember my words, if they were words, but the sense of my heart was that I was willing. Thus I was healed in another manner. For I was never again bitter about the hardships of life nor angry with God, as I have confessed to being, remembering that this had happened long before my birth into this world. Once more I could "like God." For now I knew that I myself had consented to make this earthly pilgrimage for the sake of His Son Jesus Christ.[111]

Through this experience, Agnes contends that she had received a major healing of memories, and she accepts the experience at face value. Following the account, she writes, "I am *not* expounding any theory. I am *only* stating what happened to me, as truthfully as I can. But I point out one very significant thing: *I was not in a body* [emphasis hers]."[112] She relates the incident primarily to emphasize not being in a body at the time, and she discusses the idea of preexistence only secondarily. Also, she makes a point of definitively stating she does not believe in the idea of reincarnation but views the experience in light of the immortality of the spirit.

Agnes had several beliefs and experiences defying easy categorization. She accepts a modified view of Theistic evolution at a time when many in the Evangelical movement largely considered it heretical; however, she also affirms a special creation for man and woman, maintaining the doctrine of a literal fall from grace. Based on her understanding of the redemptive work of Christ, she describes a belief in the possible attainment of the resurrection body that significantly matches the doctrine of deification as presented by notable early Church theologians. She holds a post-millenial eschatology that conforms to Renewal ideology and practice while it simultaneously contrasts with some Renewalists' common theological perspectives. She proclaims a Christian mandate toward creation with solid biblical support while surprisingly allowing for alternate forms of life on earth and in the universe. Most unusually, she believes in the possible preexistence of the human spirit. Although some of her beliefs relate more to sacramental than traditional Evangelical experiences, none of them invalidate her Christian theology.

Conclusion

In all of her works, Agnes presents an orthodox Christian theology. Although her terminology often reflects metaphysics and psychology more than religion, she maintains the basic biblical foundations of the Christian faith: her belief in the nature of the Trinity coincides with historic teachings of the Presbyterian and Episcopal denominations; she affirms a fully orthodox view of the redemptive work of Christ, including His incarnation, death, and resurrection; and she holds an inspired view of Scripture—though it is moderated with a high opinion of science. Still, she maintains a strong commitment to the core doctrines of the Christian faith. Still, Agnes describes a relationship with God emphasizing experience over dogma. Her metaphysical ideology merged with her childhood experiences in China to form a Christian lifestyle more experiential than intellectual. In some cases, Agnes describes beliefs, experiences, and theological positions foreign or contrary to the mainline denominations, some of which are occasionally associated with pantheism, spiritism, deism, and even shamanism. However, she rejected those positions and held a largely orthodox theology.

Notes

[1] The original subtitle is evident in the 2nd edition but has been shortened or removed in later editions by MacAlester Park. Subsequent printings by Ballentine Books contain no subtitle at all.

[2] Agnes Sanford, *Behold Your God*, 13-14.

[3] Agnes Sanford, *Behold Your God*, 13-14.

[4] Agnes Sanford, *Behold Your God*, 71-72.

[5] Agnes Sanford, *Behold Your God*, 9, 76.

[6] Agnes Sanford, *Behold Your God*, 127.

[7] Agnes Sanford, *Behold Your God*, 130.

[8] Mark Cartledge highlights the value of studies "conducted from within the Pentecostal community... [using] the methodology of mutual critical correlation... to evaluate claims to the Spirit's guidance"; see Mark J. Cartledge, "Practical Theology" in *Studying Global Pentecostalism: Theories & Methods*, edited by Allan Anderson, Michael Bergunder, Andre Droogers, and Cornelis Van der Laan, 268-285 (Berkeley: University of California Press, 2010), 279. Gary Greig points out that "faith in signs and wonders worked by God cannot be confused with faith in Christ and the gospel, as some critics contend. Faith in Christ's power must necessarily be faith in Chrsit Himself"; See Gary S. Greig, "The Purpose of Signs and Wonders in the New Testament: What Terms for Miraculous Power Denote and Their Relationship to the Gospel" in *The Kingdom and the Power*, edited by Gary S. Greig and Kevin N. Springer, 133-174 (Ventura: Regal Books, 1993), 151. One of the clearest descriptions of this is provided in article by Steven Land who writes, "The believer needs to be reminded once again that it is not what 'she's got,' but who has got her. It is not how much of the Spirit he has, but how much of him the Spirit has. The point is to live from the fullness of God and not from the flesh, the world, or the devil"; see Steven J. Land, "Be Filled with the Spirit: The Nature and Evidence of Spiritual Fullness," *Ex Auditu* 12 (1996): 110.

⁹ Agnes Sanford, *Behold Your God*, 131-135; additionally, see Agnes Sanford, *Sealed Orders*, 216-219.
¹⁰ Agnes Sanford, *Behold Your God*, 136.
¹¹ Agnes Sanford, *Behold Your God*, 136-137.
¹² Agnes Sanford, *Sealed Orders*, 216.
¹³ Agnes Sanford, *Sealed Orders*, 219.
¹⁴ Agnes Sanford, *Sealed Orders*, 227.
¹⁵ Agnes Sanford, *The Healing Light*, 2nd ed., 13.
¹⁶ Agnes Sanford, *Sealed Orders*, 217.
¹⁷ Agnes Sanford, *Behold Your God*, 127-140.
¹⁸ Agnes Sanford, *Behold Your God*, 133.
¹⁹ Agnes Sanford, *Behold Your God*, 134.
²⁰ Agnes Sanford, *Behold Your God*, 141-158.
²¹ Agnes Sanford, *Behold Your God*, 70.
²² Agnes Sanford, *Behold Your God*, 70-71.
²³ Agnes Sanford, *Behold Your God*, 71.
²⁴ Agnes Sanford, *The Healing Light*, 2nd ed., 55.
²⁵ Agnes Sanford, Behold Your God, 79.
²⁶ Agnes Sanford, *Behold Your God*, 82-83.
²⁷ Agnes Sanford, *Behold Your God*, 1-5, 9-13. Cf. Matt 5:45.
²⁸ William De Arteaga, *Agnes Sanford and Her Companions*, 87-88.
²⁹ Agnes Sanford, *Behold Your God*, 115-116.
³⁰ Agnes Sanford, *Behold Your God*, 116.
³¹ Agnes Sanford, *Behold Your God*, 135.
³² Agnes Sanford, *Behold Your God*, 7n1.
³³ Agnes Sanford, *The Healing Power of the Bible*, 8.
³⁴ Agnes Sanford, *The Healing Power of the Bible*, 7-9.
³⁵ Agnes Sanford, *Behold Your God*, 25.
³⁶ Agnes Sanford, *Behold Your God*, 31.
³⁷ Agnes Sanford, *Behold Your God*, 90.
³⁸ Agnes Sanford, *Behold Your God*, 13.
³⁹ Agnes Sanford, *The Healing Light*, 2nd ed., 19, 30.
⁴⁰ Joel C. Elowsky. *We Believe in the Holy Spirit*, volume 4 of *Ancient Christian Doctrine* (Downers Grove: IVP Academic, 2009), 41-42.
⁴¹ Amos Yong, *The Spirit Poured Out on All Flesh*, 280-302; Amos Yong, *In the Days of Caesar: Pentecostalism and Political Theology* (Grand Rapids: William B. Eerdmans, 2010), 347; Amos Yong, *Spirit-Word-Community: Theological Hermeneutics in Trinitarian Perspective* (Eugene: Wipf & Stock, 2002), 43.
⁴² James K. A. Smith, *Thinking in Tongues: Pentecostal Contributions to Christian Philosophy* (Grand Rapids: William B. Eerdmans, 2010), 12, 101. Additionally, see Amos Yong, *Spirit-Word-Community*, 43.
⁴³ Agnes Sanford, *Sealed Orders*, 29-30, 36.
⁴⁴ Agnes Sanford, *Creation Waits*, 41-43.
⁴⁵ Agnes Sanford, *Behold Your God*, 77.
⁴⁶ Agnes Sanford, *The Healing Light*, 2nd ed., 34-35.
⁴⁷ Agnes Sanford, *The Healing Light*, 2nd ed., 36.
⁴⁸ Agnes Sanford, *Behold Your God*, 74. Additionally, see Agnes Sanford, *Sealed Orders*, 178199.
⁴⁹ Agnes Sanford, *Behold Your God*, 75.
⁵⁰ Agnes Sanford, *Behold Your God*, 15.

⁵¹ Leanne Payne, *Restoring the Christian Soul*, 68; Peter D. Hocken, "Sanford, Agnes Mary," in Stanley M. Burgess and Ed M. Van der Maas, eds., *The New International Dictionary of Pentecostal and Charismatic Movements* (Grand Rapids: Zondervan, 2003), 1039; Francis Baltz, *Creative Intercessor*, 38; Pavel Hejzler, *Two Paradigms for Divine Healing: Fred F. Bosworth, Kenneth E. Hagin, Agnes Sanford, and Francis MacNutt in Dialogue* (doctoral dissertation, Fuller Theological Seminary, School of Theology, 2009), 34, ProQuest (DTN 3345063). Note: "healing of memories" and "inner healing" are often used interchangeably.

⁵² Agnes Sanford, *Behold Your God*, 77, 83.

⁵³ Agnes Sanford, *Sealed Orders*, 197.

⁵⁴ Agnes Sanford, *Sealed Orders*, 195. See also Francis Baltz, *Creative Intercessor*, 36-37.

⁵⁵ In *Behold Your God*, she describes a similar incident with a woman, also a concentration camp survivor, and says it helped her understand how to pray for others to receive forgiveness in their memories. It may be the same incident with changed details to protect Sammy's identity, or it may be a different incident. The two books were written fourteen years apart. See Agnes Sanford, *Behold Your God*, 110-111.

⁵⁶ Agnes Sanford, *Behold Your God*, 111.

⁵⁷ Agnes Sanford, *The Healing Light*, 2nd ed., 28.

⁵⁸ Agnes Sanford, *The Healing Light*, 2nd ed., 30-31.

⁵⁹ William De Arteaga, *Agnes Sanford and Her Companions*, 195.

⁶⁰ Stanley M. Burgess, *The Holy Spirit: Eastern Christian Traditions*, volume 2 of *The Holy Spirit* (Grand Rapids: Baker Academic, 1989), 3-4.

⁶¹ The author has previously published portions of this section in a journal article on Agnes Sanford. See Martin Dignard, "God's Faithful Freedom," 68-84.

⁶² Agnes Sanford, *Behold Your God*, 5.

⁶³ Kimberly Ervin Alexander, *Pentecostal Healing*, 38.

⁶⁴ Kimberly Ervin Alexander, *Pentecostal Healing*, 40.

⁶⁵ Agnes Sanford, *Behold Your God*, 24-25.

⁶⁶ Agnes Sanford, *The Healing Light*, 2nd ed., 19.

⁶⁷ Agnes Sanford, *Creation Waits*, 29.

⁶⁸ Agnes Sanford, *Creation Waits*, 32.

⁶⁹ Kimberly Ervin Alexander, *Pentecostal Healing*, 154-156. The term "Finished Work" in this context indicates a conviction that believers can take their "position" in Christ's completed work on the cross and wait in faith for the full effect. This is usually in contrast to the more "Wesleyan" perspective, which views salvation in terms of sanctification and process. See chapter 2 in Alexander's work.

⁷⁰ Agnes Sanford, *Behold Your God*, 102.

⁷¹ Agnes Sanford, *Behold Your God*, 117.

⁷² Agnes Sanford, *Behold Your God*, 117-118. Note: it is unclear whether "he" references Jesus, appearing briefly over 40 days before his ascension; Enoch, who walked with God and then disappeared; or Elijah, who was taken up in a flaming chariot. Agnes discusses all three in the same paragraph.

⁷³ Agnes Sanford, *Behold Your God*, 119.

⁷⁴ Irenaeus of Lyons, *Against Heresies*, 5. Preface. In Alexander Roberts, James Donaldson, and A. Cleveland Coxe, trans., *The Apostolic Fathers with Justin Martyr and Irenaeus*, vol. 1 of *The Ante-Nicene Fathers: Translations of the writings of the Fathers down to A.D. 325* (Oak Harbor: Logos Research Systems, 1997), 526.

⁷⁵ Athanasius, *Four Discourses Against the Arians*, 1. 39. In Philip Schaff and Henry Wace, eds., *Athanasius: Select Works and Letters*, vol. 4 of *The Nicene and Post-Nicene Fathers, Second Series* (Oak Harbor: Logos Research Systems, 1997), 329.

[76] William De Arteaga, *Agnes Sanford and Her Companions*, 195.
[77] Agnes Sanford, *Behold Your God*, 91.
[78] Agnes Sanford, *Behold Your God*, 91-92.
[79] Agnes Sanford, *Behold Your God*, 100-101.
[80] Agnes Sanford, *Behold Your God*, 101.
[81] Agnes Sanford, *Behold Your God*, 115-116.
[82] Agnes Sanford, *Creation Waits*, 3.
[83] Agnes Sanford, *Creation Waits*, 8.
[84] Dwight Wilson categorizes Pentecostals as mainly premillennial, dispensational, and pretribulational; see Dwight J. Wilson, "Eschatology, Pentecostal Perspectives On" in *The New International Dictionary of Pentecostal and Charismatic Movements*, edited by Stanley M. Burgess and Eduard M. Van der Maas, 601-605 (Grand Rapids: Zondervan, 2003), 601. However, an increasing numbers of scholars have been challenging this position. For example, Matthew Thompson explains that "The uncritical adoption of Scofieldian dispensationalism [by early Pentecostals] has not only left Pentecostalism bereft of its primary theological self-identification [and] it has severely undermined, both theoretically and practically, its chief spiritually distinctive experience of Spirit baptism and glossolalia"; additionally, see Matthew K. Thompson, *Kingdom Come: Revisioning Pentecostal Eschatology* (Blandford Forum, UK: DEO, 2010), 3. See also Peter Althouse and Robby Waddell, eds., *Perspectives in Pentecostal Eschatologies* (Eugene: Pickwick, 2010).
[85] Frank D. Macchia, "Pentecostal Theology" in *"The New International Dictionary of Pentecostal and Charismatic Movements*, edited by Stanley M. Burgess and Ed M. Van der Maas, 1120-1141 (Grand Rapids: Zondervan, 2002): 1138-1140.
[86] Agnes Sanford, *The Healing Light*, 2nd ed., 25.
[87] Agnes Sanford, *Behold Your God*, 10.
[88] Agnes Sanford, *Behold Your God*, 48-49.
[89] Agnes Sanford, *Creation Waits*, 1.
[90] Agnes Sanford, *Creation Waits*, 2.
[91] Agnes Sanford, *Creation Waits*, 99.
[92] Agnes Sanford, *Creation Waits*, 100.
[93] Leanne Payne, *Heaven's Calling*, 254.
[94] Agnes Sanford, *Creation Waits*, 3.
[95] Agnes Sanford, *Behold Your God*, 6-7.
[96] Agnes Sanford, *Creation Waits*, 61.
[97] Agnes Sanford, *Sealed Orders*, 144.
[98] Agnes Sanford, *Behold Your God*, 24.
[99] Agnes Sanford, *Behold Your God*, 72-73.
[100] Agnes Sanford, *Behold Your God*, 162.
[101] Agnes Sanford, *Sealed Orders*, 281.
[102] Agnes Sanford, *Sealed Orders*, 281-282.
[103] Agnes Sanford, *Sealed Orders*, 282.
[104] Agnes Sanford, *Sealed Orders*, 282.
[105] Agnes Sanford, *Sealed Orders*, 282.
[106] Agnes Sanford, *Sealed Orders*, 282.
[107] Agnes Sanford, *Sealed Orders*, 282-283.
[108] Agnes Sanford, *Sealed Orders*, 282-283.
[109] Leanne Payne, *Restoring the Christian Soul*, 76.
[110] Agnes Sanford, *Sealed Orders*, 283.
[111] Agnes Sanford, *Sealed Orders*, 283.
[112] Agnes Sanford, *Sealed Orders*, 283.

CHAPTER 6

ASSESSING HER INFLUENCE AND CRITICS

Agnes Sanford made a profound impact upon the Charismatic Movement and the Christian church through her ministry and writings. While her influence on North American Charismatic Christianity and in other English-speaking countries touched by the Charismatic Movement is evident, she likely also had a noteworthy effect outside those areas, as reflected by the translation of many of her books into numerous languages; however, tracing that influence is beyond the scope of this research. As can be shown, her influence resulted from more than her declaration that God continues to heal the sick and perform miracles, for numerous ministries had arisen in both the nineteenth and twentieth centuries to proclaim healing and miracles were still available for believers in the modern age. Agnes held a largely unique role due to her interdisciplinary approach, incorporating metaphysics, science, and psychology into her paradigm; her straightforward methodology, relying upon experimentation, observation, and accountability in her healing prayer model; and her experiential theology, reflecting the transcendence, immanence, and essential nature of God. In other words, she made a profound impact upon her audience not because she promoted healing but because of the way she promoted it. Her methodology and theology resulted in radically different assessments of her place in modern church history. An evaluation of some of the most representative material written about Agnes will indicate the common conclusions drawn from her life and writings.

Assessment by Renewal Scholars

Even when people identify an influence in their life or ministry, they cannot undeniably ascertain the exact outcome if that influence had never existed. Similarly, a person's thoughts, attitudes, and beliefs can be influenced by others irrespective of a conscious awareness of the impact by those influences. These variables make it impossible to demonstrate the exact and conclusive nature and extent of Agnes's impact on healing ministry and the Charismatic Movement. However, evaluating her recognition by historians, theologians, and independent healing ministries can provide a valid and useful indication of her impact.

Roman Catholic Charismatic scholar Peter Hocken authored the *NIDPCM* entry on Agnes as well as the prominent entry on the Charismatic Movement as a whole. He is significantly qualified to evaluate her effect on Christianity in the twentieth century.[1] He begins his entry "Sanford, Agnes Mary" with the brief sentence "Pioneer in healing ministry," and in his work on renewal in Great Britain, he references her as "an Episcopalian pioneer in the divine healing ministry."[2] As an authority on the Renewal Movement, he identifies Agnes as having a prominent role in promoting healing ministry. In the *NIDPCM* entry, he also declares, "Sanford was *the major pioneer* [emphasis added] in ministry for the healing of memories, which for her was all one with the forgiveness of sin."[3] According to his statements, Agnes did not just present healing as a viable option for churches but became significantly instrumental in advancing the use of healing prayer within many of the mainline denominations. Through her conference engagements, written works, and personal contacts, she influenced an entire movement.

Agnes promoted more than just healing ministry, however, for she considered the baptism in the Holy Spirit a vital need for the Christian Church. In his entry on Agnes, Hocken also states, "Through contacts in the Schools of Pastoral Care, Camps Farthest Out, and the Order of St. Luke, Sanford was one of the foremost promoters of renewal in the Holy Spirit within the historic churches in the English-speaking world."[4] Although she began operating in healing ministry before her own baptism in the Holy Spirit, it had a profound effect on her and became a significant part of her ministry. In the *NIDPCM* major entry "Charismatic Movement," Hocken describes Agnes as "a major influence in the spread of the Pentecostal experience within the historic church traditions."[5] She spoke of her own experiences in a manner that not only elicited interest but also assuaged fears within members of the mainline denominations. Hocken writes, "Mrs. Sanford's visits to Britain almost certainly contributed to the spread of the Charismatic movement," and at a later point, he boldly states, "Probably the person who contributed most to the spread of baptism in the Spirit with spiritual gifts among those firmly committed to their own church tradition was Agnes Sanford."[6] She initially only discussed her experience in private, but she later spoke of it more publicly when the Schools of Pastoral Care were held in Britain. She had a noticeable role within the Charismatic Movement overseas.

William De Arteaga is a notable historian and theologian in the Anglican tradition. His book *Quenching the Spirit* details the recurring tendency throughout Christian history for denominational leaders to reject Renewal movements. Henry H. Knight III, Wesleyan historian and theologian, identifies the text as "the first substantive work [on the subject] written from an independent or 'new' charismatic perspective."[7] De Arteaga mentions Agnes in this text, stating she "served as the apostle of healing to the mainline churches."[8] For a historian and theologian in the Anglican tradition, the title "apostle" carries significant weight. His wording suggests he viewed her as the foremost proponent of healing to the mainline denominations. De Arteaga later confirms his opinion of Agnes by writing the article "Agnes Sanford: Apostle of Healing, and First Theologian of the Charismatic Renewal" in which he discusses her impact. He declares,

> She played a particularly significant role in moving many Christians within the mainline churches away from cessationism and into the pastoral practice of healing prayer, and introduced many to the gifts of the Spirit. . . . [She] influenced mainline Protestants towards moderate idealism in much the same way that the ministry of Kenyon (and later Kenneth Hagin) influenced Pentecostal circles.[9]

Comparing her effect on Charismatics to Kenyon's and Hagin's influence on Pentecostals indicates he considered her impact extremely significant.

De Arteaga also describes Agnes's books as foundational for the early stages of the Charismatic Movement. In his opinion, her writings formed the basis for much of the Renewal's early theology. He states, "In the beginning years of the Renewal many of Mrs. Sanford's books served as the primary theological inspiration of the movement. *The Healing Light* was its first healing textbook."[10] De Arteaga asserts that Agnes's writings formed the theological foundation for the Charismatic Movement, especially in relation to healing, but he admits to being unable to quantify the extent of her impact. However, in the book he wrote about Agnes ten years later, he becomes even bolder in his claim of her impact upon the Church. He writes,

> [Agnes] was destined to become *the most important woman* [emphasis added] for the revival of healing prayer among the very mainline denominations who disbelieved in such prayers. In fact, she and her companions led a great campaign against cessationism and for the restoration of healing prayer and deliverance in the churches. She was also to advocate for the restoration of the gifts of the Spirit which had been recovered by the Pentecostals.[11]

His book traces the development of the Charismatic Movement and the extinguishing of the doctrine of cessationism, and he considers Agnes a primary figure for both. At least in the context of the restoration of healing to the Church, De Arteaga clearly identifies her theological contributions as not only prominent but foremost among her gender.

In this book, De Arteaga also unequivocally describes Agnes as one of the most significant theologians of the last one hundred years, declaring, "As time passes and it is easier to evaluate her work with historical perspective, it is clear that *she was one of the most important and original theologians of the twentieth century* [emphasis added]. The list of her accomplishments in the field of theology and innovations in healing ministry is astounding."[12] He then describes six accomplishments related to theology and healing ministry.

The first two accomplishments described by De Arteaga reference two of the books Agnes wrote during the early period of the Charismatic Movement, one on physical healing and one on inner healing. He writes,

> Among the books she wrote on healing, several now stand as classics in the field, especially *The Healing Light* (1947) and *The Healing Gifts of the Spirit* (1966), both of which greatly impacted the early Charismatic Renewal.
> *The Healing Light* was the first work of Western Christendom to seriously examine the energies of God and light of God as a normal presence and phenomenon for the Christian. Several writers in Eastern Orthodoxy had earlier described this phenomenon, but only as related to contemplative prayer.[13]

He does not mention *Behold Your God*, her most theological text. His first point describes "impact" without qualification. Of her early books, these two books describe a model for healing prayer, physical and emotional, in simple and practical steps. From a perspective of teaching people how to pray for the sick, her other works would not be as helpful. His second point suggests Agnes provided an important component to Western Theological discussion. Although she may have read material on Eastern Orthodox theologies in her life, she never mentions it, and her incorporation of energy and light in relation to God appears directly related to New Thought and science. Nevertheless, she does introduce these concepts through her works, which may facilitate subsequent discussion.

De Arteaga continues his list of accomplishments by identifying two specific areas of ministry directly resulting from Agnes's own healing ministry. In his opinion, both the inner healing movement as well as the Catholic Charismatic Movement owe a significant debt to Agnes not only for her writings but also for her personal ministry:

> She pioneered the ministry of inner healing prayer, and taught it to her disciples and companions in many church healing missions, CFO camps, and OSL missions where she taught and ministered.
> At a CFO camp she was introduced to Fr. Francis MacNutt, a Catholic Dominican priest. She subsequently discipled him in all that she had learned in healing, deliverance, and inner healing. MacNutt went on to become the principal theologian and writer on healing in the Catholic Charismatic Renewal, and thus passed on her theological legacy to the worldwide Catholic Charismatic Renewal.[14]

As noted, Hocken confirms De Arteaga's appraisal regarding Agnes being the pioneer and originator of the inner healing movement, and numerous inner healing ministries also affirm her importance. If she had accomplished nothing more than presenting a model for healing of memories to the church, her place in history would be deserved. However, she also influenced the Roman Catholic Church. MacNutt acknowledges Agnes in most of his books for her influence on him during his early years in the Charismatic Movement and for teaching him about healing. Although her impact on the Catholic Charismatic Renewal may qualify as indirect through MacNutt's ministry, he recognizes her influence on his own ministry as notable.

De Arteaga makes a significant point when he identifies Agnes's influence on early leadership within the Charismatic Movement. Her own ministry began prior to the Charismatic Movement and affected its base. As a fifth accomplishment, he states,

> Several years before the outbreak of the Charismatic Renewal, she and her husband founded the Schools of Pastoral Care, where ministers, priests, and lay leaders were instructed in healing prayer, deliverance/exorcism, inner healing prayer, and the gifts of the Spirit. None of these things were taught at the mainline seminaries of the time, and are often ignored even today. Many of the students taught by the Schools of Pastoral Care became leaders in the Charismatic R[enewal], especially after it broke out publically in 1960.[15]

In this respect, Agnes certainly had an impact upon leaders in numerous denominations, and her influence did begin prior to the official beginnings of the Charismatic Movement. De Arteaga does not provide a list of participants in the Schools of Pastoral Care to prove his assessment, for such a list is likely unavailable, but he provides an entirely reasonable supposition concerning subsequent leadership within the church.

De Arteaga's sixth accomplishment also seems somewhat subjective. In it, he refers to Agnes's ministry in regard to promoting and describing a Christian's assigned relationship to creation. In essence, he considers her a seminal source on a theology of healing prayer for creation. He writes,

> At her retirement home in California, she developed and wrote about an active "nature ministry," as in stilling storms and praying for plants. This has been occasionally recorded in Christian history, as in the lives of some Celtic saints, but it was Mrs. Sanford's work *Creation Waits* (1978) that articulated the *first theology* [emphasis from the source] of how to pray nature prayers.[16]

De Arteaga correctly identifies *Creation Waits* as a work describing a theology of the believer's position toward nature and creation, but he improperly limits it to the realm of prayer. Agnes uses the book to detail a more expansive position, including the attitudes, behaviors, and responsibilities required of a Christian toward the created world.

De Arteaga devotes more than one fifth of his book to discussing Agnes's impact and theology. Although he references other figures who denounced cessationism during the early Charismatic Movement, he considers her to be the most influential among them. Near the end of his discussion of her, he states,

> Just how much Agnes' ministry and writings helped bring about the Charismatic Renewal is impossible to quantify. She personally spoke to thousands about the

baptism of the Holy Spirit in the decade before the renewal broke out. She informed and touched many more through her books. Her books were especially influential in the Episcopal and Roman Catholic wings of the renewal.[17]

While some of his DeArteaga's statements seem subjective, his conclusions support a positive assessment of her influence.

Pentecostal historian Vinson Synan notes the significance of Agnes's influence on the Charismatic movement by pointing to her impact on Larry Christenson, a Lutheran pastor and author of numerous books on the Christian life. Synan authored an entry on Christenson in *NIDPCM*, describing him as "an ecumenical leader in the international charismatic movement" who also eventually "became the director of the International Lutheran Renewal Center," an organization founded to promote the Charismatic Movement in Lutheran churches.[18] He was involved not only in renewal in his own denomination but also among other churches. Christenson clearly had a major impact on the growing Charismatic Movement. According to Synan,

> Through reading the works of Agnes Sanford, Christenson became interested in Pentecostalism. In 1961 he was baptized in the Holy Spirit and spoke in tongues in a Foursquare Gospel church. Leading his church into a Pentecostal revival, he immediately became a national leader in the Lutheran charismatic renewal movement."[19]

Christenson became a participant in the Charismatic Movement through the writings of Agnes. Although the entry does not identify which of Agnes's books Christenson read, it had to be one of her early ones.[20] Through that work, he not only embraced the work of the Holy Spirit but also became a leader, promoting renewal to his entire denomination.

Christenson was clearly impacted by what Agnes wrote on healing and the gifts of the Spirit. He later mentions her specifically in his own works. In his book on the Holy Spirit, Christenson explains that the SPC "helped pastors in the English-speaking world to bring a ministry of healing into their congregations."[21] Here, he recognizes her influence not just in his own denomination but among other churches. Additionally, he identifies Agnes specifically as the originator of the ministry of "inner healing," confirming her impact in that arena.[22] Although he does not directly mention her impact on his interest in the baptism in the Spirit, she clearly precipitated it, and her healing ministry created an impression on him.

As knowledgeable historians and theologians, Hocken, De Arteaga, and Synan affirm the substantial impact Agnes made on healing ministry and the Charismatic Movement. Their writings reveal the profound effect she had upon both liturgical and mainline denominations at pivotal times during the early and formative stages of the Charismatic Movement.

Contemporary Ministries

John Gaynor Banks, an Episcopal priest, had a pivotal position both in relation to healing ministry and the Charismatic Movement. He and his wife Ethel founded The Order of St. Luke the Physician (OSL) as "an ecumenical organization dedicated to the Christian healing ministry" in 1932.[23] Although OSL had a primary focus on healing, it became an interdenominational center for people from many churches to learn about healing. As seen, both Hocken and De Arteaga attribute a great deal of Agnes's influence to the Schools of Pastoral Care, the Camps Farthest Out, and the Order of St. Luke.[24] In her autobiography, Agnes describes John Banks as one of the two people along with her doing "the healing works of Jesus."[25] Both John and Ethel Banks reference *The Healing Light* through their writings. After a meeting at her house, John published quotes from the manuscript in his *Sharing* magazine.[26] His excerpts directly led to its publication. He later describes it as "one of the most practical, genuinely inspirational and smoothly written accounts on the subject ever published."[27] He clearly found the book impressive. While discussing ways to overcome fear, he makes a profound statement about her first book. He explains, "if you read such a book as *The Healing Light* by Agnes Sanford, the reading of that book for you is religious therapy."[28] He clearly had a great deal of respect and regard for Agnes's healing ministry and at least her first book.

Glenn Clark was a physician who also had a significant role in the early stages of the Charismatic Movement. As discussed, Clark initially published Agnes's first book, *The Healing Light*, through MacalesterPark Publishing, a company he had founded for his own works on healing. De Arteaga as well as Mark Pearson identify him as one of the pioneers along with Agnes who promoted healing and denounced cessationism.[29] As well as writing books on healing, Clark founded Camps Farthest Out (CFO), which was to become a major venue for promoting the baptism and gifts of the Holy Spirit through their ongoing conferences. In his entry on the Charismatic Movement, Hocken describes the significance for Glenn Clark and the CFO; he writes,

> Another milieu in which many "mainline" Christians first heard of [the baptism of the Holy Spirit] was Camps Farthest Out (CFO), founded by Glenn Clark in 1930 to aid Christians to become "athletes of the Spirit." CFO conferences, like those of OSL, proved to be an environment receptive to the Pentecostal message, even though the organizers eventually came out against any identification with [the Charismatic Movement]. CFO gatherings, usually a week in length, gave much scope to the camp leaders, who over the years included Sanford, Tyson, Bredesen, Brown, Derek Prince, and many others.[30]

The CFOs clearly had a major part in the influence Agnes made on the early Charismatic Movement. She spoke at many of the conferences and was recognized as one of the primary leaders.

Clark did more than just found the CFOs through which Agnes spoke. He also published her first book. She recounts his reaction to the unpublished manuscript: "Upon reading it he remarked, 'This is *the best book on healing ever written* [emphasis added]. It is much better than any of mine, and I am going to see to it that it is published even if I have to publish it myself.'"[31] Agnes was not being deceptive, for Clark himself wrote the Introduction before he published it. In a pre-release recommendation, he wrote, "for those who would learn how to heal the sick this is *the best text ever written* [emphasis added]."[32] Considering he had written numerous books on healing, his statement clearly indicates the value he placed on her work. Along with Banks, Clark considered Agnes's ministry and writings a primary source for spreading the message of healing prayer during the early twentieth century.

Emily Gardner Neal was a journalist before the start of the Charismatic Movement. She originally began researching healing ministries to prove they were fake, but eventually wrote *A Reporter Finds God through Spiritual Healing* in 1956 after being convinced that many of the healings were genuine.[33] According to her own testimony, the reality of supernatural healing led to her becoming a Christian. Subsequently, she joined the Episcopal Church and started a healing ministry.[34] She wrote her second book, *God Can Heal You Now*, in 1958 to illustrate numerous examples of verified healings as well as discuss many active healing ministries of the time. Both of these books were written prior to the recognized beginning of the Charismatic Movement. Being a reporter, she carefully documented and verified the validity of healings before publishing them in her books.

In the second half of *God Can Heal You Now*, Neal describes fourteen healing ministries that she considered most significant at the time. Notably, the author lists these ministries under a section titled "Modern Apostles" and states, "Through the working of the Holy Spirit they are leading the way to a new era in Christianity—a rebirth of its pristine power, founded on a vibrant faith in the living God."[35] Of the fourteen ministries chosen to represent the healing ministry of the time, Neal mentions Agnes and discusses *The Healing Light*. According to Neal, Agnes's first book by that time "has gone into nineteen editions and has been reprinted in seven languages," and she boldly states, "I venture to say that there is no member of the laity in the United States who is wielding a greater or more widespread influence on the revival of healing within the churches than Agnes Sanford."[36] For another Episcopalian to identify Agnes as an "Apostle" is noteworthy. The author references the formation of the School of Pastoral Care in 1956 and writes, "Through this teaching center the healing ministry is being spread through the churches of America in a way not possible by any other means . . . [and participants] include Episcopalians, Methodists, Presbyterians, Lutherans, Congregationalists, Baptists, and others."[37] As a reporter, Neal's estimation of Agnes's impact confirms the profound effect she had on the healing theology and practice of the time as well as locating her in a significant position for the formative years of the early Charismatic Movement.

Clark, Banks, and Neal all had their own foundational roles in the early

Charismatic Movement, and considering their individual ministries as well as their own published works, their substantial recommendations of Agnes's first book, *The Healing Light*, supports the major importance of her work. These independent sources indicate that Agnes had a pioneering effect both on healing ministry, including originating the inner healing movement, and on promoting renewal within mainline denominations, propagating the acceptance of the gifts and baptism of the Holy Spirit within churches on a widespread scale.

Subsequent Ministries

Independent sources recognize the impact Agnes had on healing ministry as well as the early Charismatic Movement. Additionally, several notable ministries arose subsequent to and resulting from her own ministry, conference engagements, and writings. Evaluating the opinions of people influenced by Agnes and her works and who subsequently developed their own ministries or published texts on healing can aid in identifying the impact she made on the Church through personal relationships, ministry interactions, and written works.

Morton Kelsey was an Episcopal priest and Jungian analyst. He wrote numerous texts on the history of the gifts of the Spirit in the Church, and Synan lists his book *Tongue Speaking* as a source Pentecostals and Charismatics read to learn about the operation of the charismata through the centuries.[38] He also gained recognition in academic fields for his works promoting the incorporation of faith and science, especially psychology, as well as denouncing a "natural" versus "supernatural" dichotomy in a theistic worldview.[39] He also wrote *Healing & Christianity: A Classic Study*, which some consider a classic in the field of healing in Christian history. Martin Marty, a noted Lutheran historian and scholar, says of the book, "This intelligent defense of the healing potential of Christianity merits careful attention."[40] Kelsey supplies both an academic and a scholarly perspective on healing in Church history.

Agnes had a notable impact on Kelsey. In *Healing and Christianity: In Ancient Thought and Modern Times*, the first edition of the text, he attributes his own initiation into healing ministry to her works. He explains, "My introduction to the healing ministry, almost twenty-five years ago, came in a roundabout way through Agnes Sanford's first book, *The Healing Light*. . . . Later I met Mrs. Sanford and we became fast friends," and he describes her as "a wise consultant on all matters relating to sacramental healing."[41] Agnes actually attended the church that Kelsey pastored, giving his words about her even more significance. In the later edition of the book, Kelsey describes first meeting Agnes at a CFO in 1949 and declares, "Because of her book, *The Healing Light*, I began to take the healing ministry seriously. Several of her books are still in print and widely appreciated. The number of people that she influenced and led into a *sane* [emphasis from source] healing ministry would be difficult to estimate."[42] Agnes had a profound effect on Kelsey, who describes her impact as incalculable. Kelsey eventually began co-leading the Schools of Pastoral Care.[43] Through her writings and personal influence, Agnes had a profound impact on Kelsey's interest and involvement in healing.

Leanne Payne was an Anglican author of numerous books on inner healing. She founded Pastoral Care Ministries (PCM) in 1982 with a special focus on healing "gender identity" issues.[44] Some of her books focus on same-sex attractions while others discuss broader issues of emotional, psychological, and relational healing. Williams explains,

> Significantly, her books found an audience not simply among pentecostals and charismatics but also in the broader evangelical world. Her 1996 book *Restoring the Christian Soul* addressed the interconnections between Christian theology, psychology, and the healing of the emotions and received Christianity Today's "Critics' Choice" award.[45]

Payne died on Ash Wednesday, February 18, 2015. *Christianity Today* identifies her as "Prominent Leader in Pastoral Care, Healing Movement."[46] Several healing ministries developed out of her own.

Payne attributes a great deal to Agnes. In fact, she references Agnes in every one of her books except for *Real Presence*, a revision of her dissertation. In Payne's first book on inner healing, she writes, "my gratitude to Agnes Sanford . . . a magnificent trailblazer in the art of healing prayer," and she quotes liberally from Agnes in the text.[47] As discussed, although Agnes wrote and taught a great deal on physical healing, she is most often recognized for developing the inner healing movement. In her memoir, Payne also states, "all who have been blessed in prayer for healing of memories owe a great debt indeed to Agnes Sanford, who pioneered this way of prayer."[48] Payne not only references Agnes in her works but also describes her own ministry as the continuation of the Schools of Pastoral Care. De Arteaga writes, "Mrs. Payne, whose inner healing ministry focused on healing homosexuals out of their lifestyles, went on to found her own version of the Schools of Pastoral Care, called Pastoral Care Ministries."[49] Agnes had a significant influence on Payne, who's theology and practices reflect Agnes's ministry.

Canon Jim Glennon was an Anglican priest at St Andrew's Cathedral in Sydney, Australia. On September 29, 1960, he held a healing service during a women's Bible study group, and the first woman to receive prayer was healed; the Wednesday evening study then quickly evolved into a regular healing service.[50] As the news spread, the healing service became an integral part of the church. Glennon's interest in healing ministry was largely independent of the teachings on healing presented in that city by Gore and Hickson almost forty years beforehand.[51] As part of his ministry, Glennon transcribed some of his teachings into a book, *Your Healing is Within You*, which was published in 1978. The book began to have significant impact. Eventually, a separate building was purchased in 1984 as the center of the St Andrew's Healing Ministry.[52] After his retirement, he began to travel and speak in other parts of the world. He responded to an invitation to speak at All Saints Church in Florida in 1992. Due to the healings experienced during his preaching tour of the United States, the All Saints Healing Ministry was established, and the "Glennon House" was purchased and dedicated as a place people could stay for periods of time while receiving prayer.[53] The home was structured to resemble the center at St Andrew's Healing Ministry.

Agnes had a significant impact on Glennon. Prior to holding his first healing service, he had gone on a short vacation to read and relax. One of the books he took with him was *The Healing Light*. Egan writes, "what he read was to not only re-focus his life, but also lead to the development of a ministry in the Sydney Diocese during the next 50 years which was to impact the lives of thousands of people worldwide."[54] The book opened his eyes to the reality of healing, and he held his first healing service on his return. Additionally, Agnes visited St Andrew's Cathedral the next year and conducted a healing mission; it was at that point that she prayed for him to receive the baptism in the Holy Spirit.[55] Similar to her own experience, Glennon had been operating in healing ministry prior to receiving the baptism. She explained to him, "You *could* [emphasis from source] have received that fullness when you were first converted if you were believing for it, and if so that is good . . . but if you did not receive it then, you can receive it now."[56] He goes on to describe, similar to Agnes's own story, how he felt an increase in power as well as finding that things were accomplished with less effort and greater joy. Egan links two specific healing ministries in Australia and the United States to Agnes's writings and ongoing ministry.

Mark Pearson is a priest at Trinity Church in New Hampshire. He is a member of the Charismatic Episcopal Church (CEC), a denomination founded in 1992 and separate from the Episcopal Church.[57] He has written three books on living the Christian life and one book on developing a healing ministry in the Church. He and his wife Mary, a medical physician, founded The Institute for Christian Renewal in 1980, a ministry aimed at teaching Christians how to live a vibrant and balanced life incorporating the gifts of the Spirit, and New Creation Healing Center in 1992, a place where people can receive medical care in combination with healing prayer.[58] The Pearsons conduct healing conferences around the globe, indicating an active and effective ministry.

Agnes had some effect upon Pearson although the extent remains unclear. In his book, *Christian Healing: A Practical and Comprehensive Guide*, he recounts one of his parishioners telling him, "I was dramatically healed once! It was thirty years ago when Agnes Sanford prayed for me."[59] He did not follow the comment with any qualification or description of Agnes, so he may have expected his readers to recognize her name. In his discussion of inner healing, Pearson often uses the phrase "healing of memories," a term coined by Agnes and commonly associated with her.[60] His using her terminology along with referencing Payne twice suggests some basic level of awareness with Agnes's teachings. Also, in the book's introduction, the Rev. Jürgen Liias writes, "In the mainline churches, spiritual healing has been courageously pioneered by such persons as Agnes

Sanford and Glenn Clark and respectfully promoted by the Order of St. Luke."[61] Most authors are familiar with people affirmed in their own books. Pearson gives no credit to Agnes, but her works clearly influenced his ministry. Evidence of her teachings without attribution could potentially indicate her work has become part of the core practice and theology of the Charismatic Movement beyond any conscious awareness of her person.

Francis MacNutt is a Roman Catholic priest and author of several books on healing. Journalist Stephen Strang identifies him as "a pioneer in the charismatic renewal in foreign lands, particularly in Latin America among priests and other church leaders."[62] He has had a foundational impact on the Catholic Charismatic Renewal. De Arteaga describes him as "one of the founders of the Catholic Charismatic Renewal . . . [and] one of its principal healing theologians," and Thomas J. Csordas names him "the first and most widely known among American Catholic Charismatic healers."[63] His book *Healing* is considered by many to be a classic on healing. Although he is not officially recognized in the *NIDPCM* as a theologian, his education and credentials are significant.

MacNutt has had a profound impact on the Renewal Movement. He and his wife Judith founded Christian Healing Ministries (CHM) in 1980 as an interdenominational center to minister and teach healing.[64] People from numerous denominations attend their conferences and reference their books. Francis's qualifications as a theologian become clear in *The Nearly Perfect Crime: How the Church Almost Killed the Ministry of Healing*, a scholarly and practical discussion of the decline of the spiritual gifts in Church history. Concerning the book, Synan says, "MacNutt, as much as any other person in modern times, has brought the ministry of healing back to the attention of contemporary Christians in every denomination. I highly recommend this book."[65] Both in his ministry and writings, MacNutt has had a significant impact on healing ministry, not only in the Catholic Charismatic Renewal but also in the Charismatic Movement worldwide.

Agnes had a profound impact on MacNutt. He learned about healing and experienced the baptism in the Holy Spirit at a Camps Farthest Out in 1967 where she was one of the leaders. He claimed that he received the full baptism when she prayed for him, and that she also prophesied over him that he would restore healing ministry to the Roman Catholic Church.[66] In *Healing*, MacNutt mentions her repeatedly and declares, "Mrs. Sanford carried on the work of teaching and was perhaps *more responsible than anyone else* [emphasis added] for renewing the healing ministry in the mainline churches."[67] He also identifies her by name in his sequel book on healing: "In all we do we have tried to build on the foundation we first received from Mrs. Agnes Sanford and other *pioneers in the healing ministry* [emphasis added]."[68] MacNutt considered Agnes foundational not only in his own ministry but also in the emergence of the healing ministry in the mainline denominations during the early years of the Charismatic movement. Williams references MacNutt's widespread impact as well as Agnes's direct influence when he writes, "Perhaps the best known charismatic proponent of inner healing influenced by Sanford's teaching was the Roman

Catholic minister Francis MacNutt."[69] Agnes played a pivotal role in MacNutt's own ministry, which has had a profound impact upon both healing ministry and Renewal across denominational lines.

Also a Roman Catholic, Michael Scanlan is a third-order Franciscan priest. He has numerous degrees, not only in religion and theology but also the legal field. Hocken describes him as a "prominent figure in the Catholic charismatic renewal (CCR)" who has written several books on the subjects of healing, deliverance, and the gifts of the Spirit.[70] Scanlan became instrumental in the early Catholic Charismatic Renewal. He became president of the Franciscan University of Steubenville in 1974, transforming a failing college into a flourishing university.[71] Under his leadership, the institution held conferences that promoted the Renewal to clergy and students. Both Synan and Hocken recognize Scanlan and the University of Steubenville for having an instrumental impact on the Catholic Charismatic Renewal.[72] Scanlan had a notable role in promoting the Charismatic Movement in the Roman Catholic Church.

Agnes had an influence on Scanlan. In one of his book, he states, "the particular approach for healing prayers is indebted *to a significant extent* [emphasis added] to the insights of Mrs. Agnes Sanford," and he references her book *The Healing Light*.[73] However, he read more than just her first book. In his own book on inner healing, he lists both *The Healing Light* and *The Healing Gifts of the Spirit* in his bibliography.[74] Agnes clearly influenced him through her writings. Additionally, Scanlan often travelled with MacNutt, learning about healing and renewal and speaking at many of the same meetings.[75] Scanlan does not reference Agnes as often as MacNutt, nor is he as well known in ecumenical circles; however, he did have an impact on the Charismatic Movement in the Roman Catholic Church, and Agnes influenced him in relation to both physical and inner healing.

John and Paula Sandford are well known within Charismatic churches for their ministry of inner healing. De Arteaga identifies them as "certainly one of the *most influential* [emphasis added] couples of the Charismatic Renewal."[76] They have written several books on inner healing, intercessory prayer, deliverance, and restoring the family. They founded Elijah House in 1975 as an international organization for healing ministry and renewal in the Church.[77] Their ministry has focused on ministering to people as well as teaching them how to minister to others. De Arteaga says, "Thousands of students and ministers have taken its courses, either at Elijah House or via its videos, and it continues to this day as an effective school of Spirit-filled ministry."[78] Their book *The Transformation of the Inner Man* is extremely popular for advocates of the ministry of inner healing.

Agnes had a significant and direct influence on John Sandford. De Arteaga considers the ministries of the Sandfords and the MacNutts to be continuations of Agnes's own, and she describes John as her spiritual son, though they were not related.[79] Agnes mentions John several times in her autobiography. She had prayed for him in a SPC, both for physical and inner healing, and he later helped her overcome a major period of depression following Ted's death.[80] He eventually became one of the leaders of the SPCs. In his primary book on inner healing, he devotes a paragraph in the Acknowledgments to her:

> Of course no list of acknowledgments could be complete in a book concerning the healing of the inner man which does not give thanks for *the pioneering work of Agnes Sanford* [emphasis added]. Not only was she for all of us *the forerunner* [emphasis added] in the field of inner healing by prayer, but she was also our own first mentor in the Lord, our friend and advisor. It was her solid common sense which first hauled our soaring mysticism to safe moorings in sound theology, the Word of God, and earthiness.[81]

The Sandfords clearly considered Agnes the foundation for the ministry of inner healing. Additionally, the first three pages of the first chapter of the book are largely devoted to John's experiences with her and her ministry.[82] Agnes had a clear and direct impact on John Sandford, and the Sandford's ministry recognizes Agnes for its foundation.

William Vaswig was a Lutheran pastor. He founded Preaching and Prayer Ministries in 1976 for evangelism and healing prayer.[83] He also wrote *I Prayed, He Answered* to explain how Agnes taught him to pray for the sick after she healed his son from schizophrenia. He dedicated the book to her, and she in turn wrote the foreword for it.[84] The book not only describes how Sanford identified the cause of his son's illness and prayed for him but also details her meetings with medical professionals, who confirmed the healing. Vaswig discusses Agnes from the beginning of the introduction. He writes,

> In a lifetime one meets perhaps one or two people who make all the difference in the world. For me and my family, Agnes Sanford is one of those people. *The whole direction of our lives changed because of her* [emphasis added]. This book is about the difference Agnes Sanford has made. In everything from theological understanding to living out God's will in Christian caring, she is a veritable *gold mine of wisdom and motivation* [emphasis added]. Prayer doesn't mean the same to my family anymore—in either theory or practice.[85]

Agnes obviously affected his entire family. The short book does not qualify as scholarly or historical, and Preaching and Prayer Ministries is no longer active. However, by providing an example of the significant results of her individual prayers with one family, the book describes the potential for her own healing ministry to develop subsequent ministries.

Several ministries began through the prayer ministry, written works, and speaking engagements of Agnes. Both Kelsey and Payne began their ministries as offshoots and continuations of the Schools of Pastoral Care, which Agnes founded with her husband Ted. Additionally, the MacNutts and the Sandfords began teaching and healing ministries founded on their personal experiences with her. Pearson, Glennon, and Scanlan were all directly influenced through her writings, and they eventually made their own impacts on the Charismatic Movement. Although Preaching and Prayer Ministries is no longer active, Agnes had a clear and profound effect on the life and ministry of Vaswig. Through her ministry, Agnes affected countless people in numerous denominations, and those people proceeded to found ministries or develop organizations that had a profound and lasting influence on the Renewal Movement. The description of her being a "pioneer" and "forerunner" seems largely substantiated, not only for her contributions toward the ministry of physical and inner healing but also for her success in bringing the gifts and baptism of the Spirit to mainline denominations.

Negative Assessments

Not every evaluation of Agnes describes her in positive or beneficial terms. As discussed, her theology and healing paradigm included aspects from New Thought, Jungian psychology, and science—three ideologies often contradictory toward Christian faith and orthodoxy. In at least two cases, authors have associated her ministry and works with pantheism, New Age, and the occult. Although some of the interpretations and conclusions appear valid, others clearly misquote or misinterpret Agnes's statements or take them out of context. Examining the sources critical to her writings will provide further insight into her influence on the Charismatic Movement and healing ministry.

Jane Gumprecht's book, *Abusing Memory: The Healing Theology of Agnes Sanford*, provides the most critical and derogatory analysis of Agnes's works. The author, a medical doctor, identifies herself as a prior proponent of New Thought and member of the Unity School of Christianity.[86] Her background in Unity Christianity and education in medicine makes Gumprecht distinctly qualified to evaluate and discuss Agnes's writings, influenced by New Thought, psychology, and science. However, the most noteworthy of qualifications still require an honest reading and analysis of the subject matter. The negative conclusion of Gumprecht's text is obvious from the name *Abusing Memory* as well as a few of the chapter titles, such as "A Blurred Picture of Jesus," "Flirting with Spiritism," and "Turning God On." Derogatory titles become entirely appropriate if her conclusions are found to be valid. However, in the case of *Abusing Memory*, a significant and notable number of Gumprecht's interpretations, assessments, and conclusions are faulty and invalidated through inaccurate quotation, misleading attribution, and biased ideology.

Gumprecht begins her text by acknowledging many of the previous assessments of the widespread impact of Agnes's work. In the introduction to the book, she writes,

> Agnes is well-known as the mother of the Inner Healing/Healing of Memories movement. She almost single-handedly brought it out of Jungian psychology and New Thought into the Christian church. She was able to do this because of her impeccable credentials as the daughter of missionaries to China and as the wife of an Episcopalian pastor.[87]

Her statement confirms the impact Agnes made on the Church through the inner healing movement. She perhaps overstates the extent Jungian psychology influenced the inner healing movement, but the statement is relatively accurate and factual. She continues,

> Most inner healing advocates acknowledge their debt to her, and her "theology" is evident in their ministries. John Loren Sandford (no relation to her) dedicated his books to her as his beloved mentor. Morton Kelsey learned healing of memories from her as well. Karen Mains of the Chapel of the Air was trained in inner healing at the School of Pastoral Care founded by Agnes and her husband. Similarly, spiritual therapist Leanne Payne is a disciple of Agnes, as was the late Ruth Carter Stapleton. Glen Clark, who established Camps Furthest Out, published Agnes's first book, *The Healing Light*. Glen Clark's books read like Unity textbooks. *The Healing Light* was also endorsed by Theosophy, the first of the modern New Age cults.[88]

Gumprecht confirms the affirmative assessments by Sandford, Kelsey, Payne, and Clark. The author intends to disqualify the orthodoxy of Agnes's work, especially the concept of inner healing or healing of memories—not her actual impact on the Church.

In the remainder of the introduction, Gumprecht describes the Bible as her standard for evaluating doctrine, theology, and practice. She declares, "God's word is truth, and so we need to examine the basic theological foundation of Agnes Sanford's beliefs. If she taught things contrary to biblical doctrine, we must throw out the teaching, whether it appears to work or not. In the past, the name of these teachings was heresy."[89] She begins her work with the not-so-subtle implication that Agnes taught heresy. Although she then makes what appears to be a positive statement about Agnes, she immediately follows it with a very revealing negative one. She writes,

> Agnes was a loving and multi-talented woman, who believed God had given her a very important mission in life. I am sure *she thought she was a Christian* [emphasis added] because of her heritage, marriage, knowledge, and mystical experience. My intent is not to demean her as a person. Rather, I write this book in loving concern for my brothers and sisters in Christ.[90]

Although she begins with a compliment, she follows it almost immediately with clear skepticism concerning Agnes actually being a Christian. Additionally, she indicates the book will discuss "Healing of Memories in light of the second commandment."[91] These statements foreshadow a clear bias with regard to Christian orthodoxy and theology.

Gumprecht's text incorporates a stylistic approach in which otherwise innocent statements are expressed in a calumnious and accusatory fashion. While discussing Agnes's biographical information, she states, "From an early age, Agnes Sanford was in *total inner rebellion against the orthodox teaching* [emphasis added] of her missionary parents and the southern Presbyterian Church. . . .

she believed there was *something wrong with Christianity* [emphasis added]."⁹² Gumprecht misrepresents Agnes's own description of her childhood attitude in the worst possible light. Indeed, Agnes had doubts about Christianity due to the doctrine of cessationism and divisiveness among the missionaries, but her issues related to how it was being lived out and not with the Christian faith itself. From her own statement, Gumprecht describes Agnes as being in "total inner rebellion" because she identified discrepancies between the Christian faith described in the Bible and the actual lifestyles of the missionaries. In the process, the author also reveals her theological bias by identifying the doctrine of cessationism as orthodox teaching. She subsequently says, "Later, she showed a similar rebellion against the Episcopal Church, though she was married to an Episcopalian minister."⁹³ However, Agnes never makes any mention in any of her works of rejecting any of the teachings or practices of the Episcopal Church, and as reflected in *Behold Your God*, she strongly promoted the liturgy and sacraments as channels of God's presence and healing.

Gumprecht provides dubious interpretations for some of Agnes's statements to support her claim that Agnes was not a Christian. As related in her autobiography, Agnes experienced intense loneliness after her sister died of amoebic dysentery and her friend Isabell was sent away to school. Agnes writes, "It might be expected that in my loneliness I turned to the Lord. No, I didn't. I was rather fed up with the Lord, if the truth must be told."⁹⁴ Her attitude is not entirely unexpected considering the circumstances. However, Gumprecht quotes this statement as related to Agnes's prayer to the Buddhist statue in the temple:

> Perhaps the reason she *could not* [emphasis added] turn to the Lord is because, prior to the death of her baby sister, she had gone into a Buddhist temple . . . folded her hands and bowed before the "serene gilded idol" and murmered "O-me-to-fu" as the monks did. . . . Perhaps she opened herself up to a malignant spirit.⁹⁵

Agnes herself admits that the incident in the temple may have provided an open door to some type of demonic oppression, but Gumprecht goes beyond Agnes's actual words to suggest that she "could not" turn to the Lord because of demonic possession. Through a subtle use of textual phrasing, Gumprecht changes a statement of Agnes explaining her *not choosing to* turn to the Lord into her *not being able* to turn to the Lord; the two statements sound very similar but hold extremely different connotations and implications.

Agnes viewed creation as corrupted by evil due to sin, which ultimately resulted in sickness, disease, and death infecting the world. Healing, on the other hand, was God redeeming his creation from the effects of the fall. She considered the claim that God sometimes wanted sickness or suffering to be in direct opposition to his nature as described in the Bible. For her, the loving nature of God meant that he could never desire harm for his creation. As such, she attributes both doubts about God's willingness to heal and thoughts of God wanting sickness to be from the devil. Using her metaphysical terminology, Agnes writes,

> By the time we are middle-aged most of us have accumulated in the sub-conscious all manner of thought-suggestions of fear, illness, limitation and lack, every one of which is in direct contradiction to the voice of God. From this storeroom of memories there floats into the conscious mind a continual stream of doubts, fears and negations. Hence arises the destructive inner voice that says, "Oh yeah? You think this will work, do you? You're trying to kid yourself, that's all. Now don't be a fool!" and such remarks. The Bible calls this inner tempter "Satan," and suggests that powers of evil beyond the tangible forces of this world battle against us.[96]

In other words, doubts concerning God's loving nature and willingness to act according to that nature ultimately originate from the devil. However, she was pragmatic as well as idealistic. She admits, "In certain very difficult cases there are adjustments to the laws of God that cannot be made perfectly in this lifetime. Even so, we do well to strive continually toward life in our prayers, even as we strive continually toward life in our medical care."[97] She believed Christians should always view sickness and disease as results of the fall and should resist inner thoughts of accepting sickness as God's will.

The most significant aspect of Gumprecht's doubt of Agnes's Christian faith deals with a statement made in *The Healing Light* directly after Agnes admits that healing does not always occur. In this passage, Agnes describes a pivotal experience in her ministry when healing did not occur as she anticipated it would. She writes,

> I was once asked to pray for a little boy with abscessed ears. The child improved for twenty-four hours, then relapsed. I prayed with him again and the same thing happened again, more than once. Each relapse was worse than the last and he was finally taken to a hospital and operated upon for mastoid. Even the cooperation of prayer and science did not save him. The poison began to eat into the bones of the head. He was on the verge of spinal meningitis.[98]

Her methodology involved viewing prayer as an experiment, so she attempted different types of prayer, but none succeeded, and his condition worsened. She recalls,

> I found him on a certain Good Friday half-conscious and nearly blind in a darkened room. At this point Satan entered into me and I began to wonder whether it was God's will for him to die. Upon my knees I wrestled with this problem, knowing that if I were to accept God's will for a little child as blindness, agony and death, my experiments in healing were over. If I had accepted death, the child would have died. And the parents would have consoled themselves forever by thinking, "God's will be done." But I cut myself away from this convenient excuse for failure as a ship going out to sea drops its shore-lines. I telephoned to an older and more experienced prayer-worker from a neighboring city.[99]

The call provided the advice she needed, and the boy was healed. However, this was a significant point in her ministry when she was tempted to wonder if God wanted the boy to die. For Agnes, the doubts were from the devil and needed to be resisted accordingly.

Gumprecht uses Agnes's statement here to suggest demon possession and exclude the possibility of her being a Christian. Without describing the entire context of the statement, she mentions Agnes's early account of her experience in the Buddhist temple and admission that she may have opened a door for a malignant spirit. She then writes,

> Later during her healing ministry years she recorded, "At this point Satan entered me, and I began to wonder whether it was God's will for him [Ted Sanford's friend] to die." This is not a frivolous statement. The Bible records that Satan entered Judas. But I don't believe Satan can enter into Christians for they are all indwelt by the Holy Spirit of God. [The source material contains the bracketed content].[100]

Gumprecht not only relates the incident to "Ted Sanford's friend" instead of a little boy but also interprets the words out of context. Agnes makes the statement "Satan entered me" to describe the temptation to entertain thoughts she considered evil and slandering to God's character.[101] Arguably, she was not describing a moment when the devil literally entered into her but was expressing the seriousness of the struggle she experienced.

The debate over whether or not Christians can need deliverance continues to be waged within various groups within the Christian Church and Renewal Movement, and it surpasses the scope of this research. However, Gumprecht's discussion in this passage reveals her interpretive bias. Although she considers inner healing as New Age, she uses statements of other inner healing ministers to support her claim about Agnes. She states,

> Recently I had a conversation with Pastor John L. Sandford who was Sanford's "mentor as well as my pupil, my spiritual father as well as my spiritual son." He told me that he exorcised oppressive spirits from her in 1962 or 1963. This was when Agnes had been in the ministry for over ten years. In her extensive writings and in her autobiography she made ambiguous statements about her relationship to Jesus *and Satan* [emphasis added].[102]

Nowhere in her works does Agnes describe having any type of relationship with Satan beyond what is considered normative for many Christians—recognizing the devil as the tempter, the deceiver, and the one who comes to kill, steal, and destroy. Agnes does make some ambiguous statements about always knowing Jesus, being converted, and then knowing him in such a close way that she never really knew him before. Her language reveals a comparative and developing relationship with God, consistent with not only Evangelical but also Charismatic and Pentecostal theology. It does not indicate demonic possession.

Considering the metaphysical language Agnes uses in many of her works, it is not surprising Gumprecht identifies her as a pantheist. However, even in those instances, she misrepresents the meaning of the originating passages. For example, she writes,

> Sanford "entered into eternity" in her thirties when she and Ted were on vacation in a cottage by Warren's Pond in New Hampshire. There beside the "dancing waters of the lake I prayed that God's life would enter into me through the sunlight. It happened. In a time that was not time, I was beyond time—I was filled with unbearable bliss—from this time forth I knew God." Considering *God's life to be sunlight* [emphasis added] is pantheistic.[103]

As discussed previously, Agnes held an incarnational view of creation that could easily be interpreted as pantheism—except for clear, qualifying statements to the contrary. In this passage, Gumprecht declares Agnes was equating God's life to the sunlight by again using her phraseology to change the actual meaning of the quoted passage. Agnes did not pray for God's life to enter her "as the sunlight" but "through the sunlight." Gumprecht also never acknowledges or mentions the passages in which Agnes refutes pantheism.

Gumprecht makes several accurate statements about Agnes, such as the direct influence of New Thought and Jungian psychology. She also raises valid concerns for the effect those ideologies had on Agnes's theology, such as meditative practices for getting in touch with God, the preexistence of the human spirit, and the collective unconscious. However, her recurring misrepresentation of source material as well as her own biased ideology—such as considering cessationism to be an orthodox Christian doctrine and inner healing to be inherently New Age—largely negates the validity of her points. In her opinion, "God heals painful memories by enabling us to forget them."[104] Although every author has presuppositions affecting how material is evaluated and discussed, Gumprecht allows her own biases to significantly skew her discussion and warp her interpretations.

Dave Hunt and T. A. McMahon also mention Agnes in a derogatory context in their popular book, *The Seduction of Christianity*. According to the book's cover, it has sold over 500,000 copies. The authors formed The Berean Call ministry in 1985 "for the purpose of encouraging spiritual discernment among those who regarded themselves ... as *biblical* Christians [the emphasis from the source is insightful]."[105] In their self-identified role as apologists, Hunt and McMahon wrote the book in an attempt to expose what they consider to be New Age influences they believe have infiltrated the Christian church in the twentieth century. The authors correctly identify many of the sources that influenced Agnes's theology and worldview as Gumprecht does, but their methodology and preconceptions significantly undermine their conclusions.

Similar to Gumprecht, the first mention of Agnes in Hunt and McMahon's book affirms her impact upon the church. They write,

> Perhaps no woman in this century has had a larger influence upon the Christi-

anity of today than prolific best-selling author and teacher Agnes Sanford. Quoted and recommended widely by Christian leaders, Agnes Sanford was largely responsible for bringing visualization and "healing of memories" into the church.[106]

The authors do not consider their statement a compliment, for they eventually describe visualization and inner healing as New Age and occultic practices. Like Gumprecht, their critical assessment of Agnes's work discusses the content without denying the widespread impact she had on twentieth-century Christianity. In the same passage, they reference her incarnational view of creation and the source she mentions:

> After discussing the healing of the subconscious, she calls God "the very life-force existing in a radiation of an energy . . . from which all things evolved," and declares that "God is actually *in* [emphasis from the source] the flowers and all the little chirping things. He made everything out of Himself and somehow He put a part of Himself into everything.["] Sanford further states:
>
>> If anyone doubts this, considering it an unworthy female conception and too frivolous for serious consideration, let him read The Phenomenon of Man and The Divine Milieu by that great anthropologist and prehistorian, Pierre Teilhard de Chardin.
>
> Numerous other highly influential Christian authors quote Teilhard favorably without so much as a word of caution.[107]

Although the authors correctly recognize an incarnational tendency in Agnes's work, they misquote her in at least four aspects. First, they omit a closing quotation mark prior to the block quotation. Although it is likely a simple typographical error, it could reflect a notable carelessness with source quotations.

Second, and much more significantly, Hunt and McMahon place the phrase "from which all things evolved" after the phrase "the very life-force existing in a radiation of energy" even though it comes prior to it, and they imply a different context than Agnes actually intended. The actual passage from Agnes is as follows:

> "Let there be light," said the Creator in those unimaginable aeons when there was only darkness upon the face of the deep. And out of the darkness the light appeared. During all that first day the light intensified, shifting and moving and changing its form. Not from sun or moon or stars did that light appear, for they had not as yet been created. So says the Bible with that amazing inspiration which, when considered with a modicum of common sense and even the smallest knowledge of modern science, is breath-taking truth. Whence, then, came that light? Whence but from God Himself? And what was that light *from which all things evolved* [emphasis added] but the light of creativity, *the very life-force existing in a radiation of an energy* [emphasis added] akin to the light one sees with the eyes,

but existing at a higher rate of vibration? Before there were any living creatures to fly and run in that light, it brought forth the earth and the seas and plants upon the earth, each one having its seed within itself. So says the Bible and so say the sciences.[108]

As already discussed, Agnes not only believed in a form of Theistic evolution but also often references God's presence in terms of energy and light. However, her context in this passage is distinctly different. Agnes uses the phrases "the very life-force" and "from which all things evolved" not as defining God Himself but as describing the light He first spoke into existence on the first day of creation. Hunt and McMahon identify these two phrases from Agnes as defining who God is even though her context is entirely different.

Third, Hunt and McMahon immediately follow her description of creative light with her quote about God putting "a part of Himself into everything." Agnes did affirm an incarnational and sacramental view of creation; however, the placement of the second quotation following the first seems intended to present her as a pantheist—especially considering the second quotation is six pages later. Additionally, they omit a few words, without ellipsis, as well as the very next sentence in the passage, which clarifies her position. The actual passage states, "You see, God is actually *in* [emphasis hers] the flowers and the growing grass and all the little chirping, singing things. He made everything out of Himself and somehow He put a part of Himself into everything. Oh, not His whole self!"[109] Although the missing phrase "and the growing grass" is minimal, it reflects careless quotation practices. More significantly, they do not include the phrase "Oh, not His whole self!" In the quoted passage, Agnes advises mental depressives to find a place where they can connect with God, and she describes her own experience of God ministering to her as she worked in her small garden. She says, "I did not know that God spoke to me in a very gentle voice as I dug in the dirt and planted seeds . . . but I would feel a tiny bit of comfort."[110] Hunt and McMahon present Agnes's quotation out of its actual context to suggest she promoted a pantheistic view of God.

Fourth, the authors reference Agnes's comment about Pierre Teilhard de Chardin out of context. Her mention of his comment relates not to evolution as they suggest but to human creativity. Concerned that some may dismiss her suggestion as not worthy of consideration, she writes,

> It is the very plan and intention of God, then, that man created upon this earth shall continue to create. The principle of creativity carried out in fertilizer factories and power plants, in suspension bridges and schools and airplanes and automobiles is of interest to God just as the efforts of nature to bring forth dinosaurs, since discarded in favor of more practical forms of life, are of interest to God. God therefore can be a partner and helper in any honest work or play. For play also is creative: the evolving of systems of thinking and acting that stimulate thought and life.
>
> If anyone doubts this, considering it an unworthy female conception and too frivolous for serious consideration, let him read The Phenomenon of Man and

The Divine Milieu by that great anthropologist and prehistorian, Pierre Teilhard de Chardin. And let him remember that the man who wrote these books was a Jesuit priest. His contemplation of the work of God through nature and through man is neither feminine nor frivolous, and his statements of the worth to God of all endeavor of the human mind is deeply consoling.[111]

In this passage, Agnes discusses God's enjoyment of human creativity through work and play. Hunt and McMahon quote her reference to Teilhard following misrepresentations and inaccurate quotations that suggest she embraced an entirely pantheistic evolution. The authors locate her reference to this source author immediately after they describe Teilhard as being an "architect of apostasy" and "the father of the New Age" who promoted a theology in which all people can eventually evolve into godhood.[112] Although Hunt and McMahon likely believed Agnes affirmed Teilhard's theology, and her words suggest she may have done so in part, they take her words out of context in order to misrepresent her statements to their readers.

Hunt and McMahon also criticize Agnes for her use of the imagination in prayer. They mention her repeatedly in a chapter on shamanism, stating,

> "Visualization" and "guided imagery" have long been recognized by sorcerers of all kinds as the most powerful and effective methodology for contacting the spirit world in order to acquire supernatural power, knowledge, and healing. Such methods are neither taught nor practiced in the Bible as helps to faith or prayer. Those who attempt to do so are not following the leading of the Holy Spirit or the Word of God, but are practicing an ancient occult technique.... Much of the credit for bringing these occult methodologies into Christianity must go to Agnes Sanford, who has probably influenced the church, and particularly, charismatics, as much as any woman of this century.[113]

Again, the authors do not deny her impact but consider it occultic. In the chapter, they accurately identify many of the influences that affected Agnes and are reflected in her writings, such as metaphysics (New Thought) and Jungian psychology. However, they describe inner healing as a form of shamanism. For Hunt and McMahon, "Legitimate uses of the imagination would involve such things as seeing mental images of something being described in a book; designing, planning, or rehearsing something in our minds; or remembering a place or event."[114] In other words, the use of the imagination creatively—including for emotional healing—is entirely contrary to biblical orthodoxy and qualifies as witchcraft.

As expected, the authors quickly identify Agnes as a pantheist and universalist. As previously discussed, she clarifies her positions in other works, but only two sources are used—*The Healing Light* and *The Healing Gifts of the Spirit*—and are often quoted recklessly. Hunt and McMahon often prove their claims by grouping together phrases from Agnes's works regardless of the location or context. For example, three rather long sentences are indicative of their writing style throughout the entire book. They state,

> In her books, which are so blatantly pagan as to be astonishing, Agnes Sanford makes no distinction between truth and error; anything that seems to tap into what she calls "this flow of energy," this "high voltage of God's creativity," is acceptable. Saying that "we are part of God . . . He's in nature and He is nature," and calling Him that "primal Energy" and Jesus "that most profound of psychiatrists," Sanford taught that we can literally create virtues in other people by the power of our minds, heal people at a distance, and even forgive their sins through visualization. Sanford gives her approval both to "the savage dancing in the jungle . . . primitive people who create an atmosphere of faith by war paint and feathers" and to the mind-science cultists "who already have a way of faith wrought by the denial of all that is not good."[115]

Notably, the authors derive the quotations in these three sentences from seven different pages in different chapters of both books irrespective of the actual context. As already seen in discussing her influences and theology, Agnes rejected many approaches, beliefs, and practices as error, considering them unacceptable and incompatible with Christianity.

Unmistakably, Agnes makes several statements within her works that may offend some conservative Evangelicals. However, Hunt and McMahon make no effort to provide a context for some of her unusual comments. For example, the last sentence of the prior quotation comes from a paragraph in which Agnes discusses the prayer of faith. She writes,

> The crux of the prayer of faith is this: *God's power is real* [emphasis hers]. The creativity of God sent forth when the Creator said in faith, "Let there be light," still radiates through His universe. This flow of energy has been put to use in all ages, from the savage dancing in the jungle to the modern man who teaches that all else save this power of God is error. I am not writing this book, however, for primitive people who create an atmosphere of faith by war paint and feathers and drums, though I look with respect upon these early efforts to contact a power that is real. Nor am I writing for those who already have a way of faith wrought by the denial of all that is not good—though upon these also I look with respect and indeed sometimes with envy, wishing that I could grasp their theory and seeing dimly that behind it there is an area of truth. But I cannot think after this pattern for I am not of this nature. I am a graduate mental depressive and am too smashingly aware of the tragedy and horror of life to be able to look beyond it and say all is good.[116]

As already discussed, Agnes believed that all people, regardless of their knowledge of God, could receive from him if they sincerely sought after him, and she believed that healing often resulted in a subsequent personal relationship with God. This was not universalist or pluralist, for she decisively affirms the basics of the Christian faith, including Jesus Christ being the only source for redemption. Respecting uninformed-but-sincere attempts at finding God did not mean she was embracing them. She certainly does not present any type of evangelistic message in this passage, but her words do not equate to declaring she "makes no distinction between truth and error" in what she herself taught and promoted.

In the remainder of the text, Hunt and McMahon identify several authors and ministers influenced by Agnes and categorize them as Christian leaders who have also embraced occultic and New Age practices. In their opinion, some of them, such as John and Paula Sandford, Francis MacNutt, Morton Kelsey, and William Vaswig, have done so with little concern for biblical orthodoxy while a few others, such as Richard Foster and John Wimber, have been sincere but were nevertheless misled into accepting the New Age paradigm. Although the authors declare their warnings to prevent their readers from accepting Agnes's works, theology, and paradigm, they also confirm the widespread influence and impact she has had on the twentieth-century Christian Church.

Hunt and McMahon accurately identify the New Thought and Jungian roots for many of Agnes's writings. However, they discount any validity to assimilating parts of those philosophies into a Christian context. They view any use of the imagination in a creative context as inherently occultic and New Age, which categorizes a majority of Agnes's healing model as incompatible with Christianity. However, they repeatedly take quotations out of context and apply interpretations that conflict with the actual source material, and they regularly omit passages where Agnes qualifies or clarifies some of her statements when doing so would contradict the authors' conclusions. Although Hunt and McMahon provide valid cautions in certain areas, they invalidate their discussion through sensationalized language, misquoted passages, intentional misinterpretations, and even presenting source material out of its intended context. Nevertheless, they still confirm the significant extent of the impact Agnes had on the Charismatic Movement.

Gumprecht, Hunt, and McMahon discuss Agnes in extremely calumnious and critical manners. While the authors accurately identify the philosophical and ideological sources that influenced her and her works, they build their arguments on excessively biased preconceptions about inner healing and the use of the imagination. In both cases, quotations by Agnes are taken out of context and used to provide a faulty understanding of her theology and paradigm. The authors repeatedly use sensationalized language and interpret source material inconsistent with the original context of the quotations, and the misinterpretations and misquotations at times appear to be intentional. Nevertheless, both *Abusing Memory* and *The Seduction of Christianity* affirm the significant impact Agnes had on the Christian Church in the twentieth century as well as the Renewal Movement. The authors admit to her influence while attempting to identify it as a negative effect on Christian theology and practice. Additionally, the authors largely agree on the individuals impacted by her influence, such as John and Paula Sandford, Francis MacNutt, and Morton Kelsey. Even as negative assessments, these sources confirm her contributions.

Conclusion

Agnes Sanford had a significant influence in the early years of the Charismatic Movement. Through her speaking engagements, healing ministry, and written works, she affected how the Christian church of the twentieth century understands healing, both physical and emotional, as well as the Pentecostal experience, the gifts and baptism of the Holy Spirit. As historians and theologians, Hocken, De Arteaga, and Synan admit to the pioneering work Agnes accomplished, especially in relation to the inner healing movement. In their independent healing ministries, both Clark and Banks affirmed the unique and significant contribution she made through her first book, *The Healing Light*. Several ministries developed subsequently from Agnes's own ministry, promoting and continuing the work she began. Kelsey, Payne, Scanlan, and Vaswig as well as the Sandfords and MacNutts all identify Agnes as the originating source for their understanding of healing as well as their eventual ministry. Even those sources entirely critical toward Agnes, such as Gumprecht or Hunt and McMahon, affirm the unique and significant role she had upon the Christian church in the twentieth century, especially in relation to inner healing and healing prayer. Although different authors may describe her in vastly divergent tones with diverse attributions, they all confirm that Agnes Sanford had a profound, unique, and lasting effect on Christian faith and practice.

Notes

[1] Peter Hocken qualifies as a knowledgeable and highly respected Roman Catholic historian and theologian in the field of Renewal Studies. He has written several books on Renewal movements around the world and numerous articles for *The New International Dictionary of Pentecostal and Charismatic Movements* (NIDPCM), considered by many to be a primary seminal reference source for information on Pentecostal and Charismatic movements in the twentieth century. Hocken himself is discussed in *NIDPCM* for his popular and scholarly work on the Charismatic Movement as well as having "served as the president of the Society for Pentecostal Studies in 1986"; see C. M. Robeck Jr., "Hocken, Peter Dudley," in *The New Internatinoal Dictionary of Pentecostal and Charismatic Movements*, eds Stanley M. Burgess and Ed M. Van der Maas (Grand Rapids: Zondervan, 2002): 723. His inclusion in this reference affirms his qualifications. He also authored a chapter in Vinson Synan's *The Century of the Holy Spirit*, a noteworthy text by one of the top historians in the field, and Synan himself recognized Hocken for "a full treatment of worldwide developments" in the Charismatic renewal; see Vinson Synan, *The Century of the Holy Spirit*, 232, 412. Another leading historian and theologian in the field of Renewal Studies, Walter J. Hollenweger, references Hocken several times in his book *Pentecostalism: Origins and Developments Worldview*; see Walter J. Hollenweger, "Hocken, Peter" in "Index of Authors and Subjects," in *Pentecostalism: Origins and Developments World*wide (Peabody: Hendrickson, 2005), 487.

[2] P. D. Hocken, "Sanford, Agnes Mary," in *NIDPCM*, 1039; Peter Hocken, *Streams of Renewal: The Origins and Early Development of the Charismatic Movement in Great Britain* (Washington, D.C.: Word Among Us, 1986), 67.

³ P. D. Hocken, "Sanford, Agnes Mary," in *NIDPCM*, 1039.
⁴ P. D. Hocken, "Sanford, Agnes Mary," in *NIDPCM*, 1039.
⁵ P. D. Hocken, "Charismatic Movement," in *NIDPCM*, 478.
⁶ Peter Hocken, *Streams of Renewal*, 120, 181.
⁷ Henry H. Knight III, "Quenching the Spirit: Examining Centuries of Opposition to the Moving of the Holy Spirit," *Pneuma* 15 no. 2 (Fall 1993), 227.
⁸ William De Arteaga, *Quenching the Spirit: Examining Centuries of Opposition to the Moving of the Holy Spirit* (Lake Mary: Creation House, 1992), 164.
⁹ William De Arteaga, "Agnes Sanford: Apostle of Healing - Part 1 of 2," 8.
¹⁰ William De Arteaga, "Agnes Sanford: Apostle of Healing - Part 2 of 2," 4.
¹¹ William De Arteaga, *Agnes Sanford and Her Companions*, 1-2.
¹² William De Arteaga, *Agnes Sanford and Her Companions*, 2.
¹³ William De Arteaga, *Agnes Sanford and Her Companions*, 2.
¹⁴ William De Arteaga, *Agnes Sanford and Her Companions*, 2-3.
¹⁵ William De Arteaga, *Agnes Sanford and Her Companions*, 3.
¹⁶ William De Arteaga, *Agnes Sanford and Her Companions*, 3.
¹⁷ William De Arteaga, *Agnes Sanford and Her Companions*, 245.
¹⁸ Vinson Synan, "Christenson, Laurence Donald ("Larry")," in *The New International Dictionary of Pentecostal and Charismatic Movements*, eds Stanley M. Burgess and Ed M. Van der Maas, (Grand Rapids: Zondervan, 2002): 522-523; also Vinson Synan, *The Century of the Holy Spirit*, 165.
¹⁹ Vinson Synan, "Christenson, Laurence Donald ('Larry')," in *NIDPCM*, 523.
²⁰ Agnes does not discuss her baptism in the Holy Spirit in her first book, *The Healing Light*, for she had not yet had the experience. It is possible he had read *Behold Your God*, which gives a detailed description of her experience along with the results. However, all of her works discuss healing prayer.
²¹ Larry Christenson, ed. *Welcome, Holy Spirit: A Study of Charismatic Renewal in the Church* (Minneapolis: Augsburg, 1987), 282.
²² Larry Christenson, ed. *Welcome, Holy Spirit*, 285.
²³ International Order of Saint Luke the Physician, "About Us," accessed July 18, 2016, https://orderofstluke.org/en/about.html. Note: Hocken indicates the organization was founded in 1947, but his date contradicts their published history. See P. D. Hocken, "Charismatic Movement," in *NIDPCM*, 478.
²⁴ Interestingly, this is contradicted in a personal communication from Drury to Baltz on November 28, 1976: "Agnes knows nothing about the Order of St. Luke, has never been a member of it, may have spoken once or twice at their meetings but really has never had a good feeling about the Order nor seen any need for it . . . so the answer to your first questions is that Agnes probably ante-dated the Order of St. Luke and everybody connected with it, and in any case gained nothing from them or even knew that they existed until she was well established and sought-after as a speaker." However, some aspects of this communication seem to be incorrect, for Agnes clearly knew John and Ethel Banks.
²⁵ Agnes Sanford, *Sealed Orders*, 165.
²⁶ Agnes Sanford, *Sealed Orders*, 120-121.
²⁷ John Gaynor Banks, "Healing Marches On: A New Book on Healing," *Sharing* 15 (May 1947), 10.
²⁸ John Gaynor Banks, *Healing Everywhere: A Book of Healing Mission Talks* (Irvington: St. Luke's Press, 1974), 86.
²⁹ William De Arteaga, *Agnes Sanford and Her Companions*, 4, 137ff; also, see William L. De Arteaga, "From Radical Idealism to Pentecostalism," 1-22; also Mark A. Pearson,

Christian Healing: A Practical and Comprehensive Guide (Grand Rapids: Chosen Books, 2000), 11.

[30] P. D. Hocken, "Charismatic Movement," in *NIDPCM*, 478; also see William L. DeArteaga, "Glenn Clark's Camps Furthest Out: The Schoolhouse of the Charismatic Renewal," *Pneuma* 25, no. 2 (Fall 2003): 265-288. Note: Many sources reference the organization as "Camps Furthest Out," but the organization identifies itself as "Camps Farthest Out." See Camps Farthest Out, "History," accessed July 18, 2016, https://cfonorthamerica.org/node/28.

[31] Agnes Sanford, *Sealed Orders*, 120-121.

[32] John Gaynor Banks, "Healing Marches On," 10.

[33] Wade H. Boggs Jr., review of *God Can Heal You Now*, by Emily Gardner Neal, *Journal of Pastoral Care* 15, no. 3 (Fall 1961): 178.

[34] The Episcopal Church, "Neal, Emily Gardner," in "an Episcopal Dictionary of the Church," accessed November 10, 2016, http://www.episcopalchurch.org/library/glossary/neal-emily-gardiner

[35] Emily Gardner Neal, *God Can Heal You Now* (Englewood Cliffs: Prentice-Hall, 1958), 268.

[36] Emily Gardner Neal, *God Can Heal You Now*, 306.

[37] Emily Gardner Neal, *God Can Heal You Now*, 310.

[38] Vinson Synan, *The Century of the Holy Spirit*, 18.

[39] Larry Christenson, ed., *Welcome, Holy Spirit*, 161-162, 170-171.

[40] Morton Kelsey, *Healing & Christianity*, back cover promotion.

[41] Morton T. Kelsey, *Healing and Christianity: In Ancient Thought and Modern Times* (New York: Harper and Row, 1973), viii, x. Note: in the 1995 publication, Kelsey does not mention *The Healing Light* but says, "I was introduced to this ministry by the writing and example of Agnes Sanford," and "Agnes Sanford became a close friend." See Morton Kelsey, *Healing & Christianity*, 1995, xii-xiii.

[42] Morton Kelsey, *Healing & Christianity*, 1995), 191.

[43] Agnes Sanford, *Sealed Orders*, 298.

[44] P. D. Hocken, "Payne, Leanne," in *The New International Dictionary of Pentecostal and Charismatic Movements*, eds Stanley M. Burgess and Ed M. Van der Maas, (Grand Rapids: Zondervan, 2002): 959.

[45] Joseph W. Williams, *Spirit Cure*, 165.

[46] Timothy C. Morgan, "Died: Leanne Payne, 82, Prominent Leader in Pastoral Care, Healing Movement," Gleanings, in "News & Reporting," *Christianity Today*, February 20, 2015. http://www.christianitytoday.com/gleanings/2015/february/died-leanne-payne-pastoral-care-heal-lgbt-change-cslewis.html.

[47] Leanne Payne, *The Broken Image* (Grand Rapids: Baker Books, 1996), 11.

[48] Leanne Payne, *Heaven's Calling*, 217.

[49] William De Arteaga, *Agnes Sanford and Her Companions*, 237.

[50] Paul Francis Egan, "The Development of, and Opposition to, Healing Ministries," 32.

[51] Paul Francis Egan, "The Development of, and Opposition to, Healing Ministries," 33-35.

[52] Paul Francis Egan, "The Development of, and Opposition to, Healing Ministries," 160-170.

[53] Paul Francis Egan, "The Development of, and Opposition to, Healing Ministries," 148-149. Additionally, see the information at http://www.glennonhouse.org/about.htm

[54] Paul Francis Egan, "The Development of, and Opposition to, Healing Ministries," 29.

⁵⁵ Paul Francis Egan, "The Development of, and Opposition to, Healing Ministries," 66.

⁵⁶ Jim Glennon, *Your Healing is Within You*, 99.

⁵⁷ P. D. Hocken, "Charismatic Episcopal Church (CEC)," in *The New International Dictionary of Pentecostal and Charismatic Movements*, eds Stanley M. Burgess and Ed M. Van der Maas, (Grand Rapids: Zondervan, 2002): 476.

⁵⁸ Institute for Christian Renewal, "About ICR," Accessed July 19, 2016, https://christianrenewal.wordpress.com/about/; Also see New Creation Healing Center, "History," accessed July 19, 2016, http://www.newcreationhc.org/history.htm.

⁵⁹ Mark A. Pearson, *Christian Healing*, 234.

⁶⁰ Mark A. Pearson, *Christian Healing*, 7, 107-131, 349. He quotes Payne on pp. 121 and 131.

⁶¹ Mark A. Pearson, *Christian Healing*, 11.

⁶² Stephen Strang, "MacNutt, Francis Scott," in *The New International Dictionary of Pentecostal and Charismatic Movements*, eds Stanley M. Burgess and Ed M. Van der Maas (Grand Rapids: Zondervan, 2002): 856.

⁶³ William L. De Arteaga, *Agnes Sanford and Her Companions*, 22; Thomas J. Csordas, "Catholic Charismatic Healing in Global Perspective: The Cases of India, Brazil, and Nigeria," in *Global Pentecostal and Charismatic Healing*, ed Candy Gunther Brown (Oxford: Oxford University, 2011), 339.

⁶⁴ Christian Healing Ministries, "Organizational History," in "About Us," accessed July 19, 2016, reaccessed March 22, 2018, https://www.christianhealingmin.org/index.php/chm-info/about-chm.

⁶⁵ Francis MacNutt, *The Nearly Perfect Crime: How the Church Almost Killed the Ministry of Healing* (Grand Rapids: Chosen Books, 2005), back cover promotion.

⁶⁶ Francis MacNutt, *The Nearly Perfect Crime*, 93, 224-225; Agnes Sanford, *Sealed Orders*, 225-226; Stephen Strang, "MacNutt, Francis Scott," in *NIDPCM*, 855-856; David Kyle Foster, "Interview – Francis & Judith MacNutt."

⁶⁷ Francis MacNutt, *Healing* (Notre Dame: Ave Maria Press, 2009), 10-13.

⁶⁸ Francis MacNutt, *The Power to Heal* (Notre Dame: Ave Maria, 2001), 10.

⁶⁹ Joseph W. Williams, *Spirit Cure*, 103.

⁷⁰ P. D. Hocken, "Scanlan, Michael," in *The New International Dictionary of Pentecostal and Charismatic Movements*, eds Stanley M. Burgess and Ed M. Van der Maas (Grand Rapids: Zondervan, 2002): 1041.

⁷¹ Franciscan University of Steubenville, "Our History," accessed July 21, 2016, http://www.franciscan.edu/about/history/.

⁷² P. D. Hocken, "Scanlan, Michael," in *NIDPCM*, 1041; Vinson Synan, *The Century of the Holy Spirit*, 223.

⁷³ Michael Scanlan, *The Power In Penance* (Notre Dame: Ave Maria, 1979), 9-10.

⁷⁴ Michael Scanlan, *Inner Healing: Ministering to the Human Spirit through the Power of Prayer* (New York: Paulist Press, 1974), 84.

⁷⁵ Francis MacNutt, *Healing*, 13; Francis MacNutt, *The Power to Heal*, 10.

⁷⁶ William L. De Arteaga, *Agnes Sanford and Her Companions*, 247n1.

⁷⁷ Elijah House International, "About EH," accessed July 21, 2016, https://www.elijahhouse.org/page/website.aboutus.

⁷⁸ William L. De Arteaga, *Agnes Sanford and Her Companions*, 250.

⁷⁹ William L. De Arteaga, *Agnes Sanford and Her Companions*, 218, 247-260; Agnes Sanford, *Sealed Orders*, 284.

⁸⁰ Agnes Sanford, *Sealed Orders*, 278-281. William L. De Arteaga, *Agnes Sanford and Her Companions*, 249.

[81] John and Paula Sandford, *The Transformation of the Inner Man* (Tulsa: Victory House, 1982), vi.

[82] John and Paula Sandford, *The Transformation of the Inner Man*, 3-5.

[83] William L. Vaswig, *I Prayed, He Answered*, 86; Manta, "Preaching & Prayer Ministries, Inc," Accessed July 21, 2016, http://www.manta.com/c/mmj7244/preaching-prayer-ministries-inc.

[84] William L. Vaswig, *I Prayed, He Answered*, 3, 7.

[85] William L. Vaswig, *I Prayed, He Answered*, 9.

[86] Jane Gumprecht, *Abusing Memory: The Healing Theology of Agnes Sanford*, revised ed. (Moscow, ID: Canon Press, 2010), 5.

[87] Jane Gumprecht, *Abusing Memory*, 6.

[88] Jane Gumprecht, *Abusing Memory*, 6. Neither Karen Mains nor Ruth Carter Stapleton is included in this book due to inconclusive evidence of a direct link to Agnes. De Arteaga does link Stapleton to Agnes, but he does not cite evidence, and Agnes is not attributed in her works; see William L. De Arteaga, *Agnes Sanford and Her Companions*, 218-220. Also, in response to an email on May 22, 2015, President Jimmy Carter does not recall his sister ever mentioning Agnes. Endorsement by Theosophy subsequent to the publication of *The Healing Light* does not confirm the intention of the book or the author.

[89] Jane Gumprecht, *Abusing Memory*, 7.

[90] Jane Gumprecht, *Abusing Memory*, 7.

[91] Jane Gumprecht, *Abusing Memory*, 8.

[92] Jane Gumprecht, *Abusing Memory*, 13.

[93] Jane Gumprecht, *Abusing Memory*, 13.

[94] Agnes Sanford, *Sealed Orders*, 16; Jane Gumprecht, *Abusing Memory*, 14.

[95] Jane Gumprecht, *Abusing Memory*, 14-15.

[96] Agnes Sanford, *The Healing Light*, 2nd ed., 43.

[97] Agnes Sanford, *The Healing Light*, 2nd ed., 25.

[98] Agnes Sanford, *The Healing Light*, 2nd ed., 25-26.

[99] Agnes Sanford, *The Healing Light*, 2nd ed., 26.

[100] Jane Gumprecht, *Abusing Memory*, 15.

[101] A valid example of using "Satan" metaphorically is in the incident when Peter exclaims his desire to prevent Jesus from dying. Jesus responds to Peter with the exclamation, "Get behind Me, Satan!" Jesus was not declaring Peter was the devil literally but was attributing the content of his statement and intention as being contrary to God's will. See Matthew 16;22-23 and Mark 8:32-33.

[102] Jane Gumprecht, *Abusing Memory*, 15.

[103] Jane Gumprecht, *Abusing Memory*, 16.

[104] Jane Gumprecht, *Abusing Memory*, 108.

[105] The Berean Call, "About TBC – History," accessed July 25, 2016, http://www.thebereancall.org/content/about-berean-call.

[106] Dave Hunt & T. A. McMahon, *The Seduction of Christianity: Spiritual Discernment in the Last Days* (Eugene: Harvest House, 1985), 78. Dave Hunt briefly restates his opinion of Agnes in his sequel. See Dave Hunt, *Beyond Seduction: A Return to Biblical Christianity* (Eugene: Harvest House, 1987), 204ff.

[107] Dave Hunt and T. A. McMahon, *Seduction of Christianity*, 78.

[108] Agnes Sanford, *The Healing Gifts of the Spirit*, 24-25.

[109] Agnes Sanford, *The Healing Gifts of the Spirit*, 31.

[110] Agnes Sanford, *The Healing Gifts of the Spirit*, 30.

[111] Agnes Sanford, *The Healing Gifts of the Spirit*, 29.

[112] Dave Hunt and T. A. McMahon, *Seduction of Christianity*, 77.
[113] Dave Hunt and T. A. McMahon, *Seduction of Christianity*, 123-124.
[114] Dave Hunt and T. A. McMahon, *Seduction of Christianity*, 123.
[115] Dave Hunt and T. A. McMahon, *Seduction of Christianity*, 125.
[116] Agnes Sanford, *The Healing Gifts of the Spirit*, 54-55.

CHAPTER 7

THE SIGNIFICANCE OF HER MINISTRY AND THEOLOGY

Agnes Sanford is a pioneering figure in twentieth-century Christian history, especially in North America, though she did have influence elsewhere. She grew up on the Presbyterian mission field in China and had been taught that miracles had ceased after the New Testament Church. She later discovered God still healed through prayer, and her life changed. Through her healing ministry, speaking engagements, and written works, she helped countless others to recognize the reality and importance of the gifts and baptism of the Holy Spirit. As an Episcopalian, her message was accepted by numerous mainline denominations, and her books became foundational for the early Charismatic Movement. Agnes also originated the inner healing movement through her discussion of the healing of memories, and numerous subsequent ministries developed from her works. Through her influence, Agnes became part of the very foundation of the Renewal Movement in the twentieth century and beyond. Clearly, a substantive work on her was necessary for the history and future development of the Renewal Movement.

Considering the impact and influence Agnes had on healing ministry and the Charismatic Movement, very little has been written about her. She herself wrote fifteen books and six short excerpts for publication as well as other unpublished or lost works. Her first book, *The Healing Light*, became a pioneering work on healing prayer, blending metaphysical, psychological, scientific, and sacramental approaches into a simplified healing model. The book, first published in 1947, significantly informed the developing theology of the Charismatic Movement and is considered by many to be a classic on the topic of healing. She also published *The Healing Gifts of the Spirit* to describe the healing of memories, and the book became the foundation for the inner healing movement. In it, she provides a combination of psychological and sacramental steps for people dealing with depression. Agnes describes her theology in detail in *Behold Your God*, her most theological work. It gives the clearest understanding of her Christian orthodox beliefs in conjunction with her metaphysical, psychological, sacramental, and scientific worldview. Her autobiography, *Sealed Orders*, puts her ministry and works into the context of her life experiences. She reveals her struggles and accomplishments honestly and coherently. The rest of her books present different aspects of healing using instructive, meditative, and fictional genres.

Agnes maintained a Christian orthodox theology that was influenced by metaphysics, psychology, and science, sometimes integrating aspects of each into her own theology and practice. Her belief in the nature of the Trinity, the redemptive work of Christ, and the baptism in the Holy Spirit remained consistent with historical Christian doctrines and creeds, including those of Renewal Christianity even though she often used unconventional terminology. She believed the Bible was inspired and authoritative although she trusted science to interpret it. Her sacramental theology often consisted of spiritual experiences interpreted in the context of God's transcendence and immanence, sometimes making her descriptions of God's Presence in nature appear foreign to Evangelical paradigms. Also, she believed healing was intrinsically related to God's nature and design for the world. Agnes incorporated numerous distinct and unrelated perspectives into a complex-but-coherent orthodox theology.

Numerous sources recognize Agnes as a pioneer in the areas of physical healing and inner healing. She not only promoted the gifts of the Spirit within multiple mainline denominations but also advocated for the baptism in the Holy Spirit among leaders and laypersons alike. Through her works, she became a foundational influence during the formative years of the Charismatic Movement, both through her interdisciplinary approach to healing as well as her pragmatic and practical application to ministry. She combined aspects of sacramental theology, metaphysical ideology, Jungian psychology, and scientific methodology into a healing paradigm that not only was original and unique but also shaped the course of healing ministry and counseling methods in the twentieth century. Several significant ministries were born and evolved as a result of her books, conferences, and ministry events. As a result, her contributions deserve recognition.

The three books written about Agnes present radically different perspectives. *Abusing Memory* by Gumprecht provides a distinctly critical and biased discussion of her life and works. Although the author is qualified to evaluate Agnes's writings, the tendency to consistently take source material out of context largely negates its value. *I Prayed, He Answered* by Vaswig supplies a personal account of how she changed the author's life. It is positively biased with only minimal scholarly value. *Agnes Sanford and Her Companions* by De Arteaga entails the most academic discussion of her life and ministry. The author's discussion reflects some positive bias and neglects to support some of the statements or conclusions. It qualifies as the most objective of the three books but is limited in scope. Similarly, the graduate works and journal articles on Agnes provide very different perspectives of her life and ministry, but they are all limited in their content and approach. Clearly, a more comprehensive discussion of her theology and contributions was needed.

The review of current literature about her has revealed a significant lack in scholarly and comprehensive discussion of Agnes's life, ministry, writings, theology, and impact. Her written works reveal a woman who was passionate, disciplined, analytical, sensitive, creative, inspiring, and driven as well as slightly cynical, mildly sarcastic, and internally conflicted at times. Multiple sources discuss her ministry and theology without incorporating all of her writings, giving at best an incomplete and at worst an erroneous understanding of her life and beliefs. Evaluating secondary sources in the context of her entire library of works has revealed not only the profound limitation in scope but also recurrent weaknesses in their methodology and approach. Numerous authors also reference Agnes as a source or as a significant figure in her field, revealing the importance and value of her writings. Still, a complete understanding of her pivotal place in Church history did not exist. A careful and thorough examination of both primary and secondary sources along with recognition of tertiary references has provided as close to a comprehensive work as possible.

The Contributions of this Book

This text fills a notable gap in scholarship on several points. First, this study has provided significant insight into the development of Agnes's worldview, theology, and healing model. As a child on the Presbyterian mission field in China, she discovered Christians did not always live according to the example described in the Bible. Through a combination of conflicts among the Church leaders, the doctrine of cessationism, and the traumas of fear and loss, she developed a distinct cynicism toward Christianity. Her cynicism remained after her marriage to Ted Sanford, an Episcopal priest, and her move to the United States, and she began to proceed into deep depression almost to the point of suicide. Her life began to change when she saw her son healed through the laying on of hands by another priest as well as her own eventual healing from depression. She studied to learn all she could about healing prayer, and went on to develop her own healing ministry. Through speaking engagements, written books, and praying for others, she made a lasting impact on the early Charismatic Movement.

Second, although the works of Baltz, De Arteaga, and Gumprecht provide limited discussion of her life experiences and their effect on her later theology and ministry, this work has provided a more accurate account of her life as well as a context for her ministry. By incorporating several of her works along with her own autobiography, a more complete understanding of her personality and worldview became possible. In light of not only her experiences but also her recorded perceptions of events, a more trustworthy and accurate interpretation of her teachings could be accomplished than had previously been available. Therefore, this study, by accomplishing a largely comprehensive biographical examination of her life, has provided significant and unique insight into her life, ministry, and theology.

Third, Agnes's integration of New Thought teachings, especially as they were presented through the Unity School of Christianity, has been thoroughly explored and analyzed. As discussed, a metaphysical approach to healing was accepted by many believers interested in healing ministry during the early twentieth century; however, Agnes incorporated it in unique ways. As a corollary, her rejection of the more radical teachings and ideology of Christian Science and Abundant Life has been established.

Fourth, the integration of popular Jungian psychology into Agnes's healing model has been examined and discussed. At the time of her ministry, psychological theory and practice was viewed not only with extreme suspicion by Pentecostals but also with some hesitancy within Charismatic circles. This dissertation has described how she adopted valid aspects of the subconscious, rejected occultic or atheistic concepts, and maintained a solid Christian orthodoxy.

Fifth, Agnes's positive view of science and its devotion to the discovery of truth has been examined. This work has shown how she incorporated the scientific method as the basis of her healing prayer model and used scientific discoveries and principles to both support and verify the efficacy and orthodoxy of healing prayer.

Sixth, attention has been given to how these different philosophies, combined with her Presbyterian and Episcopal backgrounds, formed a distinct but orthodox theology that merged the metaphysical, the psychological, the scientific, and the sacramental into a mostly cohesive whole. Although other authors identified the ideologies that directly influenced Agnes and her theology, they did so incompletely by failing to recognize how they merged into a cohesive and coherent worldview. Of the secondary sources, only De Arteaga and Williams described the accepted position New Thought and Unity Christianity held at the time Agnes began her own healing ministry. Additionally, De Arteaga accurately recognized the additional impact of psychology and science on her paradigm although he tended to minimize the extent Agnes knew and incorporated Jungian theory into her own healing model. Any discussion of the meaning of the metaphysical, psychological, and scientific terms and concepts in her works becomes tenuous when it lacks sufficient contextualization in her Presbyterian and Episcopalian theology. Examining all the significant influences that affected her developing worldview and paradigm instead of focusing on only one or two provided a profoundly faithful understanding of her beliefs and enabled an accurate evaluation of her theology.

Seventh, this text has established Agnes's orthodoxy in relation to the Trinity and the essentiality of Jesus' redemptive work on the cross for salvation of the lost even though she held a conviction that God the Father answered the prayers of non-Christians. Also recognized by this research is that, along with her orthodox foundation, she affirmed some doctrinal beliefs that were unusual among conservative Evangelicals, such as modified versions of Theistic evolution, Post-millenialism, Eco-theology, and deification, but not among all orthodox Christians then or now. Her understanding of God's immanence and transcendence resulted in a strongly incarnational view of nature as well as a notably flexible view of time. In a less-than-mainstream way, Agnes also professed some unusual tangential beliefs, such as the preexistence of the human spirit and sentient life on other planets or even in nature. Nevertheless, she maintained a theology consistent and coherent with Christian faith.

Agnes embraced a theology that not only was orthodox but also incorporated both metaphysical and sacramental ideals. Many of the sources that discuss her ministry and works do not fully integrate how both aspects informed her beliefs. Although she admits to periods when she questioned some portions of its fundamental doctrines, she affirmed the basic orthodox tenets of the Christian faith. Additionally, examining her metaphysical and scientific perception of the world in conjunction with her understanding of Christian doctrine has revealed a theology that went beyond a primarily intellectual understanding of God's nature, Christ's redemption, the Spirit's empowerment, and the Bible's authority and essentially put those beliefs into practice. In other words, a comprehensive and thorough evaluation of her theology has indicated a lifestyle reminiscent of Christian mysticism and reflecting a faith more cohesive, coherent, and consistent than many Pentecostals or Charismatics of her time or in the present—including many others involved in healing ministry.

An eighth contribution is the examination of Agnes' promotion of the gifts and baptism of the Holy Spirit for empowerment and joy in the life of the believer. This work has described her involvement in healing ministry before and after she received her own baptism and its relation to her sacramental and metaphysical paradigm. By comparing her first book, *The Healing Light*, to her sequel on healing, *Behold Your God*, a noticeable and significant evolution in her theology has been identified.

A ninth contribution made by this research project is the establishing of the profound impact Agnes had on the Charismatic and Renewal Movements of the twentieth century. Both Hocken and De Arteaga identify her as a pioneer in healing ministry and bringing the experience of the gifts and baptism of the Holy Spirit into mainline churches, both in the United States and overseas. Synan also affirms the impact she made upon the mainline denominations through her influence on Christenson. The independent healing ministries of Clark and Banks recognized the unique and necessary contribution of her first book, occasionally elevating her work over their own. After she was published and began speaking publicly, several ministries developed out of her direct influence, such as those of Payne, the MacNutts, and the Sandfords.

Several sources have referenced the impact Agnes had on the early Charismatic Movement, both in Protestant and Roman Catholic groups in the United States and Britain. However, none of the authors have analyzed her perceived impact within all of the possible contexts. Evaluating and reviewing the statements made by scholars, other ministries, and even antagonists in relation to her influence on physical healing, inner healing, and the gifts and baptism of the Spirit within multiple mainline denominations has provided substantial evidence that Agnes affected the Renewal Movement to a profound extent—

possibly more than any other single person in the twentieth century. Although De Arteaga has identified her as an "Apostle of healing" to the mainline churches, only a thorough examination of representative statements from numerous sources could adequately support his claim—which has now been done.

Related to this, a tenth contribution is the critical analysis of Agnes's critics—namely Gumprecht, Hunt, and McMahon—who have labeled her practices as New Age, pantheistic, shamanistic, and occultic. This study has shown that although some of their suppositions are valid, such as her being influenced by New Thought and Jungian psychology, there conclusions are decisively invalidated through their repeated and largely intentional misinterpretation and misquotation.

As has been seen, both positive and negative assessments agree that Agnes had a pioneering effect on the Christian Church in the twentieth century, not just in the area of physical healing but especially in relation to the inner healing movement. Several sources have referenced the impact Agnes had on the early Charismatic Movement, both in Protestant and Roman Catholic groups in the United States and overseas. However, none of the authors have analyzed her perceived impact within all of the possible contexts. Evaluating and reviewing the statements made by scholars, other ministries, and even antagonists in relation to her influence on physical healing, inner healing, and the gifts and baptism of the Spirit within multiple mainline denominations has provided substantial evidence that Agnes affected the Renewal Movement to a profound extent. Although De Arteaga has identified her as an "Apostle of healing" to the mainline churches, only a thorough examination of representative statements from numerous sources could adequately support his claim. Through thorough evaluation, analysis, and quotation of primary and secondary source material, this work has proven this claim.

Implications for Further Study

There are significant aspects of Agnes's life and ministry that remain to be discussed and require further study. Although source authors have confirmed her profound impact on healing ministry and the Charismatic Movement, the exact nature of that impact remains to be discussed.

Agnes was raised in China before moving to the United States. Based upon her own statements in her autobiography and some of her other written works, her childhood in an Eastern culture had a noticeable impact on her theology and worldview. Although this effect has been mentioned, further study is necessary to identify the full extent of different cultures on her theology and ministry.

Additionally, her incorporation of metaphysics, science, and psychology into her healing model provides profound opportunities for dialogue between the often-seen-as-contradictory fields of science and faith. Agnes's work on the healing of memories has already significantly impacted psychologists, psychiatrists, and counselors. Her inner healing model could potentially result in a distinctly Christian psychological approach, which currently remains absent in the field. Her simplified healing model also provides opportunities for more churches and denominations to include healing ministry in their congregations, both evangelistically and pastorally. Additionally, her evidence-based approach could resolve tensions between paradigms that seem diametrically opposed.

Agnes has described the baptism of the Holy Spirit not only as being received but also as being released. Her understanding, based in metaphysical and sacramental beliefs, provides significant opportunities for resolving disagreements between traditional Pentecostal and Charismatic positions. Her conviction that God answers the prayers of non-Christians as well as believers presents exceptional opportunities for interfaith dialogue and understanding.

Although Agnes' influence on Charismatic ministries in North America and other English-speaking countries has been discussed here, examining the extent that her books have impacted non-English-speaking countries has not been possible in this work. The translation of some of her books into numerous other languages suggests a broader effect than currently recognized. Research into the influence of her writings in other languages would be certainly beneficial.

Finally, the almost unequaled level of respect and success in her ministry as a woman while simultaneously founding the Schools of Pastoral Care with her husband indicates an understanding of God's calling that is sorely needed in contemporary discussions on gender and ministry roles. Agnes serves as a model of both ministry and leadership as well as a mentor of male and female ministers.

Appendix 1

As of the original date of publication, my research involved all of the relevant extant material published by Agnes, written about her, and referencing her life, ministry, and theology. Below is my basic review of this literature as published in the dissertation that formed the draft foundation of this book. It is provided here in its entirety for those desiring to review the scholarly summary of all the major sources contributing to the work even though some of the material is duplicated in the main chapters of the book.

Primary Sources

Agnes wrote fifteen books over a period of 31 years. Although sources often categorize her texts as instructional or fictional, this dichotomy can create discrepancies. Although she clearly intended some books to teach the reader to pray for the sick, such as *The Healing Light* and *Behold Your God*, she meant other works to be more informative or devotional than instructive, such as *Twice Seven Words* or *Sealed Orders*, her autobiography. Two of her companion works, *The Healing Gifts of the Spirit* and *The Healing Power of the Bible*, blur the line between instruction, information, and theology, and her final book, *Creation Waits*, appears to be simultaneously instructional, inspirational, biographical, and theological. Her seven novels certainly qualify as fiction, but they consistently include instructions and information related to healing prayer. She also wrote six smaller works, five for journal publication and one as an educational pamphlet. Agnes strongly believed that the imagination as well as the mind was vital for fully understanding God, the Bible, theology, healing prayer, and the entire cosmos. As such, her theology and healing paradigm directly connect to her worldview, directly expressed throughout her different books. Therefore, no complete examination of Agnes can be accomplished without incorporating the entire corpus of her published works.

Agnes wrote her first book to describe a practical model for those desiring to effectively pray for the sick. *The Healing Light* (St. Paul: Macalester Park, 1947) was published over a decade prior to the recognized advent of the Charismatic

Movement.[1] It often incorporates scientific, metaphysical, and psychological language to explain spiritual concepts. Agnes describes the disillusionment and depression that almost took her life before discovering divine healing still taking place through the prayers of believers. She then outlines the process she found most effective in healing prayer. She strongly promotes the scientific method in healing, teaching people to view prayer for the sick as an experiment in channeling God's healing power to others. She recommends the reader select a specific approach depending on the type of sickness, observe the results of the prayer, make adjustments accordingly, and pray again as needed. Agnes's model reflects confidence in the scientific method as the optimal approach for understanding healing prayer. She consistently uses scientific phrases and concepts to explain her theological paradigm, making her interdisciplinary perspective apparent by incorporating psychology, medicine, and physics. Readers must remember she was describing largely original concepts with metaphysical phrases later adopted by New Age philosophies.

Agnes first published *The Healing Light* through Macalester Park Publishing, a company Glenn Clark founded for publishing his own works. Since that time, it has gone through numerous additional editions, revisions, formats, and printings. Her book has been published in at least seven countries and translated into German, French, Danish, Swedish, Finnish, and Afrikaans; additionally, an audio version is available in English, Danish, and Swedish. Although her active ministry was primarily in North America, the translation of *The Healing Light* into numerous languages suggests she has had some level of influence in other countries. Just in the United States, it has been published through Macalester Park, Logos International, Charisma Books, Walker, and Martino Publishing. In a joint arrangement with Macalester Park Publishers, Ballentine Books in Canada published a mass-marketed paperback edition in 1983; as of 1991, it has gone through thirteen printings and sold over 500,000 copies. Due to its popularity, a facsimile of the original first edition was published through Martino Publishing in 2013 as well as Benediction Classics in England in 2016. Identifying exactly how many copies of *The Healing Light* have been sold is impossible, but its popularity and impact is undeniable.

Agnes's second instructional book is a children's book on healing, prayer, and faith. *Let's Believe* (New York: Harper & Row, 1954) incorporates language and concepts understandable to small child who can read, but she intended adults to use it as a guide for teaching children about prayer and the basics of faith.[2] The text fits the genre of a bedtime reader more than a workbook, containing poems, stories, and limericks along with illustrations drawn by her husband, Ted. As Agnes explains on the back, the book often uses stories and poems with hidden meanings that may not be immediately understood by the child but that will eventually develop faith toward God in the unconscious mind. In this aspect, she creatively incorporates her understanding of the subconscious mind into her writing.

Agnes wrote a sequel to her first book for her readers seeking a deeper understanding of healing prayer. In *Behold Your God* (St. Paul: Macalester Park,

1958), she focuses on several practical disciplines to aid the reader in hearing from God, identifies the most common hindrances to prayer power, and explains how the spirit, soul, conscious, and subconscious relate to healing.[3] She dedicates a significant amount of space to describing the relationship of healing to the persons of the Trinity according to orthodox theology. Unlike her first book, this text includes diagrams to assist the reader in conceiving the nature and relationship of the spirit and soul to the body. Again, she reveals her theology and scientific methodology through her discussion of faith, healing, and forgiveness. The book uses more advanced and complex wording and sentence structure than *The Healing Light*, and the content and language indicates she expected her readers to have begun practicing healing prayer as outlined in her first work. Agnes takes a more direct approach with readers when addressing how sin hinders prayer. She clearly intended this sequel to lead her audience to a more effective level of healing prayer.

Agnes's next healing book describes how the Church can use both supernatural and natural methods to help those struggling with depression. *The Healing Gifts of the Spirit* (New York: J. B. Lippincott, 1966) relates her own experience of being depressed for many years, almost to the point of committing suicide.[4] In the book, she deftly explains the thought processes, feelings, and perspectives of people suffering from depression, writing not only for those who need healing but also to anyone seeking to pray for others. Additionally, Agnes provides warnings and cautions for those involved in praying for "the mental depressive" to avoid harming them or fostering any dependence.[5] In the text, she describes her own story with straightforward and simple language, writing the entire book from a first-person perspective. The book provides numerous practical steps to help depressed people while describing how the gifts of the Spirit operate in this context. The work combines insights from psychology, theology of the sacraments, and the healing of memories together into a discussion that comforts and encourages as much as it instructs and informs. Interestingly, Agnes devotes an entire chapter to discussing the gift of tongues in relation to healing for people with mental illness.

Agnes completed a subsequent healing text as a topical commentary on fifteen specific Bible events, characters, and parables. Each of the fifteen chapters in *The Healing Power of the Bible* (New York: J. B. Lippincott, 1969) describes the miracles and healings involved before explaining what they indicate about God's character and nature.[6] Throughout the book, she draws specific comparisons between the biblical events and common contemporary needs related to healing. The book stresses both physical and inner healing, with an increased focus on the latter. Agnes's scientific and interdisciplinary approach becomes obvious in the text, especially in relation to creation and the environment. Most of the text uses first-person language and simple wording while it simultaneously reflects solid research in biblical studies.

Agnes composed a book of meditations based first on the seven statements by Jesus on the cross and then on seven statements He made after His resurrection. The relatively short text *Twice Seven Words* (Plainfield: Logos, 1971) comprises less than 100 pages in length.[7] The author describes the book as being written to address the reader's heart directly instead of being aimed at instructing the conscious mind, and it contains small devotional excerpts, stories, poems, and prayers for the reader to process slowly over time. The text uses simple and easy to read language with very few metaphysical, scientific, or psychological terms or phrases that might be new or unfamiliar to most readers. This book would be better categorized as a devotional than an instructional text.

Agnes's autobiography describes her life from childhood through her eventual retirement from ministry. *Sealed Orders* (South Plainfield: Bridge, 1972) is the largest and one of the most significant of her published works, creating a context for her other books.[8] In it, she explains her early disillusionment with cessationism in Christianity, the depression that led her dangerously close to suicide, the eventual discovery that God still heals through prayer, the development of her own teaching and healing ministry, and her experience of the baptism of the Holy Spirit. The end of the book describes her transition from primarily teaching at the Schools of Pastoral Care she founded with her husband Ted, through his eventual death, and to her retirement from active ministry. Sources often reference this text along with *The Healing Light*. Agnes uses clear and specific language to captivate the reader, reflecting a deft and insightful skill in writing, and often utilizes humor to provide intimate knowledge of the successes, mistakes, and tragedies in her life.

Agnes published her final theological work to describe a Christian perspective toward the environment. The book *Creation Waits* (Plainfield: Logos, 1978) emphasizes the stewardship placed upon humanity to care for the rest of the created world, and the title involves a clear reference to Romans 8:19.[9] The text describes a responsibility for people to bring redemption to the fallen world, which includes animals, plants, and the earth itself. Agnes explains that God gave stewardship of the earth to Adam and Eve, and that same responsibility has remained with humanity; therefore, believers have a clear obligation to channel God's love and Presence to nature in prayer and in action. The text uses simple language to present a distinctly incarnational view of the environment, and although her books on healing promote specific theological premises, this text uniquely presents a specific and comprehensive theology of creation and the environment.

Agnes authored several novels to describe her insights into healing through a creative genre, inspired by experiences recounted in her autobiography. Her first novel, *Oh Watchman* (Philadelphia: J. B. Lippincott, 1950), describes a wounded serviceman, John Masterson, who learns about prayer from a nursing aid and gets healed.[10] The book is based on the actual story of a man Agnes prayed for in an army hospital. Her next novel, *Lost Shepherd* (Philadelphia: Lippincott, 1953), focuses on Paul Forrester, an Episcopal minister who learns about the prayer of faith from a free-thinking woman named Burnett, who in turn discovers the value of sacrament and liturgy.[11] This novel seems to loosely parallel her own discovery of sacramental healing prayer after marrying Edgar, an Episcopal priest. Her novels *Dreams Are for Tomorrow* (Philadelphia: J. B. Lippincott, 1963) and *Route 1* (Plainfield: Logos, 1975) describe other ministers learning about prayer from Forrester and teaching those skills to family, friends, and congregants.[12] Both texts seem to reflect her growing involvement in healing ministry and teaching conferences. *The Second Mrs. Wu* (Philadelphia: J. B. Lippincott, 1965) reflects Agnes's childhood in China, and *The Rising River* (New York: J. B. Lippincott, 1968) teaches about healing in a context related to Chinese culture.[13] Both texts provide insight into her early worldview. Along with these novels, Agnes wrote two children's books: *A Pasture for Peterkin* (Saint Paul: Macalester Park, 1956) and *Melissa and the Little Red Book* (Saint Paul: Macalester Park, 1976).[14] Except for *The Second Mrs. Wu*, all her novels describe prayer and faith using psychological, metaphysical, and theological concepts in simplified terms for readers seeking to learn more about prayer.

Agnes also authored five brief articles and a pamphlet for publication. She wrote "Spiritual Healing" for the Los Angeles diocese of the Episcopal Church in California.[15] The short three-page text became part of a manual for clergy and locates healing prayer solidly within the sacraments of Holy Unction and the Communion Service. In it, she encourages ministers to involve the congregation in praying for the sick. She also wrote "The Healing of Memories" for publication in *Guideposts*.[16] This short text discusses the way God heals emotional wounds in the memories through prayer. She recounts her first experience of praying this type of prayer and finishes with suggestions for people who need to pray for their own memories. Agnes wrote "Seeking Earnestly the Best Gifts" for *New Covenant* magazine.[17] This short discussion focuses on the need for Christians to desire the spiritual gifts that help others more than the gifts that benefit themselves. The article "Thy Kingdom Come" was published through the Unity School of Christianity.[18] The short article promotes a responsibility for believers to pray for the healing of creation. Agnes also wrote "Birth on Death Row" for a book of Christian experiences.[19] In it, she recounts the story of a woman who ministered healing to prisoners facing execution. Along with these articles for publication in other works, Agnes also wrote a small educational pamphlet, "How to Learn."[20] In this twelve-page work, she describes how students can study more effectively by understanding how the subconscious and conscious minds work together. Agnes also wrote material for the Schools of Pastoral Care. The handout "Homosexuality and Prayer" was given to participants to accompany the talks.[21] In it, she describes her straightforward approach to healing sexual deviation. However, most of the materials for the Schools are no longer available.

Agnes published at least fifteen books and six short articles in just over three decades. All of her works—whether instructional, fictional, or inspirational—involve clear, easy-to-read language and incorporate the subjects of prayer, healing, and faith. She consistently explains material in simple terms to make the concepts understandable and intuitive for readers, and she presents as extremely down-to-earth and practical. Throughout her books runs the conviction that God is willing to heal, and the power for healing is available to any who choose to seriously follow Him. Her acceptance of science along with faith, both through the use of the scientific method and the incorporation of psychological theory, becomes readily apparent in her writing, making her teachings attractive to many in the mainline denominations, especially during the early stages of the Charismatic Movement. The author's theology, worldview, and healing paradigm become evident in her works when they are examined as a whole and in light of the context in which they were written. However, her contributions and influences on other ministries must be identified through secondary sources as they are only minimally referenced in her books.

Secondary Sources

Agnes had a significant impact on Western Christianity even before the recognized birth of the Charismatic Movement. Her published works have been translated into at least seven languages, and her ministry has verifiably affected leaders not only in the United States but also in Australia and the United Kingdom. Numerous sources throughout the mainline denominations mention her in relation to physical healing, inner healing, prayer, and the gifts and baptism of the Holy Spirit; nevertheless, only eight substantive works—three published books and five theses and dissertations—have been written about her. None of these comprehensively discuss her life, ministry, theology, and effects on the Church but instead address specific aspects of those categories. Five journal articles in the fields of theology and psychology have also been published about her, but they are significantly limited in scope and content. The remaining mentions of Agnes range from brief chapters in topical books to a single mention of her name in an editorial column. These numerous sources provide significant insight and understanding of Agnes's theology and contributions, making them useful for developing a comprehensive work to describe her life, ministry, theology, contributions, and influence on the Church.

Published Books

William Vaswig, a Lutheran minister, wrote *I Prayed, He Answered* in 1977 as an autobiographical account of his experiences with Agnes and the beginning of his own healing ministry. In this short book, the author describes his son's healing from acute schizophrenia through Agnes's prayers, which then led him to learn about healing and begin to pray for others. He includes excerpts of case history notes for his son's major hospitalizations, the final diagnosis as being fully recovered, and a description of the meetings Agnes had with the leading psychiatrists at the psychiatric hospital. Although Vaswig wrote about physical healing in his account, the book largely focuses on emotional and psychological healing and the optimal methods of praying for those needs.

The text does not qualify as an academic or critical source on Agnes, but it does provide additional context for other sources. The brief text uses very simple language to describe the author's relationship with Agnes as well as his own learning process regarding how to pray for the sick. Although the limited scope of the source does not itself supply additional contributions toward her influence on the Charismatic Movement, it does discuss the impact Agnes had on practitioners in the field of psychology, which is confirmed by the number of mental health publications referencing Agnes as a source.

Jane Gumprecht, a physician, wrote *Abusing Memory: The Healing Theology of Agnes Sanford* in 1997 to expose what she considered to be occult influences in Agnes's theology. She explains that she began to examine Agnes's writings after she met Christians involved in inner healing, a practice she identifies as decidedly New Age and occultic. Using Agnes's own books as a source, especially focusing on her autobiography *Sealed Orders* and her main healing text *The Healing Light*, the author analyzes her childhood in China, the philosophies influencing her paradigm, different aspects of her theology, and the language used in her books. Gumprecht proves beyond a doubt that New Thought and Jungian Psychology played a significant part in the formation of Agnes's healing model and theology, which Agnes herself admits in detail in her texts. The author concludes with a warning for discerning Christians to avoid her works.

Of the three books written on Agnes, Gumprecht's text aims to be critical and succeeds at being skewed. The introduction references visualization as a Hindu practice, concedes that Agnes "thought she was a Christian," and presents a goal of exploring "healing of memories in light of the second commandment."[22] She validates her analysis by admitting prior involvement with Unity, a Christianized branch of New Thought. The author reveals her bias from beginning to end, promoting cessationism and rejecting any use of the imagination in healing prayer as valid. The author takes several of Agnes's statements out of context, interprets comments with slanted assumptions, and resorts to defamatory language. The author's rejection of significant aspects of Pentecostal or Charismatic theology along with her negative opinion of Agnes makes her text minimally useful in identifying the value of Agnes's contributions to the Church and to Renewal theology. Nevertheless, her text provides valuable insight into the philosophies often considered questionable, which did influence Agnes's theology and paradigm.

Dr. William L. De Arteaga, Anglican priest and historian, wrote the book *Agnes Sanford and Her Companions: The Assault on Cessationism and the Coming of the Charismatic Renewal* in 2015 to examine the rise and fall of the doctrine of cessationism. On the first page, he identifies Agnes as "the most important woman for the revival of healing prayer among the very mainline denominations who disbelieved in such prayers."[23] He divided the work into five sections: the first section describes the rise of cessationism in response to the heresies of Marcion; section two examines the ideologies that opposed revival and forced churches to reevaluate cessationism while section three describes the resulting response; sections four and five discuss Agnes's involvement in combatting cessationism and how her theology became foundational for the Charismatic Movement.

The text's concluding section evaluates Agnes's prayer model and theology using the criteria provided by Jonathan Edwards for identifying a true work of God.

De Arteaga uses clear and specific wording to provide a well-researched book on Agnes, and the occasional use of casual phrases or indirect sentences does not prevent his work from being both scholarly and insightful. The author approaches the work with a complimentary perspective on Agnes, and although his language sometimes reflects passion more than objectivity, he substantiates his interpretations and conclusions. He includes numerous personal communications by Agnes, providing unique insight into various aspects of her life and ministry. De Arteaga's book does not comprehensively explain her influences and theology, and he admits, "there is no published biography of [Agnes]," with the closest being a master's thesis by Francis Burkhardt Baltz.[24] A more comprehensive work remains necessary. Still, it provides extremely valuable material and insight into Agnes's influence on healing and the Renewal Movement.

None of the three books written about Agnes qualify as comprehensive. Vaswig published a laudatory text for the purpose of promoting the development of healing ministry within the Church, but it primarily focuses on emotional healing; also, it is quite brief and cannot be considered scholarly due to its non-critical nature. Gumprecht wrote a critical examination of Agnes's work and theology, but it involves an excessively biased and defamatory premise; the extent of quotations misinterpreted and taken out of context largely minimizes its value as a scholarly work. DeArteaga provided the most scholarly work on Agnes and her contributions to the Charismatic Movement, but it mainly addresses a specific context. A larger and more comprehensive work is needed.

Dissertations and Theses

Anett B. Wannamaker completed *A Psychosynthesis Study of Agnes Sanford's Practice and Theology of Prayer Healing* in 1989 as her dissertation for the Institute of Transpersonal Psychology. She examines Agnes's practice and theology of inner healing prayer through a psychological perspective, comparing her model with the psychosynthesis model developed by Robert Assagioli; she believes his model provides the best framework for understanding healing of memories. Wannamaker identifies her purpose in the introduction as "to explore those similarities and other parallels between Sanford's theology and psychosynthesis theory and practice."[25] She divides her text into three distinct sections: in the first section, she provides bibliographies of both Agnes and Assagioli along with descriptions of the two models; in section two, she describes her professional experience with Daphne, a client who received significant improvement through a prayer service led by Agnes; section three concludes the work by discussing the similar effects that healing prayer and psychosynthesis can have on an individual.

The author provides a critical and insightful examination of the subject matter while maintaining an unbiased and scholarly tone in her language, reflecting her intention to discuss the two approaches "without questioning or evaluating either."[26] Nevertheless, the interdisciplinary nature of the work necessarily examines inner healing in primarily psychological concepts, which involves the danger of misinterpretation. Although she only briefly discusses Agnes's contributions for the Charismatic Movement, her knowledge of Jungian psychology and psychosynthesis provides a valuable examination of Agnes's healing of memories theology and practice. Additionally, her work confirms the recognition and respect Agnes holds in psychological and psychiatric disciplines.

Pavel Hejzlar published *Two Paradigms for Divine Healing: Fred F. Bosworth, Kenneth E. Hagin, Agnes Sanford, and Francis MacNutt in Dialogue* in 2009. In this dissertation for Fuller Theological Seminary, the author compares and contrasts two different theological paradigms for healing, described as traditional Pentecostal and pastoral Charismatic approaches: in the former, prayer focuses on the sick person having faith that healing was accomplished in the atonement and then receiving that healing by faith; in the latter, healing involves prayer ministers identifying influences that may affect health—such as unmet emotional, psychological, social, and relational needs—and then subsequently becoming channels of God's healing power to the sick person. The author chose Fred Bosworth and Kenneth Hagin to represent the Pentecostal healing model and Agnes Sanford and Francis MacNutt to represent the Charismatic healing model.

Hejzlar provides a good critical review of primary source material, but some of his interpretations incompletely and imperfectly represent an author's actual position. For example, he identifies Agnes as a pantheist, which is a misinterpretation of her theology. The author also describes two methods or paradigms for healing, suggesting that only two approaches to healing prayer exist, which is a distinct generalization. In his introduction, he writes the following: "The two ways of ministering to the sick may well reflect two theological paradigms."[27] This generalization works for his specific comparison, but it somewhat oversimplifies the subject matter, excluding a Wesleyan Pentecostal healing theology. Nevertheless, the text provides an academic and scholarly examination of two significant paradigms for healing prayer and gives a limited discussion of Agnes's contributions toward healing ministry in contemporary Charismatic churches.

Francis Burkhardt Baltz submitted the thesis *Agnes Sanford: A Creative Intercessor* in 1979 for his Master's degree at Nashotah House. The author explains that he had read some of Agnes's books while seeking a greater effectiveness in healing prayer. He decided to attend one of her Schools of Pastoral Care where he received healing from a physical illness when she prayed for him. He writes, "[she] expresses a significant understanding of intercessory prayer for the healing of persons" so that "her influence has been widespread."[28] In his discussion, he attributes her understanding of healing prayer to her incorporation of the imagination in prayer. His text involves a biographical survey of her life, an evaluation of her published works, a description of a typical School of Pastoral Care, and numerous appendices related to her ministry and publications.[29] As noted, Baltz has provided the most complete biographical account of Agnes to date, but it is limited in scope and content.

Although Baltz attempts to discuss Agnes in an academic manner, the work reflects his personal experiences and sometimes lacks a scholarly level of objectivity and analysis. He writes relatively clearly and understandably although the text includes first-person language and occasional rough wording. Nevertheless, he incorporates an excellent level of research with valuable and applicable sources and, as De Arteaga states, provides the closest to a biography of Agnes in existence. Baltz devotes two pages to specifically discussing Agnes's influence on others. He describes her theology but only in relation to specific aspects of healing prayer. His work does not prove the extent of her contributions toward healing ministry, but it qualifies as an extremely valuable source.

Mary Ann Molinari completed *Inner Healing in the Perspective of Agnes Sanford* in 1980 as her thesis for a Master's degree at the University of St. Michael's College in Toronto. Her text aims to "situate Inner Healing in the context of Jesus' ministry and consequently in the ministry of the Church."[30] The first two chapters discuss the history and theology of inner healing in Roman Catholicism and its connection with psychology. Chapter three focuses on Agnes, explaining her background, theology, and inner healing model; almost two pages are dedicated to describing her contributions to the Catholic Charismatic Renewal. The last chapter discusses implementation in a local church body.

Molinari's short text incorporates a noticeably generous font and page format. Her writing uses relatively clear and direct wording with occasional grammatical errors and a surprising amount of casual and gendered language. She cites sources throughout, but some material lacks desired citations; for example, the chapter on Agnes averages only two citations per page. The work would be better categorized as a well-researched guide on developing an inner healing ministry in a church than an academic analysis of the topic, which is supported by the last chapter as well as the amount of the chapter on Agnes that describes how to practice her method. Nevertheless, the work does provide some useful material toward Agnes's contributions to healing ministry in churches.

Colin James Cross submitted *Agnes Sanford and the Heritage of Inner Healing* as his Master's thesis at the University of British Columbia in 1986. In this sizable work, the author analyzes the philosophy and practice of inner healing and Agnes's role in its development. His work "critiques *Inner Healing*, a psychotherapeutic ritual which aims to cure souls."[31] The first two chapters argue for a quality critique of inner healing in light of biblical orthodoxy and discusses it in light of Church history. The third chapter encompasses half the text, focusing almost exclusively on Agnes. The last two chapters describe her influence on Ruth Carter Stapleton and the Catholic Charismatic Movement.

Cross seems to attempt a critical academic analysis of the topic, but his bias is apparent from beginning to end. Early in the introduction, he states, "Christian psychology (including inner healing) is [the devil's] very own invention, a 'pseudo-science' that is riddled with deluded notions about ... shamanistic rituals ... flights of fantasy ... and words of faith," and concerning inner healing, "there seems to be much at stake, not the least of which [is] orthodoxy itself."[32] This bias permeates his analysis of Agnes's writings, misinterpreting much of it, and the recurrent disparaging language detracts from the thesis' rationality; additionally, some statements lack citation to identify the reference. Unsurprisingly, the author uses *The Seduction of Christianity* by Dave Hunt and T. A. McMahon, a source extremely disparaging toward Agnes and the concept of inner healing.[33] The thesis does reveal familiarity with psychology and inner healing principles, so it provides some useful insight and critique of the subject matter. However, Cross' discussion of Agnes's influence on Stapleton and the Catholic Charismatic Movement is its most valuable contribution to the topic.

The graduate-level works discussing Agnes vary in their scope and level of research, analysis, and scholarship. Of the three texts focusing on inner healing, Wanamaker incorporates a psychological perspective while Molinari and Cross employ a theological standpoint. Each work has clear limitations: Wanamaker's dissertation provides good analysis, but it involves an extremely narrow scope; Molinari's thesis discusses inner healing in the Church, but the work qualifies more as a practical guide than a scholarly work; Cross provides an extensive thesis with strong analysis from a particular biblical perspective, but it contains significant bias and lacks some academic discipline. The two graduate-level works addressing physical healing operate from a biblical framework. Hejzlar's dissertation compares Agnes's healing model with one Pentecostal approach while Baltz's thesis describes the core aspects of her ministry. However, these texts are also limited: Hejzlar provides an excellent review of primary texts but has a narrow scope with some questionable interpretations; Baltz shows an excellent level of research, but his work lacks the critical analysis to make it scholarly. None of the texts fully discuss Agnes's healing model, theology, and contributions.

Peer-Reviewed Journal Articles

Donald L. Clark published "Theory of Personality, Illness, and Cure Found in the Writings of Agnes Sanford and Those Acknowledging Her Influence" in the *Journal of Psychology and Theology* in 1989. After referencing a previous article, "applying the requirements of a personality theory" to faith healers in the vein of E. W. Kenyon, he identifies a similar theory for "inner healing" practitioners influenced by Agnes.[34] He identifies seven aspects associated with personality development, illness, and cure necessary to propose a personality theory and describes how the inner healing model practiced by Agnes and those acknowledging her work satisfies each aspect. He also compares the components of their theory with aspects of psychotherapy.

Clark wrote a scholarly and equitable article, analyzing source material from a psychological position without using either derogatory or laudatory language. He provides sufficient quotations from Agnes and others to support both his interpretations and conclusions. The author provides an outline of the general technique used by inner healers as well as addressing the validity of some of the primary criticisms against inner healing. The most significant and noteworthy aspect of Clark's article may be his personal communications with John and Paula Sandford, proponents of Agnes's ministry: he not only submitted questions to them for additional information while writing the article but also includes their response to his rough draft in the final version.

The article "God's Faithfulness and God's Freedom: A Comparison of Contemporary Theologies of Healing" by Henry H. Knight III was published in the *Journal of Pentecostal Theology* in 1993. The author examines several "contemporary charismatic theologies of healing" to reveal "how these theologies relate [to] God's faithfulness and God's freedom."[35] The selected models are grouped and discussed in five sections, relating to how each incorporates God's sovereignty in the process on the one hand along with certainty of the outcome on the other. For each model, he describes its theology, practice, and associated strengths and weaknesses. Knight evaluates Agnes's paradigm as emphasizing God's faithfulness over His sovereignty without reaching the extremes of the Word-Faith paradigm. After categorizing the models in relation to faithfulness and freedom, he outlines the healing theology of John Wesley in a sixth section and explains that although Wesley emphasized God's freedom over faithfulness, his theology provides a solution to the weaknesses in the other models.

Knight's article provides a scholarly discussion of healing theologies with clear and uncomplicated language. He describes the different healing models without being excessively critical and identifies the strengths and weaknesses of each—except with no clear weakness mentioned in relation to Wesley. Although Knight provides an adequate synopsis of each model, the scope of his thesis limits his descriptions; in other words, the forced dichotomy between the identified poles of God's faithfulness and freedom leads to potential oversimplification of the models. In relation to Agnes, he summarizes her model sufficiently for the purposes of the paper, but he fails to describe its complexity sufficiently and misses some of its application. His article gives a useful but limited analysis of Agnes's theology and her contribution to Renewal.

William L. De Arteaga, historian and theologian of the Charismatic Episcopal Church, wrote "Agnes Sanford: Apostle of Healing, and First Theologian of the Charismatic Renewal" as a two-part article published through *Pneuma Review* in 2006. The first part covers Agnes's biographical information and the beginning of her ministry. He states, "she played a particularly significant role in moving many Christians within the mainline churches away from cessationism and into the pastoral practice of healing prayer, and introduced many to the gifts of the Spirit."[36] The second part starts with a general synopsis of her first book, *The Healing Light*, which he describes as "the crown work of Christian New Thought" while affirming that Agnes "[used] her biblical knowledge as filter [and] eliminated the unbiblical aspects of New Thought."[37] The rest of the article describes her baptism in the Spirit, her introduction and involvement in healing ministry, and her theological influence upon the Charismatic Movement.

De Arteaga uses clear and direct language to supply an introductory discussion of Agnes for any readers unaware of her influence and contributions to the Renewal Movement. Although the text reflects the author's positive opinion of Agnes, it maintains scholarly writing and an academic tone. The author clearly intends his article as a defense against accusations of Agnes being unorthodox or occultic in her theology, reflected in his beginning the first article with a response to specific comments found in Dave Hunt's *The Seduction of Christianity*. His research provides valuable insight into her background as well as the philosophies that affected her own theology and model.

Judith Agaoglu, a clinical psychologist, published "Agnes Sanford: Pioneer in Healing Ministry and Apostle of the Healing Light of Christ" in the *Journal of Christian Healing* in 2007. She prefaces her short article by stating that many Christians seek the miracle power present in the early Church but find it largely lacking today, leaving them struggling with fear, doubt, and confusion; she writes, "Agnes Sanford has walked this very path, embracing the contradictions and searching out the mysteries of Christian healing."[38] The introduction summarizes the author's personal discovery of the effect Agnes had on the Charismatic movement. The majority of her text outlines Agnes's discovery that healing still takes place, discusses the basics of her theology, and provides an outline of her healing model. The conclusion describes the part Agnes played in healing ministry in the last century and challenges readers to embrace the same calling.

Agaoglu writes an article more casual than scholarly, using clear and simple language for a text entirely complimentary toward Agnes; nowhere does she mention or address any weaknesses or concerns that would indicate a level of critical analysis. The article mainly incorporates a first-person perspective and aims to explain and encourage readers to become more involved in healing ministry in their own churches. The author relies upon three of Agnes's texts for all of the cited information: *The Healing Light*, *Sealed Orders*, and *Behold Your God*. The text expresses the significant contribution that Agnes made toward both healing ministry and the Charismatic Renewal, but it does so without providing either specific examples or verifiable proof beyond the author's own individual perspective.

This author published "God's Faithful Freedom: Healing as an Outflow of God's Presence" in 2014 through the *Journal of Pentecostal Theology*. The work was partly in response to Knight's text, which defined healing models on a spectrum between the poles of God's sovereignty and faithfulness. The article aimed to address the weakness of an approach based on a dichotomy between sovereignty and faithfulness by suggesting that Agnes's theology resolves the apparent contradiction by identifying healing as an integral aspect of God's nature. The author also argues that validating or invalidating any healing paradigm according to potential problems may be inherently flawed: evaluations of healing models normally involve the roles of faith and personal responsibility in those seeking healing, but faith cannot be objectively measured, so the accuracy of any healing model can only be subjectively correlated with faith. The author proposes that healing models should primarily be evaluated according to their success, doctrinal cohesiveness, and correspondence to ultimate reality; Agnes's model is examined, discussed, and evaluated in light of these propositions. However, the ideologies that affected Agnes and her influences and contributions on Renewal in the Church are only briefly discussed.

Although each of these articles addresses contributions Agnes made, they all entail a limited scope. Clark's article reflects the significant role that Agnes played in the development of inner healing within the Church, but it does not address the extent that Agnes fundamentally changed the ministry of physical healing in the Charismatic Movement. Instead, he primarily examines and evaluates her model. Agaoglu's article provides more personal recommendation and discussion than scholarly analysis, but it confirms the respect Agnes had among those in the field of psychology. De Arteaga's article promotes Sanford's contributions and theology during the early Charismatic Renewal, but it does so mainly biographically. He provides an excellent but brief introductory description of her healing model and influence. Knight's article recognizes Agnes's healing model as distinctive to other approaches, but it does not discuss its influence. This author's article on Agnes discusses the importance of her theology for Renewal but does not significantly examine her influence on the Charismatic Movement. A more comprehensive analysis of Agnes's theology and contributions is necessary.

Constituent References

The book *God Can Heal You Now* by Emily Gardiner Neal was published in 1958. The author aims to teach and encourage her readers to believe in healing prayer. A short chapter in the book is dedicated to discussing Agnes and *The Healing Light*, making it one of the earliest books to cover her ministry and primary text. She begins the chapter by stating, "there is no member of the laity in the United States who is wielding a greater or more widespread influence on the revival of healing within the churches than Agnes Sanford." [39] The author summarizes Agnes's discovery of healing, her approach to healing prayer, and the development of the School of Pastoral Care ministry by her and her husband Ted. Neal uses clear and direct language with specific and effective wording to inspire her readers. Written before the recognized beginning of the Charismatic Movement by a nationally recognized journalist, the text can be considered an invaluable and original source for discussing the significant contributions Agnes made to the impending Renewal.

James T. Connelly completed *Neo-Pentecostalism: The Charismatic Revival in the*

Mainline Protestant and Roman Catholic Churches of the United States, 1960-1971 as his dissertation for the Divinity School at the University of Chicago in 1977. The sizable text provides an extensive description of the initial years of the Charismatic Revival in Protestant and Roman Catholic denominations, relying on early denominational reports, periodicals, interviews, and personal correspondence with key figures of the period. Although Agnes does not form the main subject of the text, he dedicates eight pages to discussing her. In relation to her Schools of Pastoral Care, he says, "Agnes Sanford was one of the people most responsible for making current in the historic Protestant denominations the concept of a baptism in the Spirit and the practice of glossolalia."[40] Connelly writes clearly, succinctly, and understandably, making the text scholarly, as confirmed by its use in several later sources. The early date of the work and the use of primary sources make it extremely valuable for a historical analysis to confirm Agnes's influence on the early Charismatic Movement.

Similar short sections on Agnes are found in two other dissertations in the field of Divinity. Richard Cotner submitted *Pentecost and Its Discontents* to the University of Missouri-Columbia in 2004. Approximately six pages of the text discuss Agnes's biography, ministry, writings, and influence during the early Charismatic Movement.[41] Agnes is also discussed in *Increasing Knowledge about Divine Healing within the Leadership of an Immigrant Asian Baptist Church*, submitted to the School of Theology and Missions at Oral Roberts University by KonkHogin Hagin Haokip in 2007. Almost three pages in this work describe Agnes's biography, ministry, and basic prayer model in conjunction with various other approaches to healing prayer.[42] The content in these texts provide extremely brief summaries of her life, ministry, and paradigm, but they support her inclusion as a noteworthy figure in Church history during the twentieth century.

Canon Jim Glennon, an Anglican priest, wrote *Your Healing is Within You* in 1978 based on the healing ministry he developed at St Andrew's Cathedral in Sydney, Australia. The book is a two-part work, providing both a pastoral discussion along with a scriptural defense of healing in the Christian Church. Agnes wrote the Foreword to the book, and the author devotes a page to describing his experience when she came to Australia and taught a healing mission at his church. At that time, she prayed for him to receive the infilling of the Holy Spirit. He describes the baptism in the Spirit making as much of a difference in his life as his conversion had done previously. The most significant aspects of the book are its reference to Agnes doing healing conferences over in Australia, placing her ministry on a more global scale, and the widespread his own ministry then had in Australia and abroad.

Dave Hunt and T. A. McMahon wrote *The Seduction of Christianity: Spiritual Discernment in the Last Days* in 1985 "to expose a seduction that is gathering momentum [within Christianity] . . . known as the New Age movement."[43] Many practices are labeled and identified as occult techniques nevertheless being accepted by Christians, such as psychotherapy, holistic medicine, positive confession, and others. The authors mention Agnes several times, especially discussing her in a chapter on Shamanism in which they identify her as a pantheist. They describe her methodologies as "so blatantly pagan as to be astonishing."[44] The authors also link Paul Yonggi Cho, Richard Foster, John Wimber, and Francis MacNutt, as well as many others, to occult influences. Similar statements concerning Agnes are also found in *Invasion of Other Gods: The Seduction of New Age Spirituality*, published by David Jeremiah and Carole C. Carlson in 1995.

Hunt and McMahon use very sensationalistic language to capture the reader's attention and evoke an imminent sense of danger. Their theology and hermeneutics support cessationism and the primacy of reason over spiritual experience. The work reflects a significant amount of research, but the authors often misquote and misinterpret sources. For example, after quoting Agnes as saying, "He made everything out of Himself and somehow He put a part of Himself into everything," they immediately quote her referencing Pierre Teilhard de Chardin to support their pantheistic claim.[45] However, the second quote was on an entirely different page—and discussing an entirely different subject—than the first quote. Although Hunt and McMahon use primary sources and correctly identify Agnes's influence by New Thought and Jungian psychology, the text contains too much bias and inaccuracy to be a scholarly source. Although Jeremiah and Carlson use softer language, their conclusions are identical.

The book *The Church Divided: The Holy Spirit and a Spirit of Seduction* was published in 1986 in response to *The Seduction of Christianity*. Multiple authors from various denominations contribute individual chapters and sections. De Arteaga first discusses Agnes in the section where he provides specific examples of Hunt and McMahon not only misinterpreting but also intentionally misquoting her. Robert Wise, the primary author of the text, also discusses Agnes in a separate chapter on her life and ministry. He explains that many of the concerns and misinterpretations related to her can be attributed to a nonexistence of appropriate terminology, a passion for results, and the use of psychological concepts. The authors write with direct and precise language without sensational wording, and the sections show careful and effective research and discussion. Although the sections on Agnes defend her work, they do so without ignoring valid concerns. In the same year, Thomas F. Reid, Mark Virkler, James A. Laine, and Alan Langstaff also published *Seduction?? A Biblical Response* in response to *The Seduction of Christianity*. De Arteaga mentions Agnes in a small article he authored in defense of inner healing. He refutes Hunt and McMahon's supposition that identifies visualization as an exclusively occult practice. The text seems more casual than scholarly.

Patricia E. Cerny submitted *A Psychological Evaluation of Inner Healers* as her dissertation for the Rosemead School of Psychology at Biola University in 1986. In this surprisingly brief text, the author evaluates the paradigms, practices, and theories of eight inner healing ministries and practitioners from a psychological and psychotherapeutic perspective. She dedicates five pages to Agnes to explain the main aspects of her healing of memories model along with significant aspects that relate to the categories of diagnosis, techniques, and processes.

She writes with clear and understandable wording, albeit with a surprising amount of gendered language for an APA style text. Cerny based her entire section on Agnes solely on one text, *The Healing Gifts of the Spirit*. Although she provides citations throughout, she does so casually to the point of being sloppy, resulting in at least one quotation and other references being uncited or cited so poorly that nearby pages in the source must be scanned to locate the reference. Nevertheless, the work provides some useful academic discussion and psychological evaluation of inner healing; however, specific contributions by Agnes do not form part of the discussion.

Six other dissertations in the field of psychology provide brief discussions on Agnes. Bethyl Joy Midura submitted *Psychodynamic, Existential, and Religious Views Pertaining to Psychological Healing: A Comparative Analysis* to the Rosemead Graduate School in 1981; twelve pages compare Agnes's writings with various psychotherapy models.[46] *Charismatic Christian Spiritual Healing in Two Cultural Contexts: An Existential-Phenomenological Approach* by Frank Stafford Davis was submitted to Duquesne University in 1990; three pages discuss Agnes's healing model.[47] Emmett L. Jones wrote *A Study of Traditional Prayer, Inner Healing Prayer and Psychological Well-Being among Evangelical Christians* in 1998 for the California School of Professional Psychology; five pages discussing inner healing discuss Agnes.[48] *Ethical Issues in the Use of Prayer in Clinical Practice: An Examination of Theophostic Prayer Ministry* by Linda Hunter was submitted to Regent University in 2006; four pages describe Agnes's healing paradigm.[49] Merilee Brooke Lovejoy wrote *Examining the Influence of Prayer Counseling on Client Levels of Depression, Anxiety, Spiritual Well-Being, and Surrender to God* for Seattle Pacific University in 2010; she devotes less than one page to Agnes and the development of inner healing.[50] Also submitted to Regent University was *Immanuel: Narrative Case Studies Exploring Inner Healing in Clinical Settings* by M. Elliott Hattendorf in 2014; seven pages describe Agnes's development of inner healing.[51] All these dissertations discuss Agnes as well as reference her as a source.

Peter D. Hocken, a Roman Catholic historian, wrote the book *Streams of Renewal: The Origins and Early Development of the Charismatic Movement in Great Britain*, published in 1986. He relies on extensive research and personal communications with numerous leaders from the early Renewal Movement to provide a very clear and readable history of the Charismatic Movement in Britain. Walter J. Hollenweger, a major scholar and historian of Pentecostalism, attributes Hocken with proving "the Charismatic Movement in Britain was not imported from the United States."[52] This considerable achievement for a movement often associated with North America makes the author an authority on the topic. In that light, Hocken writes, "Probably the person who contributed most to the spread of baptism in the Spirit with spiritual gifts among those firmly committed to their own church tradition was Agnes Sanford."[53] His statement indicates the substantial influence Agnes had on the Charismatic Movement not only in Britain but also in North America.

Hocken also authored a brief entry on Agnes in *The Dictionary of Pentecostal and Charismatic Movements*, published in 1988; the article was also reprinted in

The New International Dictionary of Pentecostal and Charismatic Movements in 2002. The short passage consists of three paragraphs: a short biography of Agnes's background in China before marrying Edgar Sanford and moving to the United States, a synopsis of the development of her healing ministry and the writing of her primary text on healing, *The Healing Light*, and a list of some influences and effects she had on the Charismatic Movement. Hocken describes Agnes as "one of the foremost promoters of renewal in the Holy Spirit within the historic churches ... [and] the major pioneer in ministry for the healing of memories."[54] He also mentions Agnes in the major entry "Charismatic Movement," and she is mentioned occasionally in related entries in both versions of the dictionary. The *NIDPCM* has become a recognized standard reference in the field of Renewal Studies.

Nancy A. Hardesty wrote a chapter on Agnes in *Christian Spirituality: The Essential Guide to the Most Influential Spiritual Writings of the Christian Tradition*. The edited volume by Frank N. Magill and Ian P. McGreal was published in 1988. The chapter primarily reviews Agnes's *The Healing Gifts of the Spirit*, which the author identifies as "a book on healing: physical, emotional, and spiritual."[55] Interestingly, the biographical information at the beginning of the chapter implies Agnes was still living though she had died six years earlier. The lack of citations suggests the authors did not intend the text to be academic. The author writes relatively clearly except for some surprising grammatical issues for someone as published as Hardesty. The chapter does not describe major contributions of Agnes, but its inclusion in a volume dedicated to Christianity's "Most Influential Spiritual Writings" reflects Agnes's significance.

An entry on Agnes is provided in Helen Kooiman Hosier's *100 Christian Women Who Changed the Twentieth Century*, published in 2000. The author's single-page entry on Agnes references the same source as Hocken's entry in *DPCM*, but her entry is almost identical in size, structure, and wording to Hocken's entry, suggesting she copied it from the latter instead of paraphrasing it from the former.[56] Hosier's entry does not provide any new information on Agnes's theology or contributions, but her inclusion for a selection of one hundred influential women in the twentieth century indicates importance.

Richard J. Foster and Emilie Griffin provide a short chapter on Agnes in their edited work *Spiritual Classics: Selected Readings on the Twelve Spiritual Disciplines*. They chose her as one of four authors for inclusion in a section on Prayer. After a short introductory paragraph on her life and ministry, the authors reprint excerpts from her primary work *The Healing Light* along with a selected Bible passage, discussion questions, and suggested exercises. Foster concludes the chapter by describing the influence Agnes had on him and providing an annotated bibliography of her major works for further study. The book does not provide new material on Agnes but does indicate her further influence on noteworthy authors in the fields of healing, prayer, and the development of spiritual disciplines.

William L. De Arteaga published the article "Glenn Clark's Camps Furthest Out: The Schoolhouse of the Charismatic Renewal" in *Pneuma* in 2003. He mentions Agnes several times although she does not constitute the main topic of this article. The author states, "research for this article was done . . . as I was preparing a manuscript on Agnes Sanford," and he attributes her with combatting cessationism and Idealist Cults, establishing a powerful healing ministry, and teaching others through her published writings.[57] De Arteaga reveals that Agnes had a substantial influence on multiple leaders during the early Charismatic Movement, and her writings continue to impact people.

The paper "From Radical Idealism to Pentecostalism: Three Pioneers: Glenn Clark, Rufus Moseley and Agnes Sanford," also by De Arteaga, was presented in a History Interest Group at the 2008 joint conference of the Society of Pentecostal Studies and the Wesleyan Theological Society. The content suggests the author developed it from the same material as the *Pneuma* article. After describing the Church's departure from depending on the miraculous to relying on realist philosophy, the author says Christianity only recently returned to "Faith Idealism," a position in which prayer more correctly "assumes its Biblical role."[58] He names Agnes as one of three leaders promoting Faith Idealism. De Arteaga's paper, which seems slightly unpolished, reveals how Glenn Clark, Rufus Mosely, and Agnes Sanford relied on the miraculous to inform their theology and recognized beneficial aspects of faith in metaphysical ideologies. Integral to the paper is his description of how the subjects purged heretical teachings from New Thought philosophy. The paper provides a sound argument with accurately cited material. The author provides first-hand knowledge of Agnes, making it useful in discussing her contributions to Renewal.

The *Mastering Life* website provides a transcript of an interview in 2008 with Francis and Judith MacNutt. In response to one of David Kyle Foster's questions, Francis describes meeting Agnes at a Camps Farthest Out (CFO) where he learned about healing and received the baptism of the Holy Spirit after she had prayed for him; she had also prophesied over him that God would use him to return healing to the Roman Catholic Church.[59] Judith describes reading Agnes's autobiography before meeting Francis. Although mentioned only a few times, Agnes had an evident impact on the MacNutts. Foster revised the interview and published an abbreviated form as "A Conversation with Francis and Judith MacNutt" in the online journal *The Pneuma Review* in 2014.[60] Agnes is mentioned only once in this shortened version of the interview. De Arteaga also posted the short column "Introducing Francis and Judith MacNutt" on the same website in September 2007. Although he only mentions Agnes once in this earlier post, the content indicates she had a significant effect on introducing the MacNutts to healing and to the baptism of the Holy Spirit.

Leanne Payne wrote *Heaven's Calling: A Memoir of One Soul's Steep Ascent* in 2008. In this autobiography, the author expounds on her life and ministry. As part of this account, she describes her first meeting with Agnes, their eventual work together in ministry, and the close friendship that developed. Although the text focuses on Payne's life, it provides valuable insight into Agnes's life after she completed her last book, *Creation Waits*. Payne gives a detailed description of Agnes's interactions with numerous leaders in healing ministry and the early

Charismatic Movement, including Morton Kelsey, who took over the School of Pastoral Care after Agnes retired. The text provides some insight into her contributions to Renewal, but proves especially helpful in understanding Agnes's theology in relation to Jungian psychology.

Gary Neal Hansen published *Kneeling with Giants: Learning to Pray with History's Best Teachers* in 2012. An entire chapter discusses Agnes and *The Healing Light*, summarizing and explaining the basics of the book instead of just reviewing it. He begins by explaining that people who read her books are usually polarized into loving or hating her because of her theology and her use of the imagination in prayer; however, he believes she needed to be discussed because "Sanford represents the charismatic movement."[61] He makes this bold statement based on her influence on the early Charismatic Movement, her remarkable success with healings, and her acceptance of the gifts of the Spirit after having being raised in a denomination that taught cessationism. The author provides a clear and casual text, using first-person and second-person language. Although mostly complimentary toward Agnes, Hansen does briefly discuss issues people have with her material, such as her simplification of issues related to healing, application of the scientific method to test healing prayer, and use of unorthodox terminology. The text only briefly discusses Agnes's specific contributions to Renewal.

Paul Francis Egan submitted *The Development of, and Opposition to, Healing Ministries in the Anglican Diocese of Sydney, with Special Reference to the Healing Ministry at St Andrew's Cathedral 1960-2010* as his doctoral thesis for a Faculty of Arts degree in 2012 to Macquarie University in Australia. This work warrants discussion for several reasons: first, several pages are devoted to discussing Agnes's impact on healing ministry and the Charismatic Movement during its earlies stages; second, Egan provides notable insight into the influences that contributed to the healing theology and ministry of Hollis Colwell as well as the Episcopal Church in New Jersey at the time Agnes was healed; third, the author describes the specific impact Agnes had upon Jim Glennon, an Anglican priest who developed an active and thriving healing ministry; and fourth, the work reveals at least one instance in which Agnes spoke and ministered outside of North American and England. Through his careful and extensive research, Egan links Agnes's ministry with late 19th-century Anglicanism and a healing ministry founded in Australia.

The book *Spirit Cure: A History of Pentecostal Healing* by Joseph W. Williams was published in 2013. The text examines Pentecostal healing practices by comparing them to various medical paradigms and metaphysical traditions of the early twentieth century. After mentioning Agnes's ability "to influence the trajectory of Pentecostal healing," the author states, "few had as significant an impact on pentecostals and charismatics in [regard to inner healing] as the Episcopal laywoman Agnes Sanford."[62] His entire section on inner healing discusses Agnes and those directly influenced by her, and he explains their adaptation of several specific aspects of psychology and New Thought to healing prayer; those are two of the primary influences that affected Agnes's own theology. Williams provides an extremely valuable resource on Agnes's theology by establishing a connection between certain New Thought teachings from the Unity School of Christianity and the mind-cure ideals of numerous early Pentecostal healers.

Brian Stanley wrote *The Global Diffusion of Evangelicalism: The Age of Billy Graham and John Stott* in 2013, volume five of "A History of Evangelicalism" series. He mentions Agnes in the chapter "New Charismatic and Pentecostal Movements," devoting two paragraphs to discussing her influence on the early Charismatic Movement. The author describes an increased interest in divine healing in the Americas and Europe after 1945 "owing in part to the writings and ministry of the American Episcopalian Agnes Sanford," who "had an increasing impact on Britain, as well as on the United States."[63] Although Stanley offers only a brief discussion of Agnes, he references Hocken's *Streams of Renewal* to indicate her significant influence in England. He also attributes an awareness of the baptism of the Holy Spirit among clergy to the Sanfords' ministry through the Schools of Pastoral Care and the Order of St. Luke. Stanley's text gives valuable support for Agnes's contributions within and beyond the United States.

At this point, all the available material containing any substantial discussion of Agnes has been reviewed. Discounting duplicates, these forty sources reflect Agnes's extensive effect on people in many of the mainline denominations before, during, and after the advent of the Charismatic Movement, both in the United States and overseas. Of references to Agnes in books, dissertations, papers, and interviews, authors have evenly divided their focus between her theology and her contributions. Neal and Hardesty mainly review two of her books on healing while De Arteaga and Wise explain the context of her works and argue against the defamatory assessment of Hunt and McMahon. Hansen and Foster identify Agnes as an influential teacher on prayer and provide extended passages from *The Healing Light* for their readers. Hocken and Hosier give a brief synopsis of Agnes's life, ministry, and contributions while Williams and Stanley provide a historical context for her theology and influence. Connelly and the dissertations in the field of Divinity mainly summarize Agnes's life and ministry in the context of the Charismatic Movement while Cerny and the dissertations in the field of Psychology primarily compare her inner healing ministry to models of counseling and psychotherapy. De Arteaga, Hocken, and Stanley additionally describe the contributions Agnes made to defeating cessationism and promoting the baptism of the Holy Spirit.

Acknowledgments

When an author writes a book, the dedication, acknowledgement, foreword, and preface provide an opportunity to identify significant influences and people who deserve recognition or gratitude. These can indicate the extent a person has impacted the lives of others; Agnes has certainly succeeded in doing this. Francis MacNutt, healing minister in the Roman Catholic Church and author of several books, mentions Agnes in the preface to *The Power to Heal*: "In all we do we have tried to build on the foundation we first received from Mrs. Agnes Sanford and other pioneers in the healing ministry."[64] MacNutt similarly references Agnes in every one of his major books as significantly contributing to healing ministry within the Charismatic Movement. In the preface to *Healing and Christianity*, Morton Kelsey attributes Agnes to being responsible for his introduction to the healing ministry; he succeeded her in leading the School of Pastoral Care when she retired. Some other books with similar mentions include *The Power in Penance* by Michael Scanlan, *The Transformation of the Inner Man* by John and Paula Sandford, and *Praying with Another for Healing* by Dennis Linn, Matthew Linn, and Sheila Fabricant.

Leanne Payne often discussed Agnes in her Pastoral Care Ministries schools, describing her ministry as a continuation of Agnes's own. She references Agnes in most of her books, and says, "All who have been blessed in prayer for healing of memories owe a great debt indeed to Agnes Sanford, who pioneered this way of prayer."[65] However, numerous authors reference her on more than just the topic of inner healing. John Gaynor Banks, founder of the Order of St. Luke, wrote in his book on healing, "if you read such a book as *The Healing Light* by Agnes Sanford, the reading of that book for you is religious therapy."[66] MacNutt wrote several books on healing and praying for the sick. Nevertheless, he admits to handing out *The Healing Light* to several of his own friends who were seeking a simple book on praying for the sick.[67] Glenn Clark founded Camps Farthest Out, a focal point for teaching in the early Charismatic Movement. Prior to the publication of Agnes's first book, he declared in an editorial that "for those who would learn how to heal the sick this is the best text ever written."[68] Similar noteworthy references to Agnes are found in numerous other sources, indicating the widespread impact she had not only through her ministry and personal interactions but also through her published works.

Multiple other sources also mention Agnes, but they do so too briefly to qualify for an individual and detailed review of the source; nevertheless, the content reveals her importance to the material. Numerous dedications, acknowledgments, and mentions of Agnes support her extensive contributions and influence upon other ministries although they do not provide a complete picture of her life, ministry, theology, and contributions. Although these brief mentions in various works do not comprehensively examine any of these topics on Agnes, they indicate her important impact on healing ministry, Renewal Studies, and the Charismatic Movement.

Summary

A plethora of sources mention Agnes in significant ways, yet only a handful of full-length works examine her life, ministry, contributions, or influences, none of which do so comprehensively. Of the published books and graduate texts on Agnes, none comprehensively discuss all of these aspects in a unified work. Each focuses on specific aspects of her theology or ministry, usually relying upon only some of her published work; however, a limited scope and method can only provide a limited picture of the whole. Briefer references in journal articles and textual excerpts supply more information on her impact and theology, but they do so in separation from many of the other sources, also usually depending on only one or two of her texts. These substantive secondary sources collectively offer a significantly more accurate analysis and evaluation of Agnes's life and contributions, but they may not fully reflect the extent of her influence on others. Isolated references to Agnes, such as single sentences in a text or a reflection in a book's preface, do not provide new information on her theology but certainly reflect her widespread impact within the Charismatic Movement. Bringing all of these secondary references together provides the opportunity for both a qualitative and quantitative examination and analysis of her life, ministry, theology, contributions, and impact.

Tertiary Sources

As seen, a substantial number of authors discuss or mention Agnes and her life, ministry, theology, and contributions either in works about her or in the context of a related subject. However, her impact on the twentieth century went far beyond specific ministries that developed from her teaching and theology. Many authors consider her an authority in her field and cite her accordingly. While over forty sources discuss Agnes in various contexts, more than three times that many use her works as supporting material, mainly in the fields of Theology, Counseling, and Psychology along with occasional mentions in Anthropology, Sociology, Education, History, and even Paranormal Studies. A review of some select tertiary sources will reflect her influence.

Gordon Dalbey authored an article in *The Christian Century* titled "Recovering Healing Prayer" in 1982. The brief text argues for the entire Christian Church—not just Pentecostal or Charismatic denominations—to reincorporate an active theology of physical healing. The author logically explains how healing prayer combats a secularizing tendency to rely upon science instead of faith; for this reason, a belief in physical healing with all its mystery, uncertainty, and potential shortcomings promotes a dependency upon God. For an article discussing healing prayer in light of a culture devoted to science, the author understandably cites Agnes. In this instance, however, his introduction to the quote outshines the quote itself. He calls her "perhaps the most widely acknowledged authority on healing prayer," before quoting from *The Healing Light*.[69] Dalbey only quotes from the text twice but clearly considers her an authority on the topic.

Stephen Applebaum authored "The Laying on of Health: Personality Patterns of Psychic Healers" in the *Bulletin of the Menninger Clinic* in 1993. The article attempts to identify psychological traits of practitioners involved in healing prayer. In describing the basic structure of his analysis, the author recognizes love as an aspect of healing and provides two quotes as support before continuing on with his discussion; one of the quotes is from Agnes.[70] Again, the actual quote holds less significance here than the author's selection of Agnes as one of the two sources used for the quote. Clearly, authors in the field of psychology consider Agnes a reputable reference source.

In 1984, *The Journal of Pastoral Care* published a volume focused on people involved in pastoral care. In the article "Healing Prayer and Pastoral Care," George M. Furniss describes the important place healing prayer holds in the medical field. He references Agnes's first text, *The Healing Light*, as a "seminal [source] on healing prayer," and in a footnote, he identifies it and *The Healing Gifts of the Spirit* along with two books by Glenn Clark as "the pioneering contributions on the theology of healing prayer."[71] Linda L. Sieh uses similar language to describe Agnes's first book. In "Reclaiming the Church's Healing Ministry" in *Chaplaincy Today*, she states, "one of the most exciting healers in the twentieth century was Agnes Sanford whose seminal book, The *Healing Light*, written in 1947, combined science and faith to explain her own healing ministry."[72] For authors familiar with numerous works in the fields of Psychology and Counseling to consider Agnes's first book a seminal source makes a significant point concerning her impact on those disciplines.

As reflected in these four texts, authors regularly recognize Agnes as an authority in the field of healing prayer. Her first book, *The Healing Light*, appeared more than a decade prior to the recognized beginning of the Charismatic Movement; it not only deeply influenced the movement's theology but also qualifies as a seminal source for some in the field of psychology and counseling. Along with mentions in more than twenty other journal articles, more than ninety additional books, theses, and dissertations cite and reference her books. The number of tertiary sources referencing Agnes reflects the impact she made in multiple fields through her published works and ministry.

Conclusion

A review of the literature related to Agnes Sanford reveals a largely untapped reservoir of information. Her works successfully present the concepts of healing, prayer, and faith in simple and practical concepts. Similar to C. S. Lewis, she wrote material instructive and challenging to scholars and theologians while remaining accessible and understandable by laypersons and children alike. Together, these books provide insight into her life, ministry, and theology. Although Agnes wrote fifteen books, only eight full-length texts have been written about her, none of which fully describe the impact she made on Christianity in the twentieth century. Even the scholarly examinations of her work have identifiable limitations, such as including some primary sources while excluding others in evaluating her theology, resulting in an incomplete view of her work. Additionally, some secondary sources examine Agnes's writings with such a predominantly negative bias that misinterpretations and misquoted passages produce significantly errant conclusions. Nevertheless, numerous published works mention and reference Agnes, sometimes substantially and at other times casually and in recognition of her legacy. She holds a position as an authority in healing prayer in multiple fields, which is reflected in her being cited and referenced as a seminal source in multiple disciplines.

Although a great deal has been written about Agnes, only a small amount has been published compared to her impact on psychology and theology through the early years of the Charismatic Movement. A comprehensive examination and description of her life, ministry, theology, worldview, and contributions remains necessary and vital for the field of Renewal Theology as the Christian Church proceeds in the twenty-first century. This substantial work requires incorporating both the fiction and nonfiction of her primary sources together with the scholarly and personal determinations of secondary and tertiary sources. Together, this material will provide an accurate and decisive understanding of Agnes Sanford and her legacy.

Notes

[1] The original edition includes the subtitle *On the Art and Method of Spiritual Healing from the Christian Viewpoint and in the Christian Tradition*. There is no subtitle in the mass-marketed paperback edition of *The Healing Light* (New York: Ballentine Books, 1983), which is in its thirteenth printing.

[2] The first paperback edition was printed by Harper & Row in 1976.

[3] *Behold Your God* was published in a mass-marketed paperback edition as *The Healing Touch of God* (New York: Ballentine Books, 1983) and was in its fifth printing as of 1987. Agnes considered this book as supernaturally inspired. While discussing the topic of listening to God, she says, "A great deal of the book *Behold Your God* is—well, I don't know if it is direct messages or guidance or the interpretation of tongues or what—but anyway, the words came to me *word for word*, spoken in the first person as though God were speaking; of course, in the book I had to change and say 'He" instead of 'I,' but it came directly." Agnes Sanford, *Our Need to Recognize Our Spiritual Self*, recorded at Camps Farthest Out, n.d., 50:25.

[4] The original edition of this book went through at least six printings and was published in Philadelphia by A. J. Holman Company, in New Jersey by Spire Books, and in New York by Jove Books before it was eventually published in the current paperback format by HarperSanfrancisco in 1984.

[5] Agnes often uses the phrase "mental depressive" when referencing depressed persons.

[6] The book was subsequently published in Philadelphia by A. J. Holman Compnay and in New York by Jove Books before the current paperback format was published in San Francisco by Harper & Row in 1984.

[7] The book has not gone through other editions or printings or become available as a paperback.

[8] The book has only been available as a paperback, and no other editions or printings are known. The Bridge publication was in conjunction with Logos International, so two publishers are identified.

[9] No other editions or printings of the book have been published.

[10] The book was also published through The Order of St. Luke in Indiana and has gone through at least ten printings.

[11] *Lost Shepherd* went through seven printings in hardcover before its paperback printing by Logos and Bridge Publications in New Jersey. In light of her autobiography, readers may consider Paul Forrester to be based on her husband; however, in an unpublished letter with Francis Baltz on December 31, 1977, Agnes states, "[Paul] is not in any way a reflection of Ted, who was as unlike Paul as a person could be."

[12] No additional editions or printings are available apart from the original hardcover publication.

[13] Both novels were only published once as a hardcover in the United States; however, *The Second Mrs. Wu* was also published in England, and *The Rising River* was published in Germany.

[14] While *A Pasture for Peterkin* has gone through three printings as of 1973, *Melissa & the Little Red Book* has not had any further printings or editions.

[15] Agnes Sanford, "Spiritual Healing," in *The church's Ministry of Healing: A Manual for Clergy and Laity*, presented by The Commission on Religion and Health (Los Angeles: The Episcopal Church, The Diocese of Los Angeles, 1964), 10-12.

[16] Agnes Sanford, "The Healing of Memories," *Guideposts* 24, no. 9 (November 1969): 3-6.

[17] Agnes Sanford, "Seeking Earnestly the Best Gifts," *New Covenant* 3, no. 5 (November 1973): 5-7.

[18] Agnes Sanford, "Thy Kingdom Come," 1-3.

[19] Agnes Sanford, "Birth on Death Row," in *God Ventures: True Accounts of God in the Lives of Men*, compiled by Irene Burk Harrell (Plainfield: Logos International, 1970), 102-104.

[20] Agnes Sanford, *How to Learn* (Cincinnati: Forward Movement Publications, 1965).

[21] Agnes Sanford, "Homosexuality and Prayer," *School of Pastoral Care*. Westboro: School of Pastoral Care, n.d

[22] Jane Gumprecht, *Abusing Memory*, 5-8.

[23] William DeArteaga, *Agnes Sanford and Her Companions*, 1-2.

[24] William De Arteaga, *Agnes Sanford and Her Companions*, 3.

[25] Annet B. Wannamaker, "A Psychosynthesis Study of Agnes Sanford's Practice and Theology of Prayer Healing" (doctoral dissertation, Institute of Transpersonal Psychology, 1989), 4, ProQuest (DTN DP14283).

[26] Annet Wannamaker, "A Psychosynthesis Study," 2.

[27] Pavel Hejzlar, "Two Paradigms for Divine Healing," 1.

[28] Francis Baltz, "Agnes Sanford," 1-3.

[29] As noted by De Arteaga, Baltz provides the most complete biographical account of Agnes available to date. While completing his thesis, Baltz sent letters to Agnes, and she dictated responses to him through Edith Drury, her personal attendant during her later years after she had retired from ministry. Baltz has provided this author with original correspondence received from Edith Drury; information from these letters is primarily contained in footnotes as "Personal correspondence from Drury to Baltz."

[30] Mary Ann Molinari, "Inner Healing in the Perspective of Agnes Sanford" (master's thesis, University of St. Michael's College, Toronto School of Theology, 1980), 2.

[31] Colin James Cross, "Agnes Sanford and the Heritage of Inner Healing" (master's thesis, Regent College, University of British Columbia, 1986), 5. Italicized material originally underlined in source.

[32] Colin James Cross, "Agnes Sanford and the Heritage of Inner Healing," 12, 14.

[33] Two books by Hunt and McMahon are discussed in the *Constituent References* section.

[34] Donald L. Clark, "Theory of Personality, Illness, and Cure Found in the Writings of Agnes Sanford and Those Acknowledging Her Influence," *Journal of Psychology and Theology* 17, no. 3 (Fall 1989): 236.

[35] Henry H. Knight III, "God's Faithfulness and God's Freedom," 65-89.

[36] William De Arteaga, "Agnes Sanford: Apostle of Healing, Part 1 of 2," 8.

[37] William De Arteaga, "Agnes Sanford: Apostle of Healing, and First Theologian of the Charismatic Renewal; Part 2 of 2," 4-5.

[38] Judith Agaoglu, "Agnes Sanford: Pioneer in Healing Ministry and Apostle of the Healing Light of Christ," *The Journal of Christian Healing* 23, no. 1 (Spring/Summer 2007): 5.

[39] Emily Gardiner Neal, *God Can Heal You Now*, 184.

[40] James T. Connelly, "Neo-Pentecostalism: The Charismatic Revival in the Mainline Protestant and Roman Catholic Churches of the United States, 1960-1971" (doctoral dissertation, University of Chicago, 1977), ProQuest (DTN: T-26529), 183.

[41] Richard Cotner, "Pentecost and Its Discontents" (doctoral dissertation, University of Missouri - Columbia, 2004), ProQuest (DTN: 3137689), 290-295.

[42] Konkhogin (Hagin) Haokip, "Increasing Knowledge about Divine Healing within the Leadership of an Immigrant Asian Baptist Church" (doctoral dissertation, Oral Roberts University, 2007), ProQuest (DTN 3350991), 87-90.

[43] Dave Hunt and T. A. McMahon, *Seduction of Christianity*, 7. Hunt repeats his concerns about Sanford in his sequel. See Dave Hunt, *Beyond Seduction*, 204ff.

[44] Dave Hunt and T. A. McMahon, *Seduction of Christianity*, 125.

[45] Dave Hunt and T. A. McMahon, *Seduction of Christianity*, 78.

[46] Bethyl Joy Midura, "Psychodynamic, Existential, and Religious Views Pertaining to Psychological Healing: A Comparative Analysis" (doctoral dissertation, Rosemead School of Psychology, Biola University, 1981), ProQuest (DTN 8118199), 26-29, 47-49, 83-87.

[47] Frank Stafford Davis, "Charismatic Christian Spiritual Healing in Two Cultural Contexts: An Existential-Phenomenological Approach" (doctoral dissertation, Duquesne University, 1990), ProQuest (DTN 9030679), 94-96.

[48] Emmet L. Jones, "A Study of Traditional Prayer, Inner Healing Prayer and Psychological Well-being among Evangelical Christians" (doctoral dissertation, California School of Professional Psychology - Los Angeles, 1998), ProQuest (DTN 9831023), 38-42.

[49] Linda Hunter, "Ethical Issues in the use of Prayer in Clinical Practice: An Examination of Theophostic Prayer Ministry" (doctoral dissertation, Regent University, 2008), ProQuest (DTN 3292116), 23-27.

[50] Merilee Brooke Lovejoy, "Examining the Influence of Prayer Counseling on Client Levels of Depression, Anxiety, Spiritual Well-being, and Surrender to God" (doctoral dissertation, Seattle Pacific University, 2010), ProQuest (DTN 3398991), 34-35.

[51] M. Elliott Hattendorf, "Immanuel: Narrative Case Studies Exploring Inner Healing

in Clinical Settings" (doctoral dissertation, Regent University, 2014), ProQuest (DTN 3636216), 23-30.

⁵² Peter D. Hocken, *Streams of Renewal*, 7.

⁵³ Peter D. Hocken, *Streams of Renewal*, 181.

⁵⁴ Peter D. Hocken, "Sanford, Agnes Mary" in *DPCM*, 767; see also, *NIDPCM*, 1039.

⁵⁵ Nancy A. Hardesty, "The Healing Gifts of the Spirit," in *Christian Spirituality: The Essential Guide to the Most Influential Spiritual Writings of the Christian Tradition*, ed. Frank N. Magill and Ian P. McGreal (San Francisco: Harper & Row, 1988), 622.

⁵⁶ Helen Kooiman Hosier, *100 Christian Women Who Changed the Twentieth Century* (Grand Rapids: Baker Book House, 2000), 373.

⁵⁷ William DeArteaga, "Glenn Clark's Camps Furthest Out," 265, 279, 284. Note: footnote 2 on page 265 states, "neither Glenn Clark and his CFO nor Agnes Sanford are given separate articles in the *Dictionary [of Pentecostal and Charismatic Movements]*" published in 1988, but *DPCM* does have an entry on Agnes. Also, the official name of the organization was Camps Farthest Out.

⁵⁸ William DeArteaga, "From Radical Idealism to Pentecostalism," 3.

⁵⁹ David Kyle Foster, "Interview - Francis & Judith MacNutt."

⁶⁰ The condensed interview, which is titled "A Conversation with Francis and Judith MacNutt" on *The Pneuma Review* website at http://pneumareview.com/conversation-with-francis-and-judith-macnutt/ registers with search engines as posted March 21, 2014 but has a listed date of September 20, 2007; it is unlikely the condensed version became available a year prior to the longer interview, so the later date is likely correct.

⁶¹ Gary Neal Hansen, *Kneeling with Giants: Learning to Pray with History's Best Teachers* (Downers Grove: InterVarsity Press, 2012), 177.

⁶² Joseph W. Williams, *Spirit Cure*, 84, 100.

⁶³ Brian Stanley, *The Global Diffusion of Evangelicalism: The Age of Billy Graham and John Stott*, vol. 5, *A History of Evangelicalism: People, Movements and Ideas in the English-Speaking World* (Downers Grove: IVP Academic, 2013), 183-184.

⁶⁴ Francis MacNutt, *The Power to Heal*, 10.

⁶⁵ Leanne Payne, *Heaven's Calling*, 217. Note: Sanford is not mentioned in *Real Presence*, Payne's dissertation on C. S. Lewis, which was published prior to their friendship.

⁶⁶ John Gaynor Banks, *Healing Everywhere*, 86.

⁶⁷ Francis MacNutt, *The Prayer That Heals: Praying for Healing in the Family* (Notre Dame: Ave Maria Press, 2000), 12.

⁶⁸ Glenn Clark, review of *The Healing Light*, 10.

⁶⁹ Gordon Dalbey, "Recovering Healing Prayer." *The Christian Century* 99, no. 21 (June 1982): 691.

⁷⁰ Stephen A. Appelbaum, "The Laying on of Health: Personality Patterns of Psychic Healers." *Bulletin of the Menninger Clinic* 51, no. 1 (Winter 1993): 38.

⁷¹ George M. Furniss, "Healing Prayer and Pastoral Care." *The Journal of Pastoral Care* 38, no. 2 (June 1984): 108-9.

⁷² Linda L. Sieh, "Reclaiming the Church's Healing Ministry," *Chaplaincy Today* 15, no. 2 (January 1999): 18.

BIBLIOGRAPHY

Primary Sources [chronologically]

Sanford, Agnes. *The Healing Light: On the Art and Method of Spiritual Healing from the Christian Viewpoint and in the Christian Tradition*. 2nd ed. St. Paul: Macalester Park, 1947.

———. *Oh Watchman!: A Novel*. Philadelphia: Lippincott, 1950.

———. *Lost Shepherd: A Moving Novel of Life in the Spirit*. New York: J. B. Lippincott, 1953.

———. *A Healing Mission of Agnes Sanford*. Transcribed lectures by Agnes Sanford at St. Paul's Cathedral. Detroit: Fellowship of the Concerned, 1954. 56 pages.

———. *Let's Believe*. New York: Harper & Row, 1954.

———. *A Pasture for Peterkin*. Saint Paul: Macalester Park, 1956.

———. *Behold Your God*. [St. Paul: Macalester Park, 1958]. Saint Paul: Macalester Park, 1989.

———. "Homosexuality and Prayer." *School of Pastoral Care*. Westboro: School of Pastoral Care, n.d.

———. *Dreams Are for Tomorrow*. Philadelphia: J. B. Lippincott, 1963.

———. "Spiritual Healing." In *The church's Ministry of Healing: A Manual for Clergy and Laity*, presented by The Commission on Religion and Health, 10-12. Los Angeles: The Episcopal Church, The Diocese of Los Angeles, 1964.

———. *How to Learn*. Cincinnati: Forward Movement Publications, 1965.

———. *The Second Mrs. Wu*. Philadelphia: J. B. Lippincott, 1965.

———. *The Healing Gifts of the Spirit*. New York: J. B. Lippincott, 1966.

———. *The Rising River*. New York: J. B. Lippincott, 1968.

———. *The Healing Power of the Bible*. San Francisco: Harper & Row, 1969.

———. "The Healing of Memories." *Guideposts* 24, no. 9 (November 1969): 3-6.

———. "Birth on Death Row." In *God Ventures: True Accounts of God in the Lives of Men*, compiled by Irene Burk Harrell, 102-104. Plainfield: Logos International, 1970.

———. *Twice Seven Words*. Plainfield: Logos, 1971.

———. "Thy Kingdom Come." *Weekly Unity* 63, no. 9 (June 1971): 1-3.
———. *Sealed Orders*. South Plainfield: Bridge, 1972.
———. "Seeking Earnestly the Best Gifts." *New Covenant* 3, no. 5 (November 1973): 5-7.
———. *Route 1*. Plainfield: Logos, 1975.
———. *Melissa and the Little Red Book*. Saint Paul: Macalester Park, 1976.
———. *Creation Waits*. Plainfield: Logos, 1978.

Secondary Sources [alphabetically]

Agaoglu, Judith. "Agnes Sanford: Pioneer in Healing Ministry and Apostle of the Healing Light of Christ." *The Journal of Christian Healing* 23, no. 1 (Spring/Summer 2007): 5-9.
Baltz, Francis Burkhardt. "Agnes Sanford: A Creative Intercessor." Master's thesis, Nashotah House, 1979. ProQuest (DTN 1313475).
Banks, John Gayner. *Healing Everywhere: A Book of Healing Mission Talks*. Logansport: St. Lukes Press, 1961.
Boa, Kenneth. *Conformed to His Image: Biblical and Practical Approaches to Spiritual Formation*. Grand Rapids: Zondervan, 2001.
Brown, W. Dale. "We're All So Hungry: An Interview with Frederick Buechner." *The Reformed Journal* 40, no. 3 (March 1990): 12-20.
Burgess, Stanley M., ed. *The New International Dictionary of Pentecostal and Charismatic Movements*. Grand Rapids: Zondervan, 2003.
Cerny, Patricia E. "A Psychological Evaluation of Inner Healers." PhD diss., Rosemead School of Psychology, Biola University, 1986. ProQuest (DTN 8616812).
Clark, Donald L. "Theory of Personality, Illness, and Cure Found in the Writings of Agnes Sanford and Those Acknowledging Her Influence." *Journal of Psychology and Theology* 17, no. 3 (Fall 1989): 236-244.
Clark, Glenn. Review of *The Healing Light*, by Agnes Sanford. "Healing Marches On." *Sharing* 15 (May 1947):10.
Connelly, James Thomas. "Neo-Pentecostalism: The Charismatic Revival in the Mainline Protestant and Roman Catholic Churches in the United States, 1960-1971." PhD diss., University of Chicago, 1977. ProQuest (DTN T-26529).
Cotner, Richard. "Pentecost and its Discontents." PhD diss., University of Missouri - Columbia, 2004. ProQuest (DTN 3137689).
Cross, Colin James. "Agnes Sanford and the Heritage of Inner Healing." Master's thesis, Regent College, University of British Columbia, 1986. Ottawa: National Library of Canada Microfilms, 1986.
Davis, Frank Stafford. "Charismatic Christian Spiritual Healing in Two Cultural Contexts: An Existential-Phenomenological Approach." PhD diss., Duquesne University, 1990. ProQuest (DTN 9030679).

DeArteaga, William L. "Glenn Clark's Camps Furthest Out: The Schoolhouse of the Charismatic Renewal." *Pneuma* 25, no. 2 (Fall 2003): 265-288.
———. "Agnes Sanford: Apostle of Healing, and First Theologian of the Charismatic Renewal; Part 1 of 2." *Pneuma Review* 9, no. 2 (Spring: 2006): 6-17.
———. "Agnes Sanford: Apostle of Healing, and First Theologian of the Charismatic Renewal; Part 2 of 2." *Pneuma Review* 9, no. 3 (Summer: 2006): 4-17.
———. "The Charismatic Renewal." *The Pneuma Review*. March 20, 2014. http://pneumareview.com/conversation-with-francis-and-judith-macnutt/
———. "Introducing Francis and Judith MacNutt." *The Pneuma Review*. September 21, 2007, accessed September 26, 2016. http://pneumareview.com/introducing-francis-and-judith-macnutt/
———. "From Radical Idealism to Pentecostalism: Three Pioneers; Glenn Clark, Rufus Moseley and Agnes Sanford." Paper presented at the 37th Annual meeting of the Society for Pentecostal Studies in Durham, North Carolina, March 13-15, 2008: 1-22.
———. *Quenching the Spirit: Examining Centuries of Opposition to the Moving of the Holy Spirit*. Lake Mary: Creation House, 1992.
———. *Agnes Sanford and Her Companions: The Assault on Cessationism and the Coming of the Charismatic Renewal*. Eugene: Wipf & Stock, 2015.
Dignard, Martin L. "God's Faithful Freedom: Healing as an Outflow of God's Presence." *Journal of Pentecostal Theology* 23, no. 1 (Spring 2014): 68-84.
———. "The Scientific Method in the Healing Paradigm of Agnes Sanford." Paper presented at The Holy Spirit, Science, and Theological Education Conference, Virginia Beach, March 2016.
Foster, David Kyle. "Interview – Francis & Judith MacNutt." Interview. *Masteringlife.org*. September 1, 2008. http://masteringlife.org/index.php/mastering-life/articles/miscellaneous/item/35-interview-francis-judith-macnutt
———. "A Conversation with Francis and Judith MacNutt." Interview. *The Pneuma Review*. March 20, 2014. http://pneumareview.com/conversation-with-francis-and-judith-macnutt/
Gumprecht, Jane. *Abusing Memory: The Healing Theology of Agnes Sanford*. Rev. ed. Moscow, ID: Canon Press, 2010.
Hansen, Gary Neal. *Kneeling with Giants: Learning to Pray with History's Best Teachers*. Downers Grove: InterVarsity Press, 2012.
Haokip, Konkhogin (Hagin). "Increasing Knowledge about Divine Healing within the Leadership of an Immigrant Asian Baptist Church." DMin diss., Oral Roberts University, 2007. ProQuest (DTN 3350991).
Hardesty, Nancy A. "The Healing Gifts of the Spirit." in *Christian Spirituality: The Essential Guide to the Most Influential Spiritual Writings of the Christian Tradition*, edited by Frank N. Magill and Ian P. McGreal, 622-626. San Francisco: Harper & Row, 1988.
Hattendorf, M. E. "Immanuel: Narrative Case Studies Exploring Inner Healing in Clinical Settings." PhD diss., Regent University, 2014. ProQuest (DTN 3636216).
Hegy, Pierre. "The Healing of Brokenness: A New Spirituality." Review of *The*

Healing Light and *The Healing Gifts of the Spirit*, by Agnes Sanford. In "Book Reviews" by Jeffrey K. Hadden, ed. *Journal for the Scientific Study of Religion* 17, no. 2 (June 1978): 181-184.

Hejzlar, Pavel. "Two Paradigms for Divine Healing: Fred F. Bosworth, Kenneth E. Hagin, Agnes Sanford, and Francis MacNutt in Dialogue." PhD diss., Fuller Theological Seminary, School of Theology, 2009. ProQuest (DTN 3345063).

Hocken, Peter D. "Charismatic Movement." In *The Dictionary of Pentecostal and Charismatic Movements*, edited by Stanley M. Burgess, Gary B. McGee, and Patrick H. Alexander, 130-160. Grand Rapids: Zondervan, 1988.

———. "Charismatic Movement." In *The New International Dictionary of Pentecostal and Charismatic Movements*, edited by Stanley M. Burgess and Ed M. Van der Maas, 477-519. Grand Rapids: Zondervan, 2002.

———. "Sanford, Agnes Mary." In *The Dictionary of Pentecostal and Charismatic Movements*, edited by Stanley M. Burgess, Gary B. McGee, and Patrick H. Alexander, 767. Grand Rapids: Zondervan, 1988.

———. "Sanford, Agnes Mary." In *The New International Dictionary of Pentecostal and Charismatic Movements*, edited by Stanley M. Burgess and Ed M. Van der Maas, 1039. Grand Rapids: Zondervan, 2002.

———. *Streams of Renewal: The Origins and Early Development of the Charismatic Movement in Great Britain*. Washington, D.C.: Word Among Us, 1986.

Hosier, Helen Kooiman. *100 Christian Women Who Changed the Twentieth Century*. Grand Rapids: Baker Book House, 2000.

Hunt, Dave. *Beyond Seduction: A Return to Biblical Christianity*. Eugene: Harvest House, 1987.

Hunt, David and T. A. McMahon. *The Seduction of Christianity: Spiritual Discernment in the Last Days*. Eugene: Harvest House, 1985.

Hunter, Linda. "Ethical Issues in the use of Prayer in Clinical Practice: An Examination of Theophostic Prayer Ministry." PhD diss., Regent University, 2008. ProQuest (DTN 3292116).

Jeremiah, David and Carole C. Carlson. *Invasion of Other Gods: The Seduction of New Age Spirituality*. Dallas: Word Publishing Group, 1995.

Johnson, Susanne. "Selected Bibliography on Spirituality, Formation and Direction." *Perkins Journal* 38, no. 2 (Winter 1985): 27-40.

Jones, Emmett L. "A Study of Traditional Prayer, Inner Healing Prayer and Psychological Well-being among Evangelical Christians." PhD diss., California School of Professional Psychology - Los Angeles, 1998. ProQuest (DTN 9831023).

Kelsey, Morton. *Healing and Christianity: In Ancient Thought and Modern Times*. New York: Harper and Row, 1973.

———. *Healing & Christianity: A Classic Study*. Minneapolis: Augsburg, 1995.

Knight, Henry H. III. "God's Faithfulness and God's Freedom: A Comparison of Contemporary Theologies of Healing." *Journal of Pentecostal Theology* 1, no. 2 (April 2003): 65-89.

Lovejoy, Merilee Brooke. "Examining the Influence of Prayer Counseling on

Client Levels of Depression, Anxiety, Spiritual Well-being, and Surrender to God." PhD diss., Seattle Pacific University, 2010. ProQuest (DTN 3398991).

MacNutt, Francis. *Healing*. Notre Dame: Ave Maria, 2009.

———. *The Nearly Perfect Crime: How the Church Almost Killed the Ministry of Healing*. Grand Rapids: Chosen Books, 2005.

———. *The Power to Heal*. Notre Dame: Ave Maria, 1985.

———. *The Practice of Healing Prayer: A How-To Guide for Catholics*. Frederick: The Word Among Us Press, 2010.

———. *The Prayer That Heals: Praying for Healing in the Family*. Notre Dame: Ave Maria Press, 2000.

Midura, Bethyl J. "Psychodynamic, Existential, and Religious Views Pertaining to Psychological Healing: A Comparative Analysis." PhD diss., Rosemead School of Psychology, Biola University, 1981. ProQuest (DTN 8118199).

Molinari, Mary Ann. "Inner Healing in the Perspective of Agnes Sanford." Master's thesis, University of St. Michael's College, Toronto School of Theology, 1980.

Neal, Emily Gardiner. *God Can Heal You Now*. Englewood Cliffs: Prentice-Hall, 1958.

Payne, Leanne. *Heaven's Calling: A Memoir of One Soul's Steep Ascent*. Grand Rapids: Baker Books, 2008.

Pearson, Mark A. *Christian Healing: A Practical and Comprehensive Guide*. Grand Rapids: Chosen Books, 2000.

Reid, Thomas F., Mark Virkler, James A. Laine, and Alan Langstaff. *Seduction?? A Biblical Response*. New Wilmington: Son-Rise Publications and Distribution, 1986.

Sandford, John & Paula. *The Transformation of the Inner Man*. Tulsa: Victory House, 1982.

Stanley, Brian. *The Global Diffusion of Evangelicalism: The Age of Billy Graham and John Stott*. Vol. 5 of *A History of Evangelicalism: People, Movements and Ideas in the English-Speaking World*. Downers Grove: IVP Academic, 2013.

Vaswig, William L. *I Prayed, He Answered*. Minneapolis: Augsburg Publishing House, 1977.

Wannamaker, Anett Botolfsen. "A Psychosynthesis Study of Agnes Sanford's Practice and Theology of Prayer Healing." PhD diss., Institute of Transpersonal Psychology, 1989. ProQuest (DTN DP14283).

Williams, Joseph W. "The Transformation of Pentecostal Healing, 1906-2006." PhD diss., Department of Religion, Florida State University, 2008.

———. *Spirit Cure: A History of Pentecostal Healing*. New York: Oxford University Press, 2013.

Wise, Robert, Paul Yonggi Cho, Dennis & Rita Bennett, John Wesley, Jim Glennon, Trevor Dearing, Kathryn Kuhlman, Mark Virkler, Clare Weakley, Bill De Arteaga, and M. L. Huffman. *The Church Divided: The Holy Spirit and a Spirit of Seduction*. South Plainfield: Bridge Publishing, 1986.

Tertiary Sources [alphabetically]

Ahn, Tae-Gil. "Healing Shame in a Korean Context: The Contributions of Heinz Kohut and Donald Eric Capps." PhD diss., Southern Baptist Theological Seminary, 1998. ProQuest (DTN 9917216).

Allen, Victoria S. "Listening to Your Life: Psychology and Judeo-Christian Spirituality in the Novels of Frederick Buechner." PhD diss., Catholic University of America, 1999. ProQuest (DTN 9925217).

Alsdurf, James M. "Personality Theory or Spiritual Discernment? A Reaction to Clark." *Journal of Psychology and Theology* 17, no. 3 (Fall 1989): 245-249.

Alsdurf, Jim M. and H. Newton Malony. "A Critique of Ruth Carter Stapleton's Ministry of 'Inner Healing.'" *Journal of Psychology and Theology* 8, no. 3 (Fall 1980): 173-184.

Appelbaum, S. A. "The Laying on of Health: Personality Patterns of Psychic Healers." *Bulletin of the Menninger Clinic* 51, no. 1 (Winter 1993): 33-40.

Armstrong, Priya Ananda. "An American Gurukula: A Hermeneutic Process of Healing through Learning." EdD diss., University of San Francisco, 1996. ProQuest (DTN 9627298).

Ashbrook, R. Thomas. "Mansions of the Heart: A Spiritual Formation Paradigm for the Church Based on Teresa of Avila's Seven Mansions." DMin diss., George Fox University, George Fox Evangelical Seminary, 2003. ProQuest (DTN 3080389).

Baca, Jack Willard. "A Plan for Discipleship at the Village Community Presbyterian Church." DMin diss., Fuller Theological Seminary, Doctor of Ministry Program, 2001. ProQuest (DTN 3047167).

Banks, Ethel Tulloch. "The Healing Light." *Sharing* 15 (August 1947): 3.

Banks, John Gaynor. "Healing Marches On: A New Book on Healing." *Sharing* 15 (May 1947): 10.

Baxter, Harold Jason. "Touched by Fire and Laughter: The Range of Grace in the Fiction of Flannery O'Connor and Frederick Buechner." PhD diss., Florida State University, 1983. ProQuest (DTN 8408939).

Bernardino, Nomeriano De La Cruz. "An Effective Training Program in Biblical Preaching for Filipino Pastors in Metro-Manila." DMin diss., Regent University, 2002. ProQuest (DTN 3042323).

Boggs, Wade H. Jr. "The Bible and Modern Religions: Faith Healing Cults." *Interpretation* 11, no. 1 (January 1957): 55-70.

Brooke, Avery. *Healing in the Landscape of Prayer*. Cambridge: Cowley, 1996.

Brown, Willard Dale. "Frederick Buechner: An Introduction." PhD diss., University of Missouri - Columbia, 1987. ProQuest (DTN 8728793).

Buechner, Frederick. *Now and Then: A Memoir of Vocation*. San Francisco: Harper Collins, 1983.

Burt, Paula Joan. "Emotional Healing and Deliverance for Women." DMin diss., Oral Roberts University, 1999. ProQuest (DTN 9935192).

Butera, Robert James, Jr. "A Comprehensive Yoga Lifestyle Program for People

Living with HIV/AIDS." PhD diss., California Institute of Integral Studies, 1998. ProQuest (DTN 9904980).

Cartledge, Mark J. *Practical Theology: Charismatic and Empirical Perspectives*. Studies in Pentecostal and Charismatic Issues. Waynesboro: Paternoster Press, 2003.

Castigliano, Serge A. "Implications of Paranormal Healing Phenomena for the Theory and Practice of Pastoral Counseling." PhD diss., Saint Louis University, 1981. ProQuest (DTN 8207392).

Cerny, Leonard J. II. "Reaction to a Critique of Ruth Carter Stapleton's Ministry of 'Inner Healing.'" *Journal of Psychology and Theology* 8, no. 3 (Fall 1980): 198-203.

Chordas, Thomas John. "Building the Kingdom: The Creativity of Ritual Performance in Catholic Pentecostalism." PhD diss., Duke University, 1980. ProQuest (DTN 8105655).

Christenson, Larry, ed. *Welcome Holy Spirit: A Study of Charismatic Renewal in the Church*. Minneapolis: Augsburg Publishing House, 1987.

Clark, Gary Kenneth. "A Strategy for Advancing the Spirit-Filled Renewal Movement among American Baptist Pastors through the Holy Spirit Renewal Ministries." DMin diss., Fuller Theological Seminary, Doctor of Ministry Program, 2000. ProQuest (DTN 9992514).

Clift, Jean Dalby. "The Beginning of My Healing Ministry." *American Journal of Pastoral Counseling* 6, no. 2 (January 2003): 63-66.

Colletti, Peter. "The Efficacy of Intercessory Prayer in Healing." DMin diss., Saint Mary Seminary and Graduate School of Theology, 2007. ProQuest (DTN 3258626).

Cooperstein, M. Allan. "Consciousness and Cognition in Alternative Healers: An Interim Report on Research into the Relationship of Belief, Healing, and Purported Subtle Energies." *Subtle Energies & Energy Medicine* 7, no. 3 (1996): 185-237.

Cowan, Douglas Edward. "'Bearing False Witness': Propaganda, Reality-Maintenance, and Christian Anticult Apologetics." PhD diss., University of Calgary (Canada), 1999. ProQuest (DTN NQ38462).

Craig, Steven Harland. "Integrating Faith and Practice through a Four-Dimensional Process Model of Disciple-Making." DMin diss., Fuller Theological Seminary, Doctor of Ministry Program, 2001. ProQuest (DTN 3013533).

Crane, Sidney D. "The Gift of Prophecy in the New Testament: An Inductive Study in the Exercise and meaning of the Prophetic." ThD diss., Princeton Theological Seminary, 1962. ProQuest (DTN 6205845).

Cremeens, Timothy Brant. "Marginalized Voices: The History of the Charismatic Movement in the Orthodox Church in North America 1968-1993." PhD diss., Regent University, 2011. ProQuest (3485989).

Cuthbert, Priscilla DuBose. "The Importance of both having and Giving Hope: The Cancer Survivor Volunteer's Experience of Working with Recently Diagnosed Cancer Patients." PhD diss., Union Institute, 1994. ProQuest (DTN 9502054).

Dalbey, Gordon. "Recovering Healing Prayer." *The Christian Century* 99, no. 21

(June 1982): 690-693.

Davenport, Bryan R. "Helping the Hurting: Everyday Approaches to Healing and Deliverance." DMin diss., Assemblies of God Theological Seminary, 2013. ProQuest (DTN 3602290).

Dawe, Victor Gladstone. "The Attitude of the Ancient Church toward Sickness and Healing." PhD diss., Boston University School of Theology, 1955. ProQuest (DTN 0014173).

Dawson, Connie. "John Wimber: A Biographical Sketch of His Life and Ministry in America." PhD diss., Regent University, 2012. ProQuest (DTN 3510650).

Day, Tammerie. "Constructing Solidarity: A Theology of Liberation." PhD diss., Southern Methodist University, 2009. ProQuest (DTN 3356155).

Dickens, Glynn R. "Developing a Model for the Training of Believers to Practice the Healing Ministry of Christ." DMin diss., Oral Roberts University, 2007. ProQuest (DTN 3405449).

Eddings, Donnie Rose. "A Seminar Presenting the Team Approach to Prayer for the Psychological, Spiritual, and Physical Healing of People in Foursquare Churches in Southern California." DMin diss., Oral Roberts University, 1997. ProQuest (DTN 9732810).

Egan, Paul Francis. "The Development of, and Opposition to, Healing Ministries in the Anglican Diocese of Sydney, with Special Reference to the Healing Ministry of St Andrew's Cathedral 1960-2010." PhD thesis, 2012.

Entwistle, David N. "Shedding Light on Theophostic Ministry 1: Practice Issues." *Journal of Psychology and Theology* 32, no. 1 (Spring 2004): 26-34.

Epperly, Bruce G. "A Healing Ministry for the United Church of Christ? Theological Reflections for the Twenty-First Century." *Prism* 13, no. 2 (Fall 1998): 69-77.

Estes, Ted B. "Passing on the Healing Ministry of Jesus at Claremore Christian Fellowship through Training Believers to Pray for the Sick." DMin diss., Oral Roberts University, 1996. ProQuest (DTN 9700117).

Foster, Richard J. and Emilie Griffin, eds. *Spiritual Classics: Selected Readings for Individuals and Groups on the Twelve Disciplines.* New York: HarperOne, 2000.

Furniss, George M. "Healing Prayer and Pastoral Care." *The Journal of Pastoral Care* 38, no. 2 (June 1984): 107-119.

Garzon, Fernando, Everett L. Worthington Jr., Siang-Yang Tan, & R. Kirby Worthington. "Lay Christian Counseling and Client Expectations for Integration in Therapy." *Journal of Psychology and Christianity* 28, no. 2 (Summer 2009): 113-120.

Glennon, Jim. *Your Healing is Within You.* Plainfield: Logos International, 1980.

Gunter, Paul Stewart. "A Case Study of the Prayer Ministry of Yoido Full Gospel Church." DMin diss., Dallas Theological Seminary, 1987. ProQuest (DTN 8729702).

Harrison, Sandra Marleen. "Inner Healing and Secular Psychotherapy: Methodological Similarities." PhD diss., Emory University, 1987. ProQuest (DTN 8716114).

Hejzlar, Pavel. "Two Paradigms for Divine Healing: Fred F. Bosworth, Kenneth

E. Hagin, Agnes Sanford, and Francis MacNutt in Dialogue." PhD diss., Fuller Theological Seminary, School of Theology, 2009. ProQuest (DTN 3345063).

Helming, Mary Ann Blaszko. "The Lived Experience of being Healed through Prayer in Adults Active in a Christian Church." PhD diss., Union Institute and University, 2007. ProQuest (DTN 3273550).

Hinton, Keith William. "An analytical Study of the Dynamics of Spiritual Renewal." DMis diss., Fuller Theological Seminary, School of World Mission, 1984. ProQuest (DTN 8411205).

Hocken, Peter D. "Payne, Leanne." In *The New International Dictionary of Pentecostal and Charismatic Movements*, edited by Stanley M. Burgess and Ed M. Van der Maas, 959. Grand Rapids: Zondervan, 2002.

Homan, Terry Ann. "Psychic Alternative Healing Techniques and Teaching in Anchorage, Alaska Today." Master's thesis, University of Alaska Anchorage, 1998. ProQuest (DTN 1391154).

Hughes, Wayne Richard. "Healing Touch: A Path to Transformation." Master's thesis, St. Stephen's College (Canada), 2010. ProQuest (DTN MR80130).

Hwang, Seung Hwan. "Experiencing Divine Healing through Spiritual Training." DMin diss., Oral Roberts University, 2000. ProQuest (DTN 9989298).

Jaggs, W. Kenneth. "An Analysis of Innovations in the Health Care Delivery System through a Study of Wholistic Health Centres in Hinsdale, Illinois and Windsor, Ontario." Master's thesis, University of Windsor (Canada), 1985. ProQuest (DTN ML20102).

Jewell, Suk Cha. "The Change of Attitude about Healing in Korean Immigrant Church." DMin diss., Oral Roberts University, 2005. ProQuest (DTN 3191955).

Johanson, Gregory John. "Making Grace Specific: The Renewed Chapter of Spirituality in the History of White, Mainline Protestant Pastoral Care in America." PhD diss., Drew University, 1999. ProQuest (DTN 9949072).

Johnston, Britton W. "Breaching the Sacred Walls of Illness: A Girardian Model of Forgiveness as Healing." *Journal of Spirituality in Mental Health* 12, no. 2 (Apr-Jun 2010): 118-149.

Kim, Daniel Johnguk. "A Review of Literature in the Contemporary Prophetic Movement." Master's thesis, Fuller Theological Seminary, School of World Mission, 1995. ProQuest (DTN 1377172).

Kim, Yoo-Min. "Developing a Course on Divine Healing in an Educational Setting." DMin diss., Oral Roberts University, 2003. ProQuest (DTN 3112968).

Kim, Yoon Oh. "Increasing the Biblical Knowledge of Divine Healing in a Korean Methodist Church." DMin diss., Oral Roberts University, 2006. ProQuest (DTN 3248916).

Kim, Young Jea. "A Case Study in the Healing Ministry of the New Generation Church." DMin diss., Regent University, 2001. ProQuest (DTN 3012204).

Kim-van Daalen, Lydia,Cornelia Willemina. "Emotions in Christian Psychological Care." PhD diss., Southern Baptist Theological Seminary, 2013. ProQuest (DTN 3562527).

King, Deborah. *Be Your Own Shaman: Heal Yourself and Others with 21st-Century Energy Medicine*. Carlsbad: Hay House, 2011.

Kovarik, Kathleen C. "Hearts for Healing: An Interpretive Biography of the Journey of Pioneers in Christian Inner Healing." PhD diss., Gonzaga University, 2011. ProQuest (DTN 3452827).

Kristo, Jure. "Minneapolis Conference on Mysticism and Everyday Life." *Journal of Ecumenical Studies* 16 no. 4 (Fall 1979): 823-824.

Lawson, Kevin Duwan. "Popular Television, Cultural Worldviews, and Christian Discernment." DMin diss., Biola University, 2013. ProQuest (DTN 3560642).

Learman, Jo Ann. "The Healing Debate among Lutheran Churches." *Currents in Theology and Mission* 12, no. 1 (Fall 1985): 40-44.

Lee, Keonho. "Doing Inner Healing Ministry in a Korean Way: A Communal Approach to Inner Healing." PhD diss., Fuller Theological Seminary, School of World Mission, 2003. ProQuest (DTN 3091860).

Leshan, Lawrence. *The Medium, the Mystic, and the Physicist: Toward a General Theory of the Paranormal*. New York: The Viking Press, 1974.

Liias, Jürgen W. "Charismatic Power or Military Power?" *The Christian Century* 100, no. 36 (November 1983): 1110-1113.

Linn, Dennis, Matthew Linn, and Sheila Fabricant. *Praying with Another for Healing*. New York: Paulist Press, 1984.

———. *Healing the Purpose of Your Life*. Mahwah: Paulist Press, 1999.

Lloyd, Daisy Riley. "Visual Art as an Expression of the Holy: A Pathway to Spirituality." DMin diss., United Theological Seminary, 2002. ProQuest (DTN 3061499).

Lorntz, Emery John. "Ellen G. White's Concept of Spirituality in Relation to Contemporary Christian Theology." PhD diss., New York University, 2000. ProQuest (DTN 9981430).

Marshall, Catherine. *Something More: In Search of a Deeper Faith*. New York: Avon Books, 1974.

Mawusi, Emmanuel Dale Kodzo. "African Theology. A Study of African Theology: Within an African Traditional Religion, (the Ethetaes of Ghana) and within a Comparative Study of Christian Tradition." Master's thesis, St. Stephen's College (Canada), 2003. ProQuest (DTN MQ90462).

McClymond, Michael J. Review of *Two Paradigms for Divine Healing: Fred F. Bosworth, Kenneth E. Hagin, Agnes Sanford, and Francis MacNutt in Dialogue* by Pavel Hejzler. In *Pneuma* 34, no. 1 (March 2012): 124-125.

McGuire, Randy Richard. "Catholic Charismatic Renewal: The Struggle for Affirmation (1967-1975)." PhD diss., Saint Louis University, 1998. ProQuest (9911964).

Meyer, Carolyn Suzanne. "Body Talk as Knowledge and Practice." Master's thesis, University of New Brunswick (Canada), 2000. ProQuest (DTN MQ65509).

Miers Dennie, Noelene Gladys. "A Strategy for the Ongoing Development of the Pentecostal Bible Institute Graduate in Chile." DMin diss., Fuller The-

ological Seminary, Doctor of Ministry Program, 2001. ProQuest (DTN 3003333).
Moga, Margaret M. and William F. Bengston. "Anomalous Magnetic Field Activity During a Bioenergy Healing Experiment." *Journal of Scientific Exploration* 24, no. 3 (Fall 2010): 397-410.
Muthalali, Jacob. "Teaching Lay Ministers of a Local Church to Improve their Biblical Knowledge of Divine Healing." DMin diss., Oral Roberts University, 2003. ProQuest (DTN 3081665).
Myers, Nancy Beth. "Sanctifying the Profane: Religious Themes in the Fiction of Frederick Buechner." PhD diss., University of North Texas, 1976. ProQuest (DTN 7629160).
Neff, LaVonne. *The Gift of Faith: Short Reflections by Thoughtful Anglicans*. Harrisburg: Morehouse, 2004.
Numbers, Ronald L. and Darrel W. Amundsen, eds. *Caring and Curing: Health and Medicine in the Western Religious Traditions*. New York: Macmillan Publishing, 1986.
Ogilvie, Christine Lisa. "The Development of the AIPCA: Crossing Religious and Political Boundaries." PhD diss., University of Michigan, 1999. ProQuest (DTN 9938506).
Park, Yang Hyun. "Holistic Healing Ministry: A Practical Guide for Korean Presbyterian Churches." DMin diss., Liberty University, 2012. ProQuest (DTN 3495631).
Payne, Leanne. *The Broken Image*. Grand Rapids: Baker Books, 1996.
———. *Crisis in Masculinity*. Grand Rapids: Baker Books, 1995.
———. *Healing Homosexuality*. Grand Rapids: Baker Books, 1996.
———. *Healing Presence: Curing the Soul Through Union with Christ*. Grand Rapids: Baker Books, 1997.
———. *Listening Prayer: Learning to Hear God's Voice and Keep a Prayer Journal*. Grand Rapids: Baker Books, 1999.
———. *Restoring the Christian Soul: Overcoming Barriers to Completion in Christ through Healing Prayer*. Grand Rapids: Baker Books, 1997.
Payne, William Alan. "Spiritual Healing: Its Theory and Application." RelD diss., Claremont School of Theology, 1974. ProQuest (DTN DP11737).
Perz, Susan Maria. "Contributions of Women's Embodied Knowing to Education for Leadership and Peacemaking." PhD diss., School of Theology at Claremont, 2002. ProQuest (DTN 3075580).
Podhurst, Linda Scicutella. "Scientism in Nonmedical Healing Systems." PhD diss., Rutgers The State University of New Jersey - New Brunswick, 1990. ProQuest (DTN 9034944).
Propst, L. Rebecca. "A Comparison of the Cognitive Restructuring Psychotherapy Paradigm and Several Spiritual Approaches to Mental Health." *Journal of Psychology and Theology* 8, no. 2 (Summer 1980): 107-114.
Reside, Graham Bradley. "Renovare: Professional Pilgrims in a Post-Industrial World. A Sociological Study of a Contemporary Evangelical Spiritual Formation Movement." PhD diss., Emory University, 2003. ProQuest (DTN

3080355).

Riley, Patricia J. "The Charismatic Movement in the Lutheran Church in America." PhD diss., Regent University, 2013. ProQuest (DTN 3573593).

Robbins, Stephen Walter. "A Strategy for Loving God and Neighbor in Everyday Life." DMin diss., Fuller Theological Seminary, Doctor of Ministry Program, 1998. ProQuest (DTN 9918778).

Rogge, Louis Philip. "The Relationship between the Sacrament of Anointing the Sick and the Charism of Healing within the Catholic Charismatic Renewal." PhD diss., Union Theological Seminary, 1984. ProQuest (DTN 8417499).

Salzman, Leon. "Spiritual and Faith Healing." *Journal of Pastoral Care* 11, no. 3 (Fall 1957): 146-155.

Samples, Terry Allen. "An Ethical Analysis of Multiethnic Congregations in Los Angeles." PhD diss., University of Southern California, 1997. ProQuest (DTN 9733130).

Sand, Faith Annette. "Healing as Kerygma." *Mission Studies* 7, no. 1 (January 1990): 97-100.

Sandford, John & Paula. *Healing the Wounded Spirit*. Tulsa: Victory House, 1985.

Scanlan, Michael. *Inner Healing: Ministering to the Human Spirit through the Power of Prayer*. New York: Paulist Press, 1974.

———. *The Power in Penance: Confession and the Holy Spirit*. Notre Dame: Ave Maria Press, 1975.

Schneider, George Allen. "The Effectiveness of Various Spiritual Disciplines in Facilitating the Emotional Healing Process." DMin diss., Drew University, 1982. ProQuest (DTN 8302417).

Shin, Soo Gill. "Experiencing Inner Healing through Confession and Prayer." DMin diss., Oral Roberts University, 2006. ProQuest (DTN 3250475).

Sieh, Linda L. "Reclaiming the Church's Healing Ministry." *Chaplaincy Today* 15, no. 2 (January 1999): 17-22.

Sisk, Timothy Ray. "An Introduction and Evaluation of the Third Wave Movement for Baptist International Missions Inc." DMin diss., Fuller Theological Seminary, Doctor of Ministry Program, 1996. ProQuest (DTN 9628851).

Smith, Linda L. *Called into Healing: Reclaiming Our Judeo-Christian Legacy of Healing Touch*. Arvada: HTSM Press, 2000.

Smith, Suzanne Natalie. "Developing a Soul Care Ministry in a Local Church." DMin diss., Regent University, 2007. ProQuest (DTN 3252642).

Smolik, Irene Ann. "The Glossolalic Utterance: What does it all Mean?" PhD diss., Carleton University (Canada), 2004. ProQuest (DTN NQ89895).

Son, Daniel. "Promoting Emotional Health with Biblical Wisdom." DMin diss., Trinity International University, 2013. ProQuest (DTN 3630458).

Spittler, Russell P. "Suggested Areas for Further Research in Pentecostal Studies." *Pneuma* 5, no. 2 (Fall 1983): 39-56.

Synan, Vinson. *The Century of the Holy Spirit: 100 Years of Pentecostal and Charismatic Renewal*. Nashville: Thomas Nelson, 2001.

Tan, Elizabeth Z. Bachrach. "Standing on Holy Ground: The Sacred Landscapes of Annie Dillard, Kathleen Norris, and Frederick Buechner." PhD diss., University of Massachusetts Amherst, 1995. ProQuest (DTN 9606486).

Tilley, James A. "A Phenomenology of the Christian Healer's Experience." PhD diss., Fuller Theological Seminary, School of Psychology, 1989. ProQuest (DTN 8924361).

Turyomumazima, Bonaventure. "The Church's Pastoral Approach to the Practice of Healing among the Banyankore of the Archdiocese of Mbarara: Toward an Integrated Healing Mission." PhD diss., University of Ottawa (Canada), 2005. ProQuest (DTN NR18111).

Udezue, Nancy N. "A Development of Healing Ministry Training in the Anglican Diocese of Kaduna, Nigeria." DMin diss., Regent University, 2003. ProQuest (DTN 3147421).

VandeCreek, Larry, ed. *Scientific and Pastoral Perspectives on Intercessory Prayer: An Exchange between Larry Dossey, M.D. and Health Care Chaplains*. Binghampton: Harrington Park, 1998.

Van Dragt, Bryan. "Paranormal Healing: A Phenomenology of the Healer's Experience." PhD diss., Fuller Theological Seminary, School of Psychology, 1980. ProQuest (DTN 8107422).

Walsh, Birrell Thomas. "The Practice of Praying for Others: Eight Examples from Late Twentieth-Century America." PhD diss., California Institute of Integral Studies, 1999. ProQuest (DTN 9949656).

Williams, Russell Howard. "An Empirical Investigation into the Beneficial Effects of Long-Distance Intercessory Prayer on Student Retention and Grade Point Average." PsyD diss., Spalding University, 2001. ProQuest (DTN 3027108).

Wilson, Margaret Taylor. "Developing a Nurturing Model of Pastoral Care in the Hospice Setting Based on 'Restored Image' in Genesis 1:27." DMin diss., Oral Roberts University, 2002. ProQuest (DTN 3079970).

Wimber, John and Kevin Springer. *Power Healing*. San Francisco: Harper & Row, 1987.

Wise, Robert L. *Healing of the Past: Recovering Emotional and Mental Wholeness*. Oklahoma City: Presbyterian and Reformed Renewal Ministries International, 1984.

Yale, Martin L. "A Heuristic Study of Spirituality's Meaning in Health and Wellness." EdD diss., Texas A&M University - Commerce, 2000. ProQuest (DTN 9980444).

Yoo, Chun Hyung. "The Implementation of a Healing Ministry in a Korean Methodist Church." DMin diss., Oral Roberts University, 1995. ProQuest (DTN 9629983).

Zulkosky, Patricia Ann. "The Wise Woman in Guided Imagery: A Feminist Interpretation." PhD diss., School of Theology at Claremont, 1984. ProQuest (DTN 8415918).

Audio Sources [alphabetically]

———. "Healing through the Holy Spirit." Lecture by Agnes Sanford. Santa Monica: St. Augustine's Episcopal Church, 1958. Lecture, 5 audio cassettes, 258 min.
———. "Is It God's Will to Heal?" Lecture by Agnes Sanford. Santa Monica: St. Augustine's Episcopal Church, 1958. Lecture, 1 audio cassette, 39 min.
———. "Jesus: Healer, King, and Redeemer." Lecture by Agnes Sanford. Bakersfield: Inspired Tape Library, 1958. Lecture, 3 audio cassettes, 92 min.
———. "Healing of Memories: The Forgiveness of Sins." Lecture by Agnes Sanford. Milo, IA: CFO Classics Library, n.d. Lecture, 1 audio cassette, 53 min
———. "Our Need to Recognize Our Spiritual Self." Lecture by Agnes Sanford. Milo, IA: CFO Classics Library, n.d. Lecture, 1 audio cassette, 54 min.

Supplemental Sources [alphabetically]

Alexander, Kimberly E. *Pentecostal Healing: Models in Theology and Practice*. Blandform Forum: DEO, 2006.
All Saints Healing Ministry: The Glennon House. "About the Healing Ministry." Accessed November 15, 2016. http://www.glennonhouse.org/about.htm
Althouse, Peter and Robby Waddell, eds. *Perspectives in Pentecostal Eschatologies*. Eugene: Pickwick, 2010.
Anderson, Allan. *An Introduction to Pentecostalism*. Cambridge: Cambridge University Press, 2004.
Athanasius. *Four Discourses Against the Arians*. In *Athanasius: Select Works and Letters*, edited and translated by Philip Schaff and Henry Wace. Vol. 4 of *The Nicene and Post-Nicene Fathers, Second Series*. Oak Harbor: Logos Research Systems, 1997.
Bear, James E., Jr. *The Mission Work of the Presbyterian Church in the United States in China, 1867-1899*. 5 vols. Richmond: Union Theological Seminary, 1963.
Berean Call. "About TBC – History." Accessed July 25, 2016. http://www.thebereancall.org/content/about-berean-call
Boggs, Wade H. Jr. Review of *God Can Heal You Now*, by Emily Gardner Neal. *Journal of Pastoral Care* 15, no. 3 (Fall 1961): 178-180.
Bradshaw, David. "The Divine Energies in the New Testament." *St Vladimir's Theological Quarterly* 50, no. 3 (2006): 189-223.
Burgess, Stanley M. *The Holy Spirit: Eastern Christian Traditions*. Vol. 2 of *The Holy Spirit*. Grand Rapids: Baker Academic, 1989.
Camps Farthest Out. "History." Accessed July 18, 2016. https://cfonorthamerica.org/node/28
Cartledge, Mark J. "Practical Theology." In *Studying Global Pentecostalism: Theories & Methods*, edited by Allan Anderson, Michael Bergunder, André Droogers, and Cornelis Van der Laan. 268-285. Berkeley: University of California Press,

2010.

Challis, Derek and Gloria Rawlinson, *The Book of Iris: A Life of Robin Hyde*. Auckland: Auckland University Press, 2002.

Christian Healing Ministries. "Organizational History." In "About Us." Accessed July 19, 2016; March 22, 2018. https://www.christianhealingmin.org/index.php/chm-info/about-chm

Cox, Harvey. *Fire from Heaven: The Rise of Pentecostal Spirituality and the Reshaping of Religion in the Twenty-First Century*. Cambridge: Da Capo, 1995.

Csordas, Thomas J. "Catholic Charismatic Healing in Global Perspective: The Cases of India, Brazil, and Nigeria." In *Global Pentecostal and Charismatic Healing*, edited by Candy Gunther Brown. 331-350. Oxford: Oxford University, 2011.

Cunningham, Raymond J. "Ministry of Healing: The Origins of the Psychotherapeutic Role of the American Churches." PhD diss., John Hopkins University, 1965. ProQuest (DTN 6510270).

Elijah House International. "About EH." Accessed July 21, 2016. https://www.elijahhouse.org/page/website.aboutus

Elowsky, Joel C. *We Believe in the Holy Spirit*. Vol. 4 of *Ancient Christian Doctrine*. Downers Grove: IVP Academic, 2009.

Episcopal Church. *The Book of Common Prayer: And Administration of the Sacraments and Other Rites and Ceremonies of the Church; Together with the Psalter or Psalms of David*. New York: Oxford University Press, 2007.

———. "Neal, Emily Gardner." Accessed November 10, 2016. http://www.episcopalchurch.org/library/glossary/neal-emily-gardiner

Franciscan University of Steubenville. "Our History." In "About." Accessed July 21, 2016. http://www.franciscan.edu/about/history/

Glennon House. "About." Accessed July 21, 2016. http://www.glennonhouse.org/about.htm

Greig, Gary S. "The Purpose of Signs and Wonders in the New Testament: What Terms for Miraculous Power Denote and Their Relationship to the Gospel." In *The Kingdom and the Power*, edited by Gary S. Greig and Kevin N. Springer, 133-174. Ventura: Regal Books, 1993.

Hall, Calvin S. and Vernon J. Nordby. *A Primer of Jungian Psychology*. New York: Penguin Putnam, 1999.

Hocken, Peter D. "Charismatic Episcopal Church (CEC)." In *The New International Dictionary of Pentecostal and Charismatic Movements*, edited by Stanley M. Burgess and Ed M. Van der Maas, 476. Grand Rapids: Zondervan, 2002.

———. "Scanlan, Michael." In *The New International Dictionary of Pentecostal and Charismatic Movements*, edited by Stanley M. Burgess and Ed M. Van der Maas, 1041. Grand Rapids: Zondervan, 2002.

Hollenweger, Walter J. *Pentecostalism: Origins and Developments Worldwide*. Peabody: Hendrickson, 2005.

Hope, N. V. "Warfield, Benjamin Breckenridge." In *Who's Who in Christian History*, edited by J. D. Douglas, Philip W. Comfort, and Donald Mitchell. Wheaton: Tyndale House, 1992.

Hopkins, Emma Curtis and Thomas Troward. *New Thought Classics*. Lexington: CreateSpace Independent Publishing Platform, 2013.

Institute for Christian Renewal. "About ICR." Accessed July 19, 2016. https://christianrenewal.wordpress.com/about/

International Order of St. Luke the Physician. "About Us." Accessed July 19, 2016, March 22, 2018. https://orderofstluke.org/en/about.html

Irenaeus of Lyons. *Against Heresies*. In *The Apostolic Fathers with Justin Martyr and Irenaeus*, edited and translated by Alexander Roberts, James Donaldson, and A. Cleveland Coxe. Vol. 1 of *The Ante-Nicene Fathers: Translations of the writings of the Fathers down to A.D. 325*. Oak Harbor: Logos Research Systems, 1997.

Knight, Henry H. III. "Quenching the Spirit: Examining Centuries of Opposition to the Moving of the Holy Spirit." *Pneuma* 15 no. 2 (Fall 1993): 227-231.

Kydd, Ronald A. N. *Healing through the Centuries: Models for Understanding*. Peabody: Hendrickson, 1998.

Land, Steven. "Be Filled with the Spirit: The Nature and Evidence of Spiritual Fullness." *Ex Auditu* 12 (1996): 108-120.

Macchia, Frank D. "Theology, Pentecostal." In *The New International Dictionary of Pentecostal and Charismatic Movements*, edited by Stanley M. Burgess and Ed M. Van der Maas, 1120-1141. Grand Rapids: Zondervan, 2002.

Manta. "Preaching & Prayer Ministries, Inc." Accessed July 21, 2016. http://www.manta.com/c/mmj7244/preaching-prayer-ministries-inc

Miskov, Jennifer A. *Life on Wings: The Forgotten Life and Theology of Carrie Judd Montgomery (1858-1946)*. Cleveland: CPT Press, 2012.

Morgan, Timothy C. "Died: Leanne Payne, 82, Prominent Leader in Pastoral Care, Healing Movement." Gleanings. *Christianity Today*, February 20, 2015. http://www.christianitytoday.com/gleanings/2015/february/died-leanne-payne-pastoral-care-heal-lgbt-change-cslewis.html

Mosley, Glenn R. *New Thought, Ancient Wisdom: The History and Future of the New Thought Movement*. Philadelphia: Templeton Foundation, 2006.

New Creation Healing Center. "History." Accessed July 19, 2016. http://www.newcreationhc.org/history.htm

Peace College. "History and Tradition." Accessed July 18, 2016. http://www.peace.edu/about_wpu/history

Porterfield, Amanda. *Healing in the History of Christianity*. Oxford: Oxford University Press, 2005.

Reid, W. Stanford. "The Christian and the Scientific Method." *The Westminster Theological Journal* 24, no. 1 (November 1961): 2-18.

Robeck, C. M. Jr. "Hocken, Peter Dudley." In *The New International Dictionary of Pentecostal and Charismatic Movements*, edited by Stanley M. Burgess and Ed M. Van der Maas, 723. Grand Rapids: Zondervan, 2002.

Robinson, James. *Divine Healing: The Formative Years, 1830-1890; Theological Roots in the Transatlantic World*. Eugene, Pickwick, 2011.

Ruthven, Jon. "On the Cessation of the Charismata: The Protestant Polemic of Benjamin B. Warfield." *Pneuma* 12, no. 1 (Spring 1990): 14-31.

Sandford, John A. *Healing Body and Soul: The Meaning of Illness in the New Testament and in Psychotherapy.* Louisville: Westminster/John Knox, 1992.

Schenck, Lewis Bevans. *The Presbyterian Doctrine of Children in the Covenant: An Historical Study of the Significance of Infant Baptism in the Presbyterian Church in America.* New Haven: Yale University Press, 1940.

Simmons, Dale H. *E. W. Kenyon and the Postbellum Pursuit of Peace, Power, and Plenty.* Lanham: The Scarecrow Press, 1997.

Smith, James K. A. *Thinking in Tongues: Pentecostal Contributions to Christian Philosophy.* Grand Rapids: William B. Eerdmans, 2010.

Stein, David E. "The Scientific Method after Next." *World Future Review* 4, no. 1 (Spring 2012): 34-41.

Strang, Stephen. "MacNutt, Francis Scott." In *The New International Dictionary of Pentecostal and Charismatic Movements*, edited by Stanley M. Burgess and Ed M. Van der Maas, 855-856. Grand Rapids: Zondervan, 2002.

Sun, Zhen. "Challenging the Dominant Stories about the Boxer Rebellion: Chinese Minister Wu Ting-Fang's Narrative." *Chinese Journal of Communication* 1, no. 2 (October 2008): 196-212.

Strang, Stephen. "MacNutt, Francis Scott." In *The New International Dictionary of Pentecostal and Charismatic Movements*, edited by Stanley M. Burgess and Ed M. Van der Maas, 855-856. Grand Rapids: Zondervan, 2002.

Synan, Vinson. *Aspects of Pentecostal-Charismatic Origins.* Plainfield: Logos International, 1975.

———. "Christenson, Laurence Donald ('Larry')." In *The New International Dictionary of Pentecostal and Charismatic Movements*, edited by Stanley M. Burgess and Ed M. Van der Maas, 522-523. Grand Rapids: Zondervan, 2002.

Thompson, Matthew K. *Kingdom Come: Revisioning Pentecostal Eschatology.* Blandford Forum, UK: DEO, 2010.

Tiedemann, R. G. "Baptism of Fire: China's Christians and the Boxer Uprising of 1900." *International Bulletin of Missionary Research* 24, no. 1 (January 2000): 7-8, 10-12.

Warfield, Benjamin Breckenridge. *Miracles: Yesterday and Today; True and False.* Grand Rapids: Wm. B. Eerdmans, 1953.

Westminster Confession of Faith and Westminster Shorter Catechism. New York: Krill Press, 2015. Kindle edition.

Wheeler, Edward Jewitt, Isaac Kaufman Funk, and William Seaver Woods, eds. "Polygamy and Foreign Missions." *The Literary Digest* 32, no. 24 (June 1906): 910-911.

White, Hugh Watt. *Jesus, the Missionary: Studies in the Life of Jesus as the Master, the Model, the Proto-type for All Missionaries. On Many Scriptures, Interpretations Are Given Which Have Been Worked Out on the Mission Field.* Shanghai: Presbyterian Mission Press, 1916.

———. "Polygamous Applicants for Baptism on the Mission Field." *Christian Observer* (Louisville, KY) May 16, 1906: 16-17.

———. *Demonism Verified and Analyzed.* Shanghai: Presbyterian Mission Press, 1922.

Wilson, Dwight J. "Eschatology, Pentecostal Perspectives On." In *The New International Dictionary of Pentecostal and Charismatic Movements*, edited by Stanley M. Burgess and Eduard M. Van der Maas. 601-605. Grand Rapids: Zondervan, 2003.

Woodcock, Brian A. "'The Scientific Method' as Myth and Ideal." *Science & Education* 23, no. 10 (May 2014): 2069-2093.

Yong, Amos. *In the Days of Caesar: Pentecostalism and Political Theology*. Grand Rapids: William B. Eeardmans, 2010.

———. *Spirit-Word-Community: Theological Hermeneutics in Trinitarian Perspective*. Eugene: Wipf & Stock, 2002.

———. *The Spirit Poured Out on All Flesh: Pentecostalism and the Possibility of Global Theology*. Grand Rapids: Baker Academic, 2005.

Index of Terms and Persons

Abundant life 83, 164
Adoptionism 44, 45, 53, 58, 97
Alexander, Kimberly Ervin 69
All Saints Healing Ministry 139
Athanasius 114, 127–128

Baltz, Francis Burkhardt 36, 176—77
Banks, Ethel 135, 156
Banks, John Gaynor 33, 135, 156, 190, 196
Baptism in the Holy Spirit 2, 4, 35, 99–100, 106, 109, 130, 139, 141, 155, 162
Basil of Caesarea 105
Bear, James F., Jr. 8, 15, 37–38
Bennett, Dennis 2
Berean Call 149, 159

Camps Farthest Out 11, 34, 130, 135–36, 141, 156, 187, 190, 193, 196
Carl Jung 64, 67
Cessationism 1, 2, 4, 17—18, 22, 28, 29, 38, 45, 59, 67, 102, 108, 131–132, 134, 135, 145, 148, 163, 172, 175, 180, 184, 187–89
CFO (*see* Camps Farthest Out)
CHM (*see* Christian Healing Ministries)
Christenson, Larry 134, 156
Christian Healing Ministries 51, 140, 157
Christian New Perspective 55
Christian Science 43, 51–52, 58–60, 67, 102, 164
Clark, Glenn 33–34, 40, 55, 135–36, 140, 156, 170, 187, 190, 192, 196
Colwell, Hollis 29–30, 43, 49, 56, 58, 188
Csordas, Thomas J. 140, 157
Cunningham, Raymond 52, 69

Deification (*see* Theosis) 110, 114–16, 124, 164
Deism 108, 125
Descartes, Rene 52
Deutsch, Martin 60

Eddy, Mary Baker 51–52, 58
Edison, Thomas 91
Egan, Paul Francis 40, 157, 188
Elijah House 142, 158
Exman, Eugene 33

Fillmore, Charles 53
Fillmore, Myrtle 51
Fosdick, Harry Emerson 23
Foster, Richard 153, 184
Fox, Emmett 56
Freud, Sigmund 64, 65
Friend's School 33

Gifts of the Spirit 4, 17, 32, 35, 40, 45, 65, 69, 71, 98, 131–34, 137, 140–41, 152, 159, 161–62, 169, 171, 180, 185–86, 188, 192, 196
Glennon, Jim 139, 157, 183, 188
Goldsmith, Harry 34

215

Gore, Charles 30
Gray Ladies 33
Gregory of Nazianzus 105
Gregory of Palamas 110, 115
Grier, Mark 16
Gumprecht, Jane 143, 158–59, 175, 194

Hagin, Kenneth 131, 177
Hall, Calvin S. 71
Hickson, James Moore 30
Hocken, Peter 130, 155
Hopkins, Emma Curtis 54, 69
Hunt, Dave 149, 159, 179, 181, 183, 195

Inner healing 1, 4, 14, 19, 20, 34, 64, 79, 109, 123, 127, 132–33, 135, 137–44, 148, 149, 152, 154, 158, 161–62, 165–67, 171, 174–80, 182, 184–85, 188–90, 195–96
Institute for Christian Renewal 140, 157
International Lutheran Renewal Center 134
Irenaeus of Lyons 114, 127
Jeffrey, H. B. 56
Jungian Psychology 5, 43, 63–67, 71, 95–96, 143–44, 148, 152, 162, 164, 166, 175, 177, 184, 188
Kelsey, Morton 5, 35, 65, 67, 71, 137, 144, 153–54, 156–57, 188, 190
Kenyon, E. W. 52, 69, 179
Knight, Henry H., III 39, 93, 131, 155, 180, 195
Kydd, Ronald A. N. 74, 93

Liias, Jürgen 140

Macchia, Frank 117
MacNutt, Francis 35, 50, 127, 133, 140–41, 153–54, 158, 177, 184, 190, 196
MacNutt, Judith 41, 69, 158, 187, 196

Mains, Karen 144, 158
Marty, Martin 137
McMahon, T. A. 149, 159, 179, 183, 195
Montgomery, Carrie Judd 113
Mosley, Glenn 51, 69

Neal, Emily Gardner 136, 156
New Age 5, 55, 143–44, 148, 149, 151, 153, 166, 170, 175, 183, 184
New Creation Healing Center 140, 157
New Thought 5, 30, 43–44, 51–60, 63–67, 69, 78–79, 88, 95–97, 100, 102, 103, 105, 132, 143–44, 148, 152–53, 164, 166, 175, 181, 184, 187, 189
Nordby, Vernon J. 71

Order of St. Luke 130, 135, 140, 156, 189, 190, 194

Pantheism 5, 97, 105, 107–108, 125, 143, 148
Pastoral Care Ministries 138–39, 190
Payne, Leanne 36, 40–41, 71, 127–28, 138, 144, 157, 187, 190, 196
PCM (*see* Pastoral Care Ministries)
Peace College 25–26
Pearson, Mark 135, 139
Pierre Teilhard de Chardin 149, 151, 184
Pluralism 11, 101–102
Preaching and Prayer Ministries 142–43

Quimby, Phineas P. 51

Robinson, James 6, 93
Ruthven, Jon 45, 68

Saint Mary's School 26
Sandford, John 121, 142
Sandford, Paula 141, 153–54, 158, 180, 190

Sanford, John 5, 67
Sanford, Ted 147, 163
Scanlan, Michael 141, 158, 190
Schenck, Lewis 11, 37
School of Pastoral Care 1, 3, 121, 137, 144, 178, 182, 188, 190, 194
Scientific method 5, 6, 43, 60–61, 63, 67, 70, 73, 79, 90, 93, 164, 170, 174, 188
Shamanism 125, 151–52, 184
Shanghai American School 24, 25
Simmons, Dale 52, 69
Smith, James K. A. 105, 126
Soochow Academy 27
Spiritism 5, 32, 36, 58, 64, 67, 125, 144
St Andrew's Healing Ministry 139
Stapleton, Ruth Carter 144, 158, 178
Stein, David 60
Strang, Stephen 140, 157, 158
Synan, Vinson 6, 134, 155–56, 158

Theistic evolution 104, 112, 124, 150, 164
Theophilus of Antioch 105
Theosis 114
Troward, Thomas 54, 69

Unity Christianity 5, 51–53, 55, 57–58, 67, 143, 164
Universalism 11, 101–102

Vaswig, William 142, 153, 174

Warfield, Benjamin 45, 68
Wesley, John 111, 180
White, Augusta 7
White, Hugh 7, 8, 13–14, 16
Williams, Joseph 52, 54, 69–70
Wilson, Henry B. 30
Wimber, John 153, 184
Woodcock, Brian A. 60, 70
Yong, Amos 6, 105, 126

www.ingramcontent.com/pod-product-compliance
Lightning Source LLC
Chambersburg PA
CBHW061938220426
43662CB00012B/1954